COLONIAL-ERA
CARIBBEAN THEATRE

COLONIAL-ERA CARIBBEAN THEATRE

Issues in Research, Writing and Methodology

EDITED BY JULIA PREST

LIVERPOOL UNIVERSITY PRESS

First published 2023 by
Liverpool University Press
4 Cambridge Street
Liverpool
L69 7ZU

Copyright © 2023 Liverpool University Press

Julia Prest has asserted the right to be identified as
the editor of this book in accordance with the Copyright, Designs and
Patents Act 1988.

All rights reserved. No part of this book may be reproduced, stored
in a retrieval system, or transmitted, in any form or by any means,
electronic, mechanical, photocopying, recording, or otherwise, without
the prior written permission of the publisher.

British Library Cataloguing-in-Publication data
A British Library CIP record is available

ISBN 978-1-83764-503-9 cased

Typeset by Carnegie Book Production, Lancaster
Printed and bound by CPI Group (UK) Ltd, Croydon CR0 4YY

Contents

List of Figures — vii

List of Contributors — ix

Acknowledgements — xi

Introduction, Julia Prest — 1

Part I: The Pan-Caribbean

1 *Studying the Colonial Caribbean: Combining Geographical and Imperial Approaches*, Dexnell Peters — 19

2 *Mobility as a Lens for Reading the History of Opera in the Colonial Caribbean*, Charlotte Bentley — 37

3 *Multilingual Approaches to Colonial-Era Caribbean Theatre Research: Challenges and Interventions*, Susan Thomas — 61

Part II: Approaches

4 *Connecting Metropole and Colony? Harlequin Travels to Suriname*, Sarah J. Adams — 87

5 *Problems of Framing: National or Colonial Approaches to Blackface Performance?* Jill Lane — 111

6 *Contextualizing Late Eighteenth-Century Jamaican Oratorio: Obstacles and Opportunities*, Wayne Weaver — 135

Part III: Sources and Gaps

7 *Silences in the Archive: The Mysterious One-Night Stand of John Fawcett's* Obi; or, Three-Finger'd Jack *in Kingston, Jamaica (1862)*, Jenna M. Gibbs   161

8 *Using Military Documents to Study Colonial-Era Theatre and Performance in Saint-Domingue*, Logan J. Connors   183

9 *Uncovering Connections between Theatre and Slavery: Runaway Advertisements in Colonial Saint-Domingue and Beyond*, Julia Prest   205

10 *Knowledge Exchange Theatre and the Colonial Caribbean: Creating* Placeholder, Catherine Bisset, Flavia D'Avila and Jaïrus Obayomi   231

Index   257

List of Figures

Cover image: Nicolaas Visscher II, *Map of Central America and the Caribbean region*, 1681. Atlas of Mutual Heritage, Koninklijke Bibliotheek, The Hague. Retrieved through Wikimedia Commons.

Figure 1: Cornelis Troost, *Arlequin, tovenaar en barbier: De bedrogen rivalen*, 1738. The Hague: Mauritshuis. Inventory number 183. Retrieved through Wikimedia Commons.   93

Figure 2: *Catherine Bisset in rehearsal* (photograph: Flavia D'Avila)   235

Figure 3: *Catherine Bisset in* Placeholder *(1), November 2021* (photograph: Chris Scott)   239

Figure 4: *Catherine Bisset in* Placeholder *(2), November 2021* (photograph: Chris Scott)   241

List of Contributors

Sarah J. Adams: Postdoctoral Researcher in Literary Studies, Ghent University and Antwerp University

Charlotte Bentley: Lecturer in Music, Newcastle University

Catherine Bisset: Actor-writer and Head of the Justice Analytical Unit at the Scottish Government

Logan J. Connors: Professor of Modern Languages and Literatures, University of Miami

Flavia D'Avila: Theatre director and Artistic Director of Fronteiras Theatre Lab

Jenna M. Gibbs: Associate Professor of History, Florida International University

Jill Lane: Associate Professor of Spanish and Portuguese, Latin American and Caribbean Studies, New York University

Jaïrus Obayomi: Director and dramaturg, occasional performer, writer and translator

Dexnell Peters: Lecturer in Caribbean and Atlantic History, University of the West Indies, Mona Campus

Julia Prest: Professor of French and Caribbean Studies, University of St Andrews

Susan Thomas: Professor of Musicology, University of Colorado Boulder

Wayne Weaver: PhD student in Music, University of Cambridge

Acknowledgements

I am grateful to the Royal Society of Edinburgh, who awarded me a Research Network Grant (2021–23) to set up the Colonial-Era Caribbean Theatre and Opera Network (CECTON) and undertake the discussions and activities that underpin this volume. I would like to thank all the CECTON-ites, each of whom made valuable oral contributions to our discussions and then equally valuable written contributions in their respective chapters here. It is a risky business creating a new group from scratch, but we were fortunate in finding ourselves eagerly exchanging ideas within minutes of our first Teams meeting starting—and that sense of a shared enterprise has lasted throughout the process. (I hope it may continue into the future as well.) I am especially grateful to Flavia D'Avila, Catherine Bisset and Jaïrus Obayomi, who made creating a new theatre piece based on our research under considerable time pressure while social distancing was still in place look easy (I know it wasn't). Thank you to Sam Osborn, who acted as an additional pair of eagle eyes when I was preparing the manuscript; to Chloe Johnson of Liverpool University Press, who responded patiently and helpfully to my many queries; and to the anonymous readers for their helpful suggestions. My heartfelt thanks to Roy Dilley, who was there every step of the way. I dedicate this book to the memory of my father John Prest who, upon first hearing of my interest in what he—as a historian of Britain—called the 'West Indies', promptly presented me with a copy of Eric Williams's excellent book *From Columbus to Castro*. I would have enjoyed discussing it all with you.

Introduction

Julia Prest

In this volume, we have chosen to focus on theatre in what we are calling the 'colonial-era Caribbean'. The term 'colonial-era' is used to suggest some historical parameters (which of course varied across different parts of the Caribbean region) and a corresponding system of governance and unequal power relations; the term is also used to call that same system into question by suggesting that not everything in the colonial era was strictly 'colonial' in practice. One purpose of the term is thus to situate our volume within a broad timeframe: while some chapters cover a longer period, most of our case studies are taken from the eighteenth or nineteenth centuries, when Caribbean colonialism was at its height. Another purpose is to create space for departures from—and challenges to—colonial structures within that timeframe. If the adjective 'colonial' (as opposed to 'colonial-era') suggests the dominance of one culture over another, it leaves little room for cultural productions—such as local, Creole works or local adaptations of metropolitan works—that are not straightforward examples of such dominance, but that also emerged during the age of colonialism.

We are focussing on the Caribbean—broadly understood—rather than on, say, the Atlantic world in order to ask in what ways the theatre traditions that arose across different parts of this smaller but undeniably rich and complex region were similar or different. Distinctions between academic disciplines make comparisons within and across, for instance, the 'English Atlantic' or the 'French Atlantic' more obvious and thus more common, and several studies of this kind have proven extremely fruitful. Elizabeth Maddock Dillon's monograph *New World Drama: The Performative Commons in the Atlantic World, 1649–1849* offers a sophisticated analysis of the political dynamics of theatre and its publics in England, Jamaica and the United States.[1] Her account of the paradox of

---

[1] Durham, NC and London: Duke University Press, 2014.

'intimate distance', which led Europeans in the colonies to assert their intimacy with the metropole while maintaining rhetorical distance from the non-white bodies present in the colonies in which they lived, is especially thought-provoking.[2] Joseph Roach's influential monograph *Cities of the Dead: Circum-Atlantic Performance* explores a wide range of performance cultures from the 'circum-Atlantic' or 'Atlantic rim', focussing particularly on London and Louisiana.[3] In particular, Roach develops a persuasive theory of the triangular relationship between memory, performance and substitution according to which cultural production and reproduction across time and space work via a process of 'surrogation': gaps or absences created by loss 'through death or other forms of departure' are filled with substitutes or surrogates that are never quite the same as what they are supposed to be replacing.[4] More recently, Jeffrey Leichman and Karine Bénac-Giroux's edited collection *Colonialism and Slavery in Performance: Theatre and the Eighteenth-Century French Caribbean* has opened up the discussion in relation to the 'French' Caribbean, arguing in favour of a transatlantic continuum between metropolitan France and its Caribbean colonies.[5]

Our focus on the Caribbean region aims to cut across more academic boundaries (both perceived and genuine). We are not suggesting that the Caribbean approach is the only one that is viable, nor even that it is necessarily the best one. We do not argue in favour of a homogeneous colonial-era Caribbean theatre tradition or set of traditions. Rather, our goal is to identify areas of overlap and difference across a region that is smaller than the whole of the Atlantic but more wide-ranging than the Atlantic—or Caribbean—associated with a single nation or empire. Based on the understanding that the colonial-era Caribbean was never as fragmented as we, in our respective departments and institutions, now are, this volume seeks to offer—individually and collectively—new theatre scholarship with a particular emphasis on methodological challenges.[6]

Theatre, including—but not restricted to—public theatre, was an important feature of the Caribbean region in the colonial era. Playhouses were built in many towns including Port-au-Prince, Cap-Français and

[2] Dillon, *New World Drama*, 16, 56–57.
[3] New York: Columbia University Press, 1996.
[4] Roach, *Cities of the Dead*, 2.
[5] Oxford University Studies in the Enlightenment (Liverpool: Liverpool University Press, 2021).
[6] In that regard, our volume may be understood to complement Baz Kershaw and Helen Nicholson (eds), *Research Methods in Theatre and Performance* (Edinburgh: Edinburgh University Press, 2011).

Saint-Marc in Saint-Domingue (now Haiti); Kingston, Spanish Town and Montego Bay in Jamaica; Havana, Santiago and Santa Clara in Cuba, as well as in Saint-Pierre (Martinique), Paramaribo (Suriname) and New Orleans (Louisiana), among others. While some theatres relied heavily on visiting troupes, others enjoyed troupes of actors who worked locally on a short-term or sometimes a long-term basis. Audiences were usually mixed but segregated, with a disproportionately small number of seats allocated to people of colour, including some people of solely African ancestry. The theatrical repertoire was wide-ranging and encompassed, among other genres, spoken comedies, tragedies, *drames* and pantomimes as well as ballets, tragic opera, *opéra-comique*, zarzuela, musical comedies and ballad opera. Although the repertoire was mostly imported from Europe, works and their performances were adapted to local conditions to a greater or lesser extent, and some new works were also created in the Caribbean colonies. These signal the emergence of a modest but important 'Creole' or local theatre tradition even within colonial-era playhouses. Outside the playhouse, private theatre was also performed, and people of African descent gave theatrical performances of various kinds—including *vodou* rituals in Saint-Domingue and Jonkanoo in Jamaica—within their communities. Some African-inspired performances also made their way into the public playhouse, usually via white portrayals of what was heralded as 'black' performance. Although these performances drew on—and perpetuated—racial stereotypes, they also inadvertently acknowledged the power of local black performance by seeking, precisely, to control that power. Churches, too, hosted semi-theatrical productions including performances of oratorio—a musical genre related to opera that was normally based on religious themes but not staged. Colonial-era Caribbean theatre is thus a very rich area of study. It is also one that has not yet received the full scholarly attention that it deserves, partly owing to the suspicion that it can provoke. As one respected theatre practitioner asked me a couple of years ago, 'why study the theatre of the colonial era when there is postcolonial theatre to study?' It is a fair question and one that I shall attempt to answer below.

This volume began with some principles and a set of research challenges, coupled with some practical constraints and opportunities. Its foundational challenge lies in the double-bind that any researcher of the colonial-era Caribbean faces: the majority of research in this area, including its theatre traditions, is single-authored and addresses only a small portion of the field. As scholars, we are trained—and, to a certain extent, obliged—to specialize and draw on the skills that we each possess or can reasonably develop. But our research also exists within a broader Caribbean context. On one hand, then, no single researcher can accrue the depth and breadth of knowledge or expertise required to tackle the whole of the colonial-era Caribbean alone.[7] However this is defined, it necessarily covers a wide range of interconnected historical, geographical, linguistic and cultural traditions, all displaying the influence (but not the full control) of a set of European empires in similar and different ways. But these connections also mean that, even to understand our own portion of the colonial-era Caribbean (in my case, the theatre of the 'French' Caribbean and especially that of the colony of Saint-Domingue in present-day Haiti), we need, ideally, to understand other traditions in the region and their particular contexts. Certainly, our research would be enhanced by meeting others who are tackling similar questions in relation to similar, colonial Caribbean situations in order to share knowledge and understanding, but also—and in particular—to debate the shared methodological challenges that scholars of the field face. These are many and complex, but can be summarized, in our case, as *how best to research and write responsibly about colonial-era Caribbean theatre today?* This seemingly simple question is the one that we seek to address, if only partly, in the present volume. Our question encompasses both practical research challenges, such as those posed by the Caribbean archive, and ethical challenges, such as the need to avoid adopting a colonial approach to the colonial era and to do what we can to tackle the unequal power relations that characterize it. It also encompasses an issue that is implicit in any study of colonial-era theatre: what does it all mean for theatre performance today?

Group discussions of the kind envisaged above do not happen as seamlessly or as frequently as they should. The relatively small number of scholars of colonial-era Caribbean theatre are scattered across a diverse array of academic disciplines (including Modern Languages, History, Theatre Studies, Caribbean Studies, Latin-American Studies, African-Diaspora Studies, English Literature, Anthropology, Music and Dance, Early-Modern Studies, Eighteenth-Century Studies, Nineteenth-Century Studies, Comparative Literature) and language areas (including English, French, Spanish, Portuguese, Danish, Dutch, Swedish and several Creoles). As a result, we are spread so thinly across the various conferences at which we might otherwise expect to meet that, even after many years working in the field, we may never meet face-to-face or

---

[7] I do not wish to suggest that the problem is unique to scholars of the colonial-era Caribbean. Similar issues undoubtedly arise in relation to the postcolonial Caribbean as well.

even necessarily encounter each other's valuable work. To put it another way, our fragmentation is inconsistent with the many ways in which our fields of study are interconnected. Yet, apart from the occasional panel at a bigger umbrella conference, meetings and exchanges between scholars of colonial-era Caribbean theatre rarely occur and must be contrived.

The opportunity to arrange a group exchange focussed on colonial-era Caribbean theatre arose thanks to the Royal Society of Edinburgh's Research Network scheme. An RSE Research Network grant allowed me to create a small network, the Colonial-Era Caribbean Theatre and Opera Network (CECTON) and, in the first instance, to bring together a group of scholars for an initial, online discussion workshop in April 2021. As a means of teasing out the dynamics of our own, small network, we began by reading the introduction to Jeppe Mulich's excellent monograph *In a Sea of Empires: Networks and Crossings in the Revolutionary Caribbean*, in which he makes the crucial point that the many different networks at play in the colonial-era Caribbean cut across official networks as they were prescribed by its various imperial nations.[8] Indeed, this trans-imperial understanding is very much in keeping with what we were hoping to achieve within our own trans-disciplinary network. As we compared notes on our respective areas of expertise, the question of comparative methodologies quickly emerged as a key issue, within both our colonial-era sources and our own discussions. It was especially useful, therefore, to reflect on Mulich's view of the 'dual challenge of comparison' and his invitation to allow 'space for native comparisons' without 'reifying the categorical units being critiqued'.[9] Not all comparisons are invidious.

Another key issue is the relationship between metropole and colony. For this, we returned to a foundational essay by Frederick Cooper and Anne Laura Stoler in the introduction to their *Tensions of Empire* volume, in which they urge scholars to move beyond the colonizer/colonized dichotomy and to treat metropole and colony as a 'single analytic field'.[10] Although this is not always the ideal solution either—a more pioneering option today would be to treat the colony independently of the metropole or to approach things from a Caribbean

---

[8] Cambridge: Cambridge University Press, 2020.
[9] Mulich, *Sea of Empires*, 5–6.
[10] Ann Laura Stoler and Frederick Cooper, 'Between Metropole and Colony: Rethinking a Research Agenda', in Frederick Cooper and Ann Laura Stoler (eds), *Tensions of Empire: Colonial Cultures in a Bourgeois World* (Berkeley: University of California Press, 1997), pp. 1–56 (4).

perspective—it was useful to reflect on how ground-breaking their volume was at the time and to gauge how far (or not) we have travelled since. One important point highlighted by Cooper and Stoler that is still highly relevant to scholars today relates to the colonial archive. As they put it, 'colonial archives [...] are themselves cultural artifacts, built on institutional structures that erased certain kinds of knowledge, secreted some and valorized others'.[11] Turning more specifically towards theatre, we then discussed questions relating to the colonial theatre archive (and what to do with it today) as recently explored in the Indian context by Bishnupriya Dutt.[12] In a thought-provoking piece, she unpicks and challenges the traditional divide between theatre, which is often perceived as a colonial import, and performance, which is often perceived as local. Like most—perhaps all—dichotomies, this division, as Dutt points out, overlooks the space in between, the overlaps and the hybrid. The final text that we discussed together was Tracy Davis's article on 'the context problem' in historical theatre research.[13] Davis begins with one of the defining challenges that all theatre researchers (at least of the pre-electronic era) face: that of working on a phenomenon that is, by definition, ephemeral. Although contextualization is a highly important tool to help meet this challenge, she reminds us that context is a subjective notion (how do we decide which gaps to fill and how to fill them?) and its methods 'doomed to incompleteness'.[14] We thus opened up some of the key methodological questions that we would go on to tackle in this volume, finding some common ground and points of reference as well as some key areas of difference. Our discussion workshop was followed in August 2021 by a conference workshop at which we shared early drafts of what would become our respective chapters here.[15] Our volume thus showcases what happens when a group of theatre researchers whose expertise lies in different but related areas come together, compare notes and then go away and write about our area of expertise in light of our broader discussions.

In an ideal world, a group publication on colonial-era Caribbean

[11] Stoler and Cooper, 'Between Metropole and Colony', 17.
[12] Bishnupriya Dutt, 'Rethinking Categories of Theatre and Performance: Archive, Scholarship, and Practices (a Post-colonial Indian Perspective)', in Tracy C. Davis and Peter W. Marx (eds), *The Routledge Companion to Theatre and Performance Historiography* (London: Routledge, 2020), pp. 86–103.
[13] Tracy C. Davis, 'The Context Problem', *Theatre Survey*, 45.2 (2004), pp. 203–09.
[14] Davis, 'The Context Problem', 206.
[15] The conference workshop was scheduled to take place in person at the University of St Andrews, Scotland, but was moved online owing to COVID-19.

theatre would also be written collaboratively, each chapter the result of a detailed conversation between the authors. A fairly recent example of a successful collaboration between two scholars with related but different expertise is *The Plantation Machine: Atlantic Capitalism in French Saint-Domingue and British Jamaica*, by Trevor Burnard and John Garrigus.[16] Their study illuminates similarities and differences between the neighbouring colonies, but ultimately illustrates that 'more unites Jamaica and Saint-Domingue than separates them'.[17] The authors note that the imperative to be fully immersed in both sets of archives made 'coauthorship necessary'.[18] But their fascinating account of how that co-authorship worked is both inspiring and, for most of us, frustratingly beyond reach. They write of having been 'a part of the other's daily and weekly work life for ten years' and of a process that involved poring over each other's texts, 'editing and organizing the text one after the other and then discussing the results from our different time zones'.[19] They describe the exercise as having been 'very enjoyable' but also 'a bit cumbersome'.[20] Although, with one exception, our chapters are single-authored and none of them is the result of the kind of long-term, in-depth collaboration outlined by Burnard and Garrigus, they do at least bear the imprint of two sets of group discussions (and some careful editorial curation). The hope is that, as a result, they are more than just the sum of their parts.

Of course, the welcome opportunity to bring a group of people together under the new banner of the Colonial-Era Caribbean Theatre and Opera Network came with some inevitable restrictions. Financial and practical constraints limited the size of the group to ten scholars plus two theatre practitioners. From the point of view of having in-depth discussions and putting together an edited collection, twelve people was a good number—one that allowed for a balance between breadth and depth. It was not such a good number from the point of view of inclusivity and, when putting the group together, I had to be very selective as I sought to balance a range of regional and other expertise alongside different academic disciplines and career stages. I was, with regret, unable to invite scholars who do not speak or write in English as we were not in a position to fund interpreters or translators. The question of language is the subject of our third chapter, partly to

---

[16] Philadelphia: University of Pennsylvania Press, 2016.
[17] Burnard and Garrigus, *The Plantation Machine*, 8.
[18] Burnard and Garrigus, *The Plantation Machine*, 11.
[19] Burnard and Garrigus, *The Plantation Machine*, 349.
[20] Burnard and Garrigus, *The Plantation Machine*, 349.

highlight this very issue; in addition, we have opted throughout the volume to include all non-English quotations in their original language, followed by English translations, in order to mitigate its monolingualism. I was also unable to invite a number of other excellent scholars who would have made fine contributions to the discussions and the volume.

Although wary of dividing up the Caribbean along purely imperial or linguistic lines, I was mindful of the need to include different geographies, histories and languages when forming the group. In the end, the founding members of the network and contributors to the present volume comprised, crudely, two experts on the 'British' Caribbean (Gibbs and Weaver), two on the 'French' Caribbean (Connors and Prest) and two on the 'Spanish' Caribbean (Lane and Thomas), as well as one on the 'Dutch' Caribbean (Adams) and one whose principal expertise is New Orleans—sometimes known as the northernmost Caribbean city (Bentley). In addition, Peters is an expert on the colonial-era Caribbean *as a region*, while D'Avila, whose contribution is co-authored with theatre practitioners Bisset and Obayomi, is experienced in practice-as-research, with a particular interest in syncretic theatre and that of Latin America (a region that of course overlaps with the Caribbean). From a theatrical perspective, our combined interests and expertise span music theatre, military theatre and spoken drama of various types, as well as oratorio and the practice of making new theatre from old traditions. Although it does not (and, indeed, cannot) aim to be exhaustive, our volume does constitute the most wide-ranging contribution on the topic of colonial-era Caribbean theatre to date.

The practical updating of the (hi)story of colonial-era theatre goes some way to answering the theatre practitioner's question outlined above: one reason we study colonial-era theatre (apart from the fact that we find it interesting and important) is that our research can also be used to create new theatre for today's audiences—theatre that is at once entertaining, thought-provoking and informative, perhaps even transformative. There are at least two models for this kind of updating of colonial-era theatre for a would-be postcolonial world: the careful adaptation and decolonization of a colonial-era work and/or the creation of new works. The first model is the one recently followed by, among others, Dr Karine Bénac in her new adaptation of the anonymous three-act comedy, *Les Veuves créoles* (The Creole Widows) from 1768—the first play known to have been written in Martinique. *Les Veuves créoles* was performed in Saint-Domingue on at least two occasions in the eighteenth century but it has not, as far as we know, been performed anywhere since then.[21] In Bénac's version, premiered at the Schœlcher campus of the Université des Antilles, Martinique in April 2022 and renamed *Des Veuves créoles* (From the Creole Widows), the enslaved figure of Marie-Rose, who is silent in the original play, becomes—crucially—a speaking role whose views frame the performance. The production combined colour-blind and, especially, colour-conscious casting (most of the performers were of Afro-Caribbean heritage) and portions of the script are in Martinican Creole. Feedback questionnaires and an enthusiastic feature in the local press confirm that this adaptation of a colonial-era play was well received by local audiences.[22] The second model is the one followed by our network, and it is outlined in the chapter summaries below.

Like the Caribbean region, our chapters could be categorized and subdivided in many different ways. We have avoided grouping them by region or empire (two chapters on Saint-Domingue appear side by side only because they address related *methodological* concerns); we have also avoided ordering them chronologically as this might suggest a false sense of linearity. Instead, we have ordered them broadly by the type of methodological concern that they address. In this way, they fall into three parts: the first group (Chapters One to Three) tackles broad issues—conceptualizing the Caribbean, mobility and language—that take the reader across the Caribbean region; the second group (Chapters Four to Six) explores different approaches to colonial-era Caribbean theatre—comparative, national, colonial and contextual—via case studies that are at once focussed yet broad in their implications; and the third group (Chapters Seven to Nine, which pave the way for Chapter Ten) are concerned primarily with widening our range and use of sources and particularly with ways of filling (apparent) gaps and silences within our archives. Chapter Ten outlines the possibility of creating new theatre based on academic research in order to fill even more of the gaps and also to bridge another gap: that between historical theatre research and modern theatre practice.

Returning to *Part I: The Pan-Caribbean*, the curtain-raiser to the volume is Peters's chapter 'Studying the Colonial Caribbean: Combining

---

[21] Anon., *Les Veuves créoles*, comédie, ed. Julia Prest (Oxford: Modern Humanities Research Association, 2017).

[22] 'En images: les étudiants du campus brûlent les planches' (3 May 2022) <https://www.martinique.franceantilles.fr/regions/centre/en-images-les-etudiants-du-campus-brulent-les-planches-606063.php>.

Geographical and Imperial Approaches' (Chapter One). Peters considers what geographical areas the colonial Caribbean might be understood to comprise (is it defined primarily by land or by sea?) and how the region, however it is defined, has been approached by historians of the Caribbean in the twentieth and twenty-first centuries. He identifies a welcome shift away from traditional imperial approaches towards more regional approaches, taking us from the important foundational work of Eric Williams's *From Columbus to Castro: The History of the Caribbean, 1492–1969*[23] to Mulich's *In a Sea of Empires*, published exactly 50 years later. We have much to learn from Mulich's exploration of the inter-imperial microregion (in his case, the Leeward Islands), which convincingly demonstrates how, even on a relatively small scale, the Caribbean was a place of inter-imperial mobility, networks and exchange. As Peters observes, a strictly imperial approach to the study of theatre in the colonial-era Caribbean would distort our understanding of travelling performers (and, one might add, travelling audience members). He advocates a combined imperial and geographical approach to the study of the colonial-era Caribbean—one that allows space for the fluidity that characterized the region and cuts across its national and other boundaries. In particular, he advocates for the kind of themed study that we have produced here as a means of providing broad but focussed accounts of a region—and era—that resists easy categorization.

Bentley's chapter, 'Mobility as a Lens for Reading the History of Opera in the Colonial Caribbean' (Chapter Two), extends the geographical or regional approach to the colonial-era Caribbean by following the journeys of two individuals who worked in opera: the opera manager Max Maretzek (1821–97), and the pianist Louis Moreau Gottschalk (1829–69), both of whom have left quite detailed accounts of their experiences. Bentley questions the notion of the operatic 'circuit' which, although useful, suggests more stability and repeatability than is strictly accurate, certainly in the case of the nineteenth-century Caribbean. Maretzek and Gottschalk take Bentley and her readers to performances in New Orleans, Mexico and Havana, and on unplanned detours (necessitated by the outbreak of war in New Granada) via St Thomas, Puerto Rico, Trinidad and Barbados as well as Martinique, Guadeloupe and the Guianas. As her wide-ranging account demonstrates very clearly, strict notions of national, imperial and geographical boundaries within the Caribbean region were of less consequence for her travellers than more

---

[23] New York: Vintage Books, 1970.

practical issues such as financial gain (or loss) and the impact on travel—and performance opportunities—of the civil war in Caracas.

The third chapter dealing overtly with pan-Caribbean issues is Susan Thomas's 'Multilingual Approaches to Colonial-Era Caribbean Theatre Research: Challenges and Interventions' (Chapter Three). Thomas highlights the 'monolingual fallacy', which was a tool of colonialism and remains a modern misapprehension: what we call, say, the 'Spanish' or hispanophone Caribbean was never uniquely Spanish-speaking, nor should we assume that writing about the colonial-era Caribbean in English (another colonial language) is anything close to ideal. As she observes, the colonial-era Caribbean was a multilingual space—a place where numerous languages were spoken, and new Creoles were developed. Some theatre pieces were written in Creole. Although these languages are unequally represented in the sources that have made their way down to us, Thomas rightly notes that in order to undertake good theatre research in the field, we need—ideally—to have access to more than just one or two of those languages. This is where collaboration and translation come in. Collaboration offers the opportunity to pool and share our resources and thereby negotiate linguistic and other boundaries, while translation can offer some opportunities for reparation—Thomas prefers the 'foreignizing' approach to translation over the 'domesticating' approach, as the foreign elements in a translation remind readers that it is (only) a translation, a shadow of the real thing. We acknowledge the irony of having a chapter promoting collaboration that is single-authored, but perhaps that only serves to underline the urgency of the call for more collaboration.

Part II: Approaches opens with a chapter that addresses one of the most vexed issues of all: the relationship between (European) metropole and (Caribbean) colony. Historically, this relationship—and its assumed dynamics—has played a significant role in the neglect of colonial-era Caribbean theatre, with many people (from the colonial era to the present day) assuming that the metropole offers the model to which the colony necessarily aspires but of which it always falls short. Why study the inferior copy when you can study the model? We eschew the metropolitan model–Caribbean copy paradigm but acknowledge that much of the theatre performed in the colonial Caribbean was imported from Europe. In 'Connecting Metropole and Colony? Harlequin Travels to Suriname' (Chapter Four), Sarah J. Adams explores what unites and separates theatre performance in metropole and colony, treating each on their own terms and using the fascinating case of the black-masked figure of Harlequin as her case study. Adams demonstrates how Harlequin was racialized both in the Netherlands and in Suriname, but argues that his racialization in the theatre in Paramaribo was more richly textured and probably more threatening—at least to the colonial authorities who, for obvious reasons, had much to fear from the portrayal of the insubordination of black figures, especially when those figures used magical practices. Her account thus sheds light on the theatre traditions of both metropole and colony while also making a strong case for the distinctiveness of the latter.

Theatrical portrayals of blackness are also central to Jill Lane's chapter 'Problems of Framing: National or Colonial Approaches to Blackface Performance?' (Chapter Five). Specifically, she problematizes received wisdom about blackface as a national tradition. Bringing (Cuban) *teatro bufo* into conversation with (American) minstrelsy, Lane carefully unpicks the ways in which blackface performance came to be understood as an inherently national form, despite sharing many characteristics across different nations. As a mode grounded in racial impersonation (rather than the full integration of people of different racial ancestries), blackface performance emerges not so much as a national phenomenon, but above all as a colonial one that in fact transcended national boundaries. It was, in turn, used as a means of creating a (false) national narrative about what it meant to be Cuban or American. Lane argues that, in the context of slave societies, all performances of blackness are racial and therefore questionable—a view that would apply to all types of blackface performance across the colonial-era Caribbean.

The third chapter in this section on approaches is Wayne Weaver's 'Contextualizing Late Eighteenth-Century Jamaican Oratorio: Obstacles and Opportunities' (Chapter Six), which engages in another form of dialogue—this time between the oratorios of Jamaican-born composer Samuel Felsted, and local debates in Kingston, Jamaica, about nationhood, whiteness and racial difference. Although oratorio (a genre most closely associated with Handel) is commonly understood to sit part-way between sacred music and opera, it is clear from Felsted's scores and libretti that he conceived of his oratorios in theatrical terms. As Weaver argues, Felsted's musical and textual settings of the trials of the Jewish people, based on Old Testament accounts, will have had very different resonances in colonial Kingston from those of similar texts telling similar stories back in Europe. In particular, questions of belonging (or not), difference and slavery will have resonated strongly with people of African ancestry, but also with other marginalized groups including the local Jewish population (which was extensive) and with other 'white others', including Felsted himself who was an Anabaptist, not an Anglican. As Weaver suggests, the relationship between Felsted's experience of Kingston society and his libretti is surely a reciprocal—and therefore a specifically Caribbean—one.

Part III: Sources and Gaps opens with Jenna M. Gibbs, 'Silences in the Archive: The Mysterious One-Night Stand of John Fawcett's *Obi; or, Three-Finger'd Jack* in Kingston, Jamaica (1862)' (Chapter Seven). Here Gibbs asks why, despite the work's popularity elsewhere in the 'British' Atlantic, John Fawcett's pantomime *Obi; or Three Finger'd Jack,* was only given a single, barely documented performance in 1862 in Kingston, and how we can find out more about this performance. She explores three ways into the conundrum: the first is to use top-down sources—paradoxically—to recover information about life further down the social scale. The second is to use non-theatrical contextual evidence, notably in relation to *obeah* (a Caribbean belief-system drawing on magic rituals) and Jonkanoo—an African-derived parade that persisted in Jamaica and which features in a scene in the pantomime.[24] Gibbs's third method is to (re)consider how we as modern researchers perceive (and thus, perhaps, also create) the silences and gaps that we then seek to fill. As she acknowledges, many questions inevitably remain unanswered. But even without details about audience composition and response (key questions for many theatre researchers), we can uncover one principal explanation for the apparent wariness among local theatre producers to stage this work: as was the case for Adams's reading of Harlequin in Suriname, Fawcett's portrayal of Jonkanoo, with its overtones of black resistance (especially in the era that followed the Haitian Revolution and during that of the American Civil War) was considered dangerous by the colonial authorities.

Gibbs's chapter on missing sources is followed by two chapters on sources that are underused by theatre researchers. In 'Using Military Documents to Study Colonial-Era Theatre and Performance in Saint-Domingue' (Chapter Eight), Logan J. Connors offers an important reminder of the strong military dimension to the colonial-era Caribbean, including its theatre productions at which the military were a significant presence, and which were funded in part by the military. Military sources of interest to the theatre researcher range from official archival documents to more personal documents written by civilians about members of the military—soldiers and sailors—who had connections, direct and indirect, to the theatre. Although these sources are rich and numerous, Connors reminds us that official military sources were of course tools of the colonial regime, while failures or perceived problems

---

[24] See Davis, 'The Context Problem', for an interesting account of how context is also a contested notion.

tend to be overrepresented in such documentation. He rightly cautions against taking them all at face value and, following Stoler, counsels reading these (and perhaps all) sources both along and against the grain.[25] As we would expect, the military documented local efforts at policing society, including at the theatre, with oppressive measures put in place to control the behaviour of free and enslaved people of colour in particular; but they also documented the misdemeanours of, notably, poor white soldiers. This too is part of the colonial picture.

Chapter Nine considers one particular type of source as a means of writing enslaved people (back) into the (hi)story of colonial-era Caribbean theatre. In 'Uncovering Connections between Theatre and Slavery: Runaway Advertisements in Colonial Saint-Domingue and Beyond', I explore what can—and cannot—be uncovered from a type of source that is a staple for researchers of slavery but not for theatre researchers: the runaway advertisement. Such advertisements appeared in the same newspapers as—and often in close proximity to—advertisements for upcoming theatre performances, and some were posted by people who identified themselves explicitly as *slave-owning theatre-makers*. Although their advertisements were intended as tools of re-enslavement, they can be mined by the modern researcher for the scraps of information that they provide about enslaved individuals who otherwise slip through the archival cracks. Although the details are frustratingly thin—and can usefully be supplemented by informed speculation, as advocated by Saidiya Hartman,[26] and by additional sources and context—they do provide an undeniable bridge between theatre-making and slavery. They also hint at the contributions made to theatre-making by enslaved people—both as domestic servants and, occasionally, as professionals practising a trade.

Our volume culminates in a chapter outlining another method of filling in the gaps: the creation of a new theatre. 'Knowledge Exchange Theatre and the Colonial Caribbean: Creating *Placeholder*' (Chapter Ten), co-authored by Catherine Bisset, Flavia D'Avila and Jaïrus Obayomi, outlines and reflects on the process of writing and performing a piece inspired by research undertaken by members of the CECTON network. As the chapter authors note, what made *Placeholder* different from other plays inspired by academic research was the emphasis in the research in question on methodology. The team were particularly drawn to our

---

[25] Ann Laura Stoler, 'Colonial Archives and the Arts of Governance', *Archival Science*, 2 (2002), pp. 87–109.

[26] Saidiya Hartman, 'Venus in Two Acts', *Small Axe*, 12.2 (June 2008), pp. 1–14.

discussions about what is—and is not—found in the archive, especially the gaps surrounding the lives of enslaved people and what we do about those gaps. They were also inspired by hearing about a performer of mixed racial ancestry, called Minette, who performed in the playhouse in Port-au-Prince, and about the practice of domestic servants holding seats at various playhouses for their 'masters'. These details provided some scaffolding around which to build their own piece of evidence-based speculation or Knowledge Exchange Theatre, which was premiered at the Scottish Storytelling Centre in Edinburgh in November 2021 and performed again at the Byre Theatre in St Andrews in February 2022. Both performances were live-streamed to mixed audiences in the UK and across the world. The chapter provides a fascinating account of the process of creation that could serve as a model for future, similar endeavours seeking to retell—and decolonize—old stories in ways that speak meaningfully to today's audiences. It also includes a link to a recording of the first performance, which allows our readers to experience some of the effects of this particular approach to researching colonial-era Caribbean theatre—one that has already reached a diverse audience that extends far beyond the confines of academia. Audience response, as demonstrated by questionnaires, private correspondence and reviews (and outlined in the chapter), confirms that *Placeholder* provoked interest in—and increased understanding of—the colonial-era Caribbean and its theatre traditions. This, then, is a compelling reason for studying colonial-era Caribbean theatre.

Bibliography

Anon. *Les Veuves créoles*, comédie, ed. Julia Prest (Oxford: Modern Humanities Research Association, 2017).

Burnard, Trevor and John Garrigus. *The Plantation Machine: Atlantic Capitalism in French Saint-Domingue and British Jamaica* (Philadelphia: University of Pennsylvania Press, 2016).

Davis, Tracy C. 'The Context Problem', *Theatre Survey*, 45.2 (2004), pp. 203–09.

Dillon, Elizabeth Maddock. *New World Drama: The Performative Commons in the Atlantic World, 1649–1849* (Durham, NC and London: Duke University Press, 2014).

Dutt, Bishnupriya. 'Rethinking Categories of Theatre and Performance: Archive, Scholarship, and Practices (a Post-colonial Indian Perspective)', in Tracy C. Davis and Peter W. Marx (eds), *The Routledge Companion to Theatre and Performance Historiography* (London: Routledge, 2020), pp. 86–103.

'En images: les étudiants du campus brûlent les planches' (3 May 2022) <https://www.martinique.franceantilles.fr/regions/centre/en-images-les-etudiants-du-campus-brulent-les-planches-606063.php>.

Hartman, Saidiya. 'Venus in Two Acts', *Small Axe,* 12.2 (June 2008), pp. 1–14.

Kershaw, Baz and Helen Nicholson (eds). *Research Methods in Theatre and Performance* (Edinburgh: Edinburgh University Press, 2011).

Leichman, Jeffrey and Karine Bénac-Giroux (eds). *Colonialism and Slavery in Performance: Theatre and the Eighteenth-Century French Caribbean,* Oxford University Studies in the Enlightenment (Liverpool: Liverpool University Press, 2021).

Mulich, Jeppe. *In a Sea of Empires: Networks and Crossings in the Revolutionary Caribbean* (Cambridge: Cambridge University Press, 2020).

Roach, Joseph. *Cities of the Dead: Circum-Atlantic Performance* (New York: Columbia University Press, 1996).

Stoler, Ann Laura. 'Colonial Archives and the Arts of Governance', *Archival Science,* 2 (2002), pp. 87–109.

Stoler, Ann Laura and Frederick Cooper. 'Between Metropole and Colony: Rethinking a Research Agenda', in Frederick Cooper and Ann Laura Stoler (eds), *Tensions of Empire: Colonial Cultures in a Bourgeois World* (Berkeley: University of California Press, 1997), pp. 1–56.

Williams, Eric. *From Columbus to Castro: The History of the Caribbean, 1492–1969* (New York: Vintage Books, 1970).

Part I

The Pan-Caribbean

One

Studying the Colonial Caribbean: Combining Geographical and Imperial Approaches

Dexnell Peters

In 1799 Henry Bolingbroke travelled to the newly acquired British colony of Demerara (present day Guyana). In Georgetown, the capital city of the north-eastern South American colony, he twice witnessed some performers from the United States. Bolingbroke noted how they travelled from North America to places like Grenada, Barbados and Demerara and 'unpacked their portable theatre', to perform select scenes from the plays of Shakespeare.[1] The performers did not restrict themselves to the British territories but also visited the French Caribbean islands where local performers of African descent were enlisted to take on some parts. Similarly, the Venezuelan entertainer Louis Britto travelled the region seeking to make a living at the turn of the nineteenth century. In 1804, he left his hometown of Cumana for Puerto Rico and Martinique, returning home a decade later. His return was short-lived on account of the Spanish-American Wars of Independence. He continued to put on shows in Trinidad and in the southern Caribbean. Six months after he arrived on Trinidad, a relative of Louis's, Francisco Anthony Britto, together with his wife and his company of rope-dancers, appeared in the *Essequebo and Demerara Royal Gazette*, giving notice of their intention to leave the colony in August (and then again in October).[2] These two brief examples illustrate how performers crisscrossed the Caribbean from both North and South America and across imperial boundaries (a subject that is discussed at greater length in Chapter Two of this volume). Furthermore, they highlight the strong relationships that existed between the Caribbean islands and nearby territories

---

[1] Henry Bolingbroke, *A Voyage to the Demerary: Containing a Statistical Account of the Settlements There, and of Those on the Essequebo, the Berbice, and Other Contiguous Rivers of Guyana* (London and Norwich: R. Phillips Stevenson and Matchett, 1807), pp. 42–43.

[2] 'Secretary's Office', *Demerary and Essequebo Royal Gazette*, 15 August 1815.

on the American mainland and the porous borders of regions of the Atlantic world.

This chapter will explore some of the methodological approaches to studying the colonial Caribbean and consider the best approach to fully reveal the lives of all the people who lived in, moved around within or passed through the Caribbean during the colonial era. It will first reflect on the traditional 'imperial' approach before exploring geographical and trans-national approaches, including situating the Caribbean within the broader context of the Atlantic world. These later approaches have led to some positive developments, but there is still a need to sharpen the focus more, as in the present volume on colonial-era theatre, in order to ensure a greater understanding of this complex early modern region. One way of achieving this is to pay more attention to the shifting trans-imperial Greater Caribbean region, which includes both mainland American territories washed by the Caribbean Sea (as in Chapter Four of this volume, in which theatre in the then Dutch colony of Suriname is discussed) and the islands. Combining imperial and geographical approaches through the lens of this region can better follow the natural contours of regional processes in the Caribbean that were shaped by global, imperial, regional and local contexts. It allows us to pay more attention to the various zones of interaction that emerged within the wider region (including those where places such as New Orleans, Curaçao, St Eustatius and Trinidad served as key nodes in the Gulf, southern and northern Greater Caribbean subregions) and how these different areas interacted over time. Such an approach, tracing the naturally developing zones of interaction that helped to shape islands and surrounding mainland territories in different ways, should help us gain a deeper understanding of the colonial Caribbean. Although not all of the areas discussed in this introductory chapter were home to a theatre tradition during the colonial era, it is worth considering the colonial Caribbean as a concept before focussing in subsequent chapters on some of the areas in which theatre did become prominent.

Traditionally, the Caribbean has been divided up into several imperial zones with separate imperial and, later, national historiographies. Historians have therefore divided the region into European-defined geographical and cultural zones. As a result, histories of the region have clearly demarked a 'British', 'French', 'Spanish' and 'Dutch' Caribbean as part of much broader imperial networks.[3] The process of colonialism

---

[3] For some examples of regional imperial histories, see Kenneth R. Andrews, *The Spanish Caribbean: Trade and Plunder, 1530–1630* (New Haven, CT: Yale University Press, 1978); Philip P. Boucher, *France and the American Tropics*

was indeed important to the development of the Atlantic world and the early modern Caribbean, and should therefore continue to be given attention. This must, however, be done increasingly from a less Eurocentric perspective, de-emphasizing a primary focus on the ways Europeans shaped and defined the region. Carrie Gibson's regional history *Empire's Crossroads* tries to address this issue, noting that after 1492 the Caribbean was marked by the 'encounter between Europeans and other peoples'.[4] It also makes it clear that this did not mean that Europeans made the islands what they have become but rather started 'a process both destructive and constructive', that has helped shape their development today.[5] Overview regional studies of the Caribbean have continued to divide the region into distinct imperial zones but have focussed increasingly on key themes and the comparative or shared processes that shaped the region.

Nevertheless, some important limitations to the imperial approach remain, especially in exploring aspects of the Caribbean's history that do not neatly fit into an imperial context or that sit outside key imperial priorities. The imperial approach has, for example, given short shrift to indigenous communities who factor less and less in early modern European records of the Caribbean, especially regarding the islands. As a result, imperial histories have tended to begin with the Columbian exchange, ignoring pre-contact periods, and even within the colonial period indigenous people often fade out of the picture over time. Yet, as David Weber very interestingly points out, 'in the late 1700s independent Indians still had effective dominion over at least half of the actual land mass of what is today continental Latin America, from Tierra del Fuego to present day Mexico'.[6] These independent, indigenous groups did not have a uniform interaction with Spaniards

---

to 1700: Tropics of Discontent? (Baltimore, MD: Johns Hopkins University Press, 2008); Richard S. Dunn, *Sugar and Slaves: The Rise of the Planter Class in the English West Indies, 1624–1713* (Chapel Hill, NC: University of North Carolina Press, 1972); Cornelis Christiaan Goslinga, *The Dutch in the Caribbean and in the Guianas, 1680–1791*, Vol. 19 (Assen, Netherlands; Dover, NH: Van Gorcum, 1985); Neville Hall, *Slave Society in the Danish West Indies: St Thomas, St John and St Croix* (Barbados, Jamaica and Trinidad: University of the West Indies Press, 1992).

[4] Carrie Gibson, *Empire's Crossroads: A History of the Caribbean from Columbus to the Present Day* (New York: Atlantic Monthly Press, 2014), p. xviii.

[5] Gibson, *Empire's Crossroads*, xviii.

[6] David J. Weber, *Bárbaros: Spaniards and their Savages in the Age of Enlightenment* (New Haven, CT: Yale University Press, 2005), p. 12.

in the Americas. In some areas, they threatened Spanish hegemony. Moreover, some forcefully made Spaniards accept their autonomy and even extracted tribute from them.[7] Some treatment of interactions with indigenous people has been noted in the imperial approach when they were involved in major conflicts, but still indigenous people often slip through the cracks.

Snippets of the activities of indigenous people can be seen in colonial records, but they quickly disappear if only viewed through an imperial lens. For example, in 1794 missionaries operating at Hoop, located by the Corentyn River on the mainland of Dutch Guiana, observed a group of indigenous people whom they described as 'Arawaks' arrive at the mission. They noted among these indigenous people a 'Spanish Indian' named Martin who was a native of Trinidad.[8] Martin had been an overseer of Christian Arawaks at St Michael on the Orinoco River, on the Spanish mainland. He left his post and ended up at the Hoop mission. By the turn of the nineteenth century, in the midst of a British-ruled island, there continued to be transient indigenous people. In 1800 a 'Guyacaree Indian', as the colonial records describe him, from Margarita helped transport three German refugees from Trinidad to the mainland. Accused of being complicit with the German deserters, he was executed without trial.[9] The ease with which Indians moved around Trinidad, even if it involved dangers and hardship, is apparent. The stories of these groups of indigenous people who moved across the British, Spanish and Dutch southern Caribbean imperial boundaries could not be fully traced through any single imperial lens.

The same remains the case for the travelling performers that introduced this chapter. They did not see their audiences as bound to any one imperial sphere of influence. Rather, they built networks that expanded across imperial boundaries. Bolingbroke's knowledge of the North American performers and their tour of the Greater Caribbean is evidence of the spread of information across the trans-imperial region. He described how well received the performers were across the British and French Caribbean and that there was enough demand for stays of three months. We also learn that in the French colonies they sometimes enlisted people of African descent to perform some roles in 'maritime

---

[7] Weber, *Bárbaros*, 9.
[8] *Periodical Accounts Relating to the Missions of the Church of the United Brethren Established Among the Heathen*, Vol. 1 (London: W. M'Cowall for the Brethren's Society for the Furtherance of the Gospel among the Heathen, 1790), p. 379.
[9] Thomas Courtenay, *Letters of Decius, in Answer to Criticism upon the Political Account of Trinidad* (London: John Morton, 1808), p. 35.

companies'.[10] The lives of these performers could not be effectively traced from the imperial approach.

It is these limitations that have given rise to some newer trans-imperial and geographical approaches to studying the colonial-era Caribbean. Historians and other researchers have increasingly attempted to write more cohesive, trans-imperial, regional accounts of the Caribbean. Eric Williams's *From Columbus to Castro* was an early attempt at a pan-Caribbean history of the region. Although the book did not consider the pre-contact period, it sought to include the whole region, paying particular attention to the British, Spanish, French and later American-influenced spheres of the Caribbean. Williams's intent in writing the book was clear: he sought to provide a well-defined sense of the major international forces shaping the region's history 'from Columbus to Castro' and to advocate for regional integration among all the units of the Caribbean as the most important way forward.[11] Later regional histories, such as Franklin Knight's, began their narrative with a pre-Hispanic or pre-Columbian period. While Knight recognized that imperial subregions existed, he noted that the 'Caribbean does form a cohesive geographic and cultural area, although one that is neither uniform nor united'.[12] For Knight, the region witnessed many more common experiences than differences, if not always at the same time. Therefore, he proposed that comparisons of the Caribbean should be systadial (at the same stage) and not synchronic (at the same time). In the case of the institution of slavery, for example, there was tremendous diversity of experience in the form, scale and scope that it took on across the region. Yet at one stage or the other, slavery played a fundamental role. Whether pertaining to the initial enslavement of indigenous people, the large-scale enslavement of people of African descent or the role enslaved persons played in particular colonial industries, the institution of slavery shaped the whole region. Much more deliberate efforts at trans-imperial histories of the region have come from collaborative, edited volumes that have provided more deliberate comparative focus and efforts to synthesize the overall Caribbean experience. The UNESCO *General History of the Caribbean* series covered the regions through five chronological and thematic themes that spanned the pre-Columbian era to the twentieth century, and paid separate attention

---

[10] Bolingbroke, *A Voyage to the Demerary*, 43.
[11] Eric Williams, *From Columbus to Castro: The History of the Caribbean, 1492–1969* (New York: Vintage Books, 1970).
[12] Franklin Knight, *The Caribbean, the Genesis of a Fragmented Nationalism* (New York: Oxford University Press, 1978), p. ix.

to the indigenous people and slave societies of the region alongside a consideration of methodology and historiography. The series drew on historians working on the various parts and in the varied languages of the Caribbean, and aimed to be a 'marker towards a fully integrated Caribbean history'.[13] More recently, Stephan Palmié and Francisco Scarano's 40-chapter edited volume on the history of the Caribbean attempted a feat similar to the UNESCO series, aiming to produce a more updated synthesis of recent scholarship.[14] The book includes efforts to compare experiences across different imperial subgroups, people groups and geographies.

Beyond attempts at more integrated regional histories, other scholars have sought to situate the region within a broader global context. Some have argued that the Caribbean stood at the centre of the emerging Atlantic world during the early modern period. Eric Williams described the Caribbean as the 'cockpit of Europe'.[15] He saw it as being at the centre of an international arena of power politics. Philip Morgan similarly noted that:

> the Caribbean has the dubious distinction of being the first region in the Americas to be introduced to slavery, sugarcane and the plantation system. Nowhere was the influence of this unholy trinity more systematically and intensely felt [...] Arguably then, the Caribbean was the focal point of overseas European expansion in the early modern world.[16]

As a result, Morgan argues that it is crucial to study the region within the broader context of the Atlantic world. Indeed, there has been a fine range of work highlighting the significance of situating the region in this broader context.[17] Recent works on the Haitian Revolution provide

---

[13] Franklin Knight (ed.), *General History of the Caribbean: The Slave Societies of the Caribbean* (Basingstoke: UNESCO Publishing, 1997), p. xi.

[14] Stephan Palmié and Francisco Scarano (eds), *The Caribbean: A History of the Region and its Peoples* (Chicago: University of Chicago Press, 2013).

[15] Williams, *From Columbus to Castro*, chapter 7.

[16] Philip Morgan, 'The Caribbean Islands in Atlantic Context, circa 1500–1800', in Felicity A. Nussbaum (ed.), *The Global Eighteenth Century* (Baltimore, MD and London: Johns Hopkins University Press, 2003), pp. 52–64.

[17] Two early significant works were Cyril Lionel Robert James, *The Black Jacobins: Toussaint L'Ouverture and the San Domingo Revolution* (New York: Vintage Books, 1989), which connected the French Revolution with the Haitian Revolution, and Eric Williams's *Capitalism and Slavery* (Chapel Hill, NC: University of North Carolina Press, 1944), which explored the contributions

a good example of this as they seek to situate the revolution within broader Atlantic and global contexts, and most specifically within the Atlantic Age of Revolutions. Historians have sought to identify the influences of the revolutionary era on the Haitian Revolution and in turn establish its wider impact within and beyond the Atlantic world.[18]

Alongside this broader context, there is also a need to sharpen focus a bit more to ensure greater understanding of this significant early modern region. This process requires paying more attention to what exactly the colonial Caribbean region is. Definitions of the region have largely focussed on the islands within the Caribbean Sea. Barry Higman's *A Concise History of the Caribbean* confined his analysis to the islands in order to simplify the task. He acknowledged larger regional conceptions such as the Greater Caribbean but noted that 'they have validity for some periods and patterns of development but not for all'.[19] He confined the narrative to the islands to set limits and provide an ecological coherence that could enable an attempt to write a systematic comparative history. Perhaps more commonly, regional histories have tended to include the Guianas and Belize as part of the Caribbean. Frank Moya Pons notes that 'because of longstanding economic and social connections, some regions, like the Guianas and Belize are normally considered to have shared their history with the Caribbean'.[20] Similarly, the UNESCO *General History of the Caribbean* defined the region as

of Caribbean slavery to the British economy. More recently, see Alejandro de la Fuente, *Havana and the Atlantic in the Sixteenth Century* (Chapel Hill, NC: University of North Carolina Press, 2008); Douglas Hamilton, *Scotland, the Caribbean, and the Atlantic World, 1750–1820* (Manchester: Manchester University Press, 2005); Adrian Leonard and David Pretel (eds), *The Caribbean and the Atlantic World Economy Circuits of Trade, Money and Knowledge, 1650–1914* (London: Palgrave Macmillan, 2015).

[18] Matthew J. Clavin, *Toussaint Louverture and the American Civil War: The Promise and Peril of a Second Haitian Revolution* (Philadelphia: University of Pennsylvania Press, 2010); Laurent Dubois, 'An Atlantic Revolution', *French Historical Studies*, 32.4 (2009), pp. 655–61; David Geggus, 'The Haitian Revolution in Atlantic Perspective', in Philip Morgan and Nicholas Canny (eds), *The Oxford Handbook of the Atlantic World* (New York: Oxford University Press, 2011), pp. 533–49; David P. Geggus (ed.), *The Impact of the Haitian Revolution in the Atlantic World* (Columbia, SC: University of South Carolina Press, 2001); David Geggus and Norman Fiering (eds), *The World of the Haitian Revolution* (Bloomington: Indiana University Press, 2009).

[19] Barry Higman, *A Concise History of the Caribbean* (New York: Cambridge University Press, 2010), p. xi.

[20] Frank Pons, *History of the Caribbean* (Princeton, NJ: Markus Wiener Publishers, 2012).

'encompassing not only the islands but also the coastal part of South America, from Colombia to the Guyanas and the riverine zones of Central America, insofar as these parts of the mainland were the homes of people engaged from time to time in activities which linked their lives with those of people in the islands'.[21] Ultimately, the decision about which territories to consider as part of the region has been strongly connected to the imperial tradition of studying Caribbean history. The inclusion of the Guianas and Belize has more to do with the fact that they were outliers on the Central and South American mainland—they were not part of Iberian America and were, by imperial affiliation, more connected to the islands. More concrete definitions of the Caribbean have therefore been determined by some clear imperial boundaries.

Exploring a broader and somewhat looser definition of the region that caters more to changes over time and that takes greater advantage of the innovations within the fields of global and trans-national history can be a useful way of considering the region. French Caribbean historian Oruno Lara, for example, emphasizes the need to consider other territories whenever they seem to shed light on the Caribbean. He argues that definitions should be seen as 'situational, fluid and shifting according to the period, and the theme, being studied'.[22] We should therefore pay more attention to when and how islands and surrounding mainland territories come into the picture.

The concept of the 'Greater Caribbean' offers a way to integrate the histories of some of the well-established regions of the Americas and to truly understand how the region was constituted across the early modern period. The region was perhaps most significantly conceived with one main thematic focus: the institution of slavery. American anthropologist Charles Wagley first delineated a 'Plantation America' which spatially covered from Brazil to the North American South.[23] The key characteristic of this region was the prevalence of the plantation system and slavery, centred mainly in the Caribbean and connected primarily to non-white labour and towards the production of key commodities such as sugar, coffee, cacao and cotton. As David Gaspar

---

[21] Knight (ed.), *General History*, vi.
[22] Oruno Lara, *Caraïbes en construction: espace, colonisation, résistance* (Montpellier: Publications du Cercam, 1992), cited in Bridget Brereton, 'Regional Histories', in Barry Higman (ed.), *General History of the Caribbean*, Vol. 6: *Methodology and Historiography of the Caribbean* (London and Oxford: UNESCO Publishing and Macmillan Education, 1999), p. 321.
[23] Charles Wagley, 'Plantation America: A Culture Sphere', in Vera Rubin and Verne Ray (eds), *Caribbean Studies: A Symposium* (Seattle, WA: University of Washington Press, 1960), pp. 3–13.

and David Geggus note, there was an 'interconnectedness about this wider region in which networks of trade and mobility of the free and the enslaved populations made it possible for news to spread from one corner to another and to produce results that could clearly transcend national, linguistic and geographical boundaries'.[24] The concept of a Plantation America has since been expanded to consider other key aspects that drew the region together.[25]

A focus on the Greater Caribbean emphasizes the nature of relationships that were fully experienced across all territories washed by the Caribbean Sea. Newer research has challenged the boundaries of the region and put into question previous geographical understandings of imperial zones. Matthew Mulcahy, for example, has recently made a claim for Barbados, Jamaica, the British Leeward Islands, South Carolina and the Georgia Lowcountry to be considered a distinct region known as the 'British Greater Caribbean'. As he notes, the Carolina and Georgia Lowcountry with 'an economy focused on rice production and a majority population of enslaved Africans, has long been viewed as a place apart from the other mainland colonies, its history and experiences often seemed too different, too distinct to fit into larger narratives concerning

---

[24] David Barry Gaspar and David Geggus (eds), *A Turbulent Time: The French Revolution and the Greater Caribbean* (Bloomington: Indiana University Press, 1997), p. viii.

[25] For current works on the Greater Caribbean, see Ernesto Bassi, *An Aqueous Territory: Sailor Geographies and New Granada's Transimperial Greater Caribbean World* (Durham, NC: Duke University Press, 2016); Matthew Mulcahy, *Hubs of Empire: The Southeastern Lowcountry and British Caribbean* (Baltimore, MD: Johns Hopkins Press, 2014); Stuart B. Schwartz, *A Sea of Storms: A History of Hurricanes in the Greater Caribbean from Columbus to Katrina* (Princeton, NJ: Princeton University Press, 2016); John Robert McNeill, *Mosquito Empires: Ecology and War in the Greater Caribbean, 1620–1914* (Cambridge: Cambridge University Press, 2010); Matthew Mulcahy, *Hurricanes and Society in the British Greater Caribbean, 1624–1783* (Baltimore, MD: Johns Hopkins University Press, 2008); Gaspar and Geggus (eds), *A Turbulent Time*; Stuart McCook, 'The Neo-Columbian Exchange: The Second Conquest of the Greater Caribbean, 1720–1930', *Latin American Research Review*, 46(S) (2011), pp. 11–31; Lara Putnam, 'Borderlands and Border-Crossers: Migrants and Boundaries in the Greater Caribbean, 1840–1940', *Small Axe*, 18.1 (2014), pp. 7–21; Nathalie Dessens, 'From Saint Domingue to Louisiana: West Indian Refugees in the Lower Mississippi Region', in Bradley Bond (ed.), *French Colonial Louisiana and the Atlantic World* (Baton Rouge: Louisiana State University Press, 2005), 265–90; Aline Helg, *Liberty and Equality in Caribbean Colombia, 1770–1835* (Chapel Hill, NC: University of North Carolina Press, 2004).

the 13 colonies as anything other than exceptions'.[26] Mulcahy argues rather that the Lowcountry had more of a shared history with the Caribbean and developed as social and economic extensions of Barbados. His concept of the British Greater Caribbean has been further supported by recent work from Paul Pressly, who makes a similar claim for Georgia sharing connections to the Caribbean until the American Revolution initiated a process that oriented the territory more towards the North American mainland.[27]

Recent work on the early 'Spanish' Caribbean has emphasized that, far from being a backwater, the Caribbean islands were well intertwined in regional Spanish networks with the mainland colonies. A recent edited volume by Ida Altman and David Wheat has argued that the early Spanish Caribbean should certainly include 'coastal Spanish settlements from eastern Venezuela to the Gulf of Mexico'.[28] They divide the region into four, overlapping, geographical quadrants:

(i) the major islands or Greater Antilles (Hispaniola, Puerto Rico, Cuba and Jamaica)

(ii) the south-eastern Caribbean, consisting of Venezuela and neighbouring islands such as Curaçao, Margarita and Trinidad

(iii) the south-western mainland including Panama and the provinces of Cartagena de Indias and

(iv) the Gulf region, comprising western Cuba, Yucatan, Veracruz and Florida.[29]

While these works have been useful in helping to reconceptualize regional intra-imperial networks in the Caribbean, there is perhaps greater fruit to be yielded from studies that step beyond specific imperial contexts to more precisely explore the broader processes across the trans-imperial Greater Caribbean. It is this approach that can best reveal the lives of those such as Venezuelan entertainer Louis Britto, who regularly performed across nearby Caribbean islands.

[26] Mulcahy, *Hubs of Empire*, 3.
[27] Paul Pressly, *On the Rim of the Caribbean: Colonial Georgia and the British Atlantic World* (Athens: University of Georgia Press, 2013).
[28] Ida Altman and David Wheat (eds), *The Spanish Caribbean and the Atlantic World in the Long Sixteenth Century* (Lincoln: University of Nebraska Press, 2019).
[29] Altman and Wheat (eds), *The Spanish Caribbean*, xvi.

Recent works have begun to unpack the greater connections within the region, including Jeppe Mulich's *In a Sea of Empires: Networks and Crossings in the Revolutionary Caribbean*, which provides rich details on the politically polyglot Leeward Islands and makes a claim for an inter-imperial microregion marked by a multiplicity of intersecting networks and significant border-crossing that supported processes of regional integration.[30] Ada Ferrer's recent work in *Freedom's Mirror*, which examines the impact of the Haitian Revolution on Cuba, is another example of a study incorporating richer subregional context alongside broader Atlantic-wide processes.[31]

Other studies have explored the nature of interactions into the surrounding mainland territories. Shannon Dawdy's *Building the Devil's Empire: French Colonial New Orleans* and Cécile Vidal's *Caribbean New Orleans: Empire, Race, and the Making of a Slave Society* connect Louisiana to wider Greater Caribbean networks.[32] Linda Marguerite Rupert's *Creolization and Contraband: Curaçao in the Early Modern Atlantic World* pays particular attention to rich relationships emerging between Curaçao and Venezuela.[33] Ernesto Bassi's recent work *An Aqueous Territory* argues for a 'transimperial Greater Caribbean', a region configured by the crisscrossing of sailors across the political borders of the Caribbean Sea. He traces the connections between the Caribbean coast of New Granada, the Greater Antilles, Curaçao and St Thomas, arguing that a de facto free trade zone emerged.[34] Similarly, Julius Scott's *The Common Wind* traces the spread of information across closely developed regional networks that allowed free and enslaved people of African descent to remain well informed of events across the Greater Caribbean.[35] Scott elaborates on the web of commerce, including both legal and illicit trade, that knitted the region's islands and nearby mainland territories together.

My own research focusses on the development of a subregion— the Greater Southern Caribbean—that developed in a new way from

---

[30] Jeppe Mulich, *In a Sea of Empires: Networks and Crossings in the Revolutionary Caribbean* (Cambridge: Cambridge University Press, 2020).

[31] Ada Ferrer, *Freedom's Mirror: Cuba and Haiti in the Age of Revolution* (New York and Cambridge: Cambridge University Press, 2014).

[32] Shannon Lee Dawdy, *Building the Devil's Empire: French Colonial New Orleans* (Chicago: University of Chicago Press, 2008); Cécile Vidal, *Caribbean New Orleans: Empire, Race, and the Making of a Slave Society* (Chapel Hill, NC: University of North Carolina Press, 2020).

[33] Athens: University of Georgia Press, 2012.

[34] Bassi, *An Aqueous Territory*.

[35] Julius Sherrard Scott III, *The Common Wind: Afro-American Currents in the Age of the Haitian Revolution* (London: Verso, 2020).

the mid-eighteenth century and which began to fracture from the immediate post-emancipation period. The second half of the eighteenth century saw the growth of the Windward Islands, the southern Dutch Antilles and the southern rimland. These developments, together with the continued importance of well-established Barbados, make it possible to conceive of a new zone of interaction, encompassing Venezuela and its offshore islands, the Guianas, Trinidad and Tobago, and the Lesser Antillean chain from Dominica to the Grenadines. Although focussed on a broader region, my ongoing research is largely premised on the belief that the island of Trinidad and the South American mainland colony Demerara (now Guyana), despite significant differences, both experienced sudden and dramatic development from the late eighteenth century which helped to consolidate a polyglot, cross-imperial and interconnected region.

Other studies have moved beyond specific locales to explore significant themes or phenomena. For example, a number of environmental histories have recently defined a Greater Caribbean as well, including Stuart B. Schwartz's *A Sea of Storms* and John Robert McNeill's *Mosquito Empires*.[36] These works conceptualize the region through the shared experience of environmental phenomena such as hurricanes and disease.

While trans-national histories of the Greater Caribbean are including more indigenous actors, there remains room for much more focussed attention on indigenous communities.[37] It has become clear from scholars of the pre-contact period that 'the Caribbean Sea during the pre-colonial period did not separate, but rather linked communities, supporting mobility and exchange'.[38] There needs to be more focus on how pre-existing regional networks persisted into the colonial era. Archaeologists such as Arie Boomert and Irving Rouse have argued for the rich integration of mainland territories with the islands at all

---

[36] Schwartz, *A Sea of Storms*; McNeill, *Mosquito Empires*. See also Mulcahy, *Hurricanes*.

[37] Recent work on the Red Atlantic has deliberately made efforts to bring indigenous communities to the forefront of Atlantic History. See Jace Weaver, *The Red Atlantic: American Indigenes and the Making of the Modern World, 1000–1927* (Chapel Hill, NC: University of North Carolina Press, 2014).

[38] Corinne Hofman and Eithne Carlin, 'The Ever-Dynamic Caribbean: Exploring New Approaches to Unraveling Social Networks in the Pre-Colonial and Early Colonial Periods', in Eithne Carlin and Simon van de Kerke (eds), *Linguistics and Archaeology in the Americas: The Historicization of Language and Society* (Leiden and Boston, MA: Brill, 2010), p. 108.

corners of the Caribbean—and especially in the southern Caribbean near north-east South America—that persisted into the Age of Revolutions.

Perhaps one concern with a broader and looser definition of the Caribbean is the fear of shifting focus away from central activities within the Caribbean Sea and further infusion with continental narratives. At the heart of a broader definition of the Caribbean must remain a vantage point from the Caribbean Sea and its islands. In considering the early Spanish Caribbean, Altman argues that 'nearly all the elements that later would characterize the complex societies of the Spanish American mainland [...] existed in the islands within fifteen to twenty years of Columbus's arrival in 1492'.[39] Spanish civil and ecclesiastical institutions were established, a diverse population had to be managed and a coerced labour system developed. Altman also reveals the early source of policies related to family and colonization. She notes that the policies of Spanish officials in the early Spanish Caribbean reveal that they saw marriage and family as crucial to social stability and economic prosperity. Similarly, Jack Greene describes Barbados as 'the cultural hearth of the British Greater Caribbean'.[40] The sugar revolution, which first touched down in Barbados, had a significant impact. Chiefly, the plantation complex took shape and would later spread to the British Leeward Islands and into British mainland America. For Bassi, the trans-imperial Greater Caribbean spans mostly the South American coastal regions and the islands of the Caribbean. To sharpen focus is to trace much more closely the boundaries of the Greater Caribbean over time seen from different vantage points.

Travelling performers such as the Britto family and other troupes like the ones our British traveller observed in Demerara sailed across an extended Caribbean region. Coming from different cardinal points across mainland America, they crisscrossed traditional regions and imperial spheres of the Americas as they travelled up and down the islands of the Caribbean Sea. Their stories reveal the usefulness of our combining imperial and geographical approaches as modern scholars. A combined approach has the potential to better follow the natural contours of regional processes in the Caribbean shaped by global, imperial, regional and local contexts. It allows us to pay more attention to the various zones of interaction that emerged within the wider region and to the ways in which different parts of the region interacted with

[39] Ida Altman, 'Marriage, Family, and Ethnicity in the Early Spanish Caribbean', *The William and Mary Quarterly*, 70.2 (April 2013), pp. 225–50.
[40] Jack Greene, 'Colonial South Carolina and the Caribbean Connection', *South Carolina Historical Magazine*, 88.4 (1987), pp. 192–210.

each other over time. Far from suggesting strict, broad definitions, the region appears to have been a site of fluidity and fluctuations at times and of stability at other times—something that needs to be clarified more. Broad regional histories accounting for all these nuances may be a difficult feat to accomplish, but—collectively—individual works continuing to piece together the dynamics of the region at different times and places will help significantly. Furthermore, single-themed volumes exploring the region provide an opportunity to explore some of these nuances of shifting boundaries and the natural relationships or zones of interaction that emerged and that may look different across different themes. A focus on theatre in the colonial Caribbean in specific locations but contextualized by the wider Caribbean ecosystem can assist the process of complicating—and clarifying—our understanding of the internal dynamics and shifting definitions of the region over time.

Bibliography

Altman, Ida. 'Marriage, Family, and Ethnicity in the Early Spanish Caribbean', *William and Mary Quarterly*, 70.2 (2013), pp. 225–50.

Altman, Ida, and David Wheat (eds). *The Spanish Caribbean and the Atlantic World in the Long Sixteenth Century* (Lincoln: University of Nebraska Press, 2019).

Andrews, Kenneth. *The Spanish Caribbean: Trade and Plunder, 1530–1630* (New Haven, CT: Yale University Press, 1978).

Bassi, Ernesto. *An Aqueous Territory: Sailor Geographies and New Granada's Transimperial Greater Caribbean World* (Durham, NC: Duke University Press, 2016).

Bolingbroke, Henry. *A Voyage to the Demerary: Containing a Statistical Account of the Settlements There, and of Those on the Essequebo, the Berbice, and Other Contiguous Rivers of Guyana* (London and Norwich: R. Phillips Stevenson and Matchett, 1807).

Bond, Bradley. *French Colonial Louisiana and the Atlantic World* (Baton Rouge: Lousiana State University Press, 2005).

Boucher, Philip. *France and the American Tropics to 1700: Tropics of Discontent?* (Baltimore, MD: Johns Hopkins University Press, 2008).

Brereton, Bridget. 'Regional Histories', in Barry Higman (ed.), *General History of the Caribbean*, Vol. 6: *Methodology and Historiography of the Caribbean* (London and Oxford: UNESCO Publishing and Macmillan Education, 1999), pp. 308–42.

Clavin, Matthew. *Toussaint Louverture and the American Civil War: The Promise and Peril of a Second Haitian Revolution* (Philadelphia: University of Pennsylvania Press, 2010).
Courtenay, Thomas. *Letters of Decius, in Answer to Criticism upon the Political Account of Trinidad* (London: John Morton, 1808).
Dawdy, Shannon Lee. *Building the Devil's Empire: French Colonial New Orleans* (Chicago: University of Chicago Press, 2008).
de la Fuente, Alejandro. *Havana and the Atlantic in the Sixteenth Century* (Chapel Hill, NC: University of North Carolina Press, 2008).
Dessens, Nathalie. 'From Saint Domingue to Louisiana: West Indian Refugees in the Lower Mississippi Region', in Bradley Bond (ed.), *French Colonial Louisiana and the Atlantic World* (Baton Rouge: Louisiana State University Press, 2005), pp. 265–90.
Dubois, Laurent. 'An Atlantic Revolution', *French Historical Studies*, 32.4 (2009), pp. 655–61.
Dunn, Richard. *Sugar and Slaves: The Rise of the Planter Class in the English West Indies, 1624–1713* (Chapel Hill, NC: University of North Carolina Press, 1972).
Ferrer, Ada. *Freedom's Mirror: Cuba and Haiti in the Age of Revolution* (New York and Cambridge: Cambridge University Press, 2014).
Gaspar, David and David Geggus (eds). *A Turbulent Time: The French Revolution and the Greater Caribbean* (Bloomington: Indiana University Press, 1997).
Geggus, David. 'The Haitian Revolution in Atlantic Perspective', in Philip Morgan and Nicholas Canny (eds), *The Oxford Handbook of the Atlantic World* (New York: Oxford University Press, 2011), pp. 533–49.
Geggus, David (ed.). *The Impact of the Haitian Revolution in the Atlantic World* (Columbia, SC: University of South Carolina Press, 2001).
Geggus, David and Norman Fiering (eds). *The World of the Haitian Revolution* (Bloomington: Indiana University Press, 2009).
Gibson, Carrie. *Empire's Crossroads: A History of the Caribbean from Columbus to the Present Day* (New York: Atlantic Monthly Press, 2014).
Goslinga, Cornelis Christiaan. *The Dutch in the Caribbean and in the Guianas, 1680–1791* (Assen, Netherlands; Dover, NH: Van Gorcum, 1985).
Greene, Jack. 'Colonial South Carolina and the Caribbean Connection', *The South Carolina Historical Magazine*, 88.4 (1987), pp. 192–210.
Hall, Neville. *Slave Society in the Danish West Indies: St Thomas, St John and St Croix* (Barbados, Jamaica and Trinidad: University of the West Indies Press, 1992).
Hamilton, Douglas. *Scotland, the Caribbean and the Atlantic World, 1750–1820* (Manchester: Manchester University Press, 2005).
Helg, Aline. *Liberty and Equality in Caribbean Colombia, 1770–1835* (Chapel Hill, NC: University of North Carolina Press, 2004).
Higman, Barry. *A Concise History of the Caribbean* (New York: Cambridge University Press, 2010).

Hofman, Corinne and Eithne Carlin. 'The Ever-Dynamic Caribbean: Exploring New Approaches to Unraveling Social Networks in the Pre-Colonial and Early Colonial Periods', in Eithne Carlin and Simon van de Kerke (eds), *Linguistics and Archaeology in the Americas: The Historicization of Language and Society* (Leiden and Boston, MA: Brill, 2010), pp. 107–22.

James, Cyril Lionel Robert. *The Black Jacobins: Toussaint L'Ouverture and the San Domingo Revolution* (New York: Vintage Books, 1989).

Knight, Franklin. *The Caribbean, the Genesis of a Fragmented Nationalism* (New York: Oxford University Press, 1978).

Knight, Franklin (ed.). *General History of the Caribbean: The Slave Societies of the Caribbean* (Basingstoke: UNESCO Publishing, 1997).

Lara, Oruno. *Caraïbes en construction: espace, colonisation, résistance* (Montpellier: Publications du Cercam, 1992).

Leonard, Adrian and David Pretel (eds). *The Caribbean and the Atlantic World Economy: Circuits of Trade, Money and Knowledge, 1650–1914* (London: Palgrave Macmillan, 2015).

McCook, Stuart. 'The Neo-Columbian Exchange: The Second Conquest of the Greater Caribbean, 1720–1930', *Latin American Research Review*, 46(S) (2011), pp. 11–31.

McNeill, John. *Mosquito Empires: Ecology and War in the Greater Caribbean, 1620–1914* (Cambridge: Cambridge University Press, 2010).

Morgan, Philip. 'The Caribbean Islands in Atlantic Context, circa 1500–1800', in Felicity Nussbaum (ed.), *The Global Eighteenth Century* (Baltimore, MD: Johns Hopkins University Press, 2003), pp. 52–64.

Mulcahy, Matthew. *Hubs of Empire: The Southeastern Lowcountry and British Caribbean* (Baltimore, MD: Johns Hopkins University Press, 2014).

Mulcahy, Matthew. *Hurricanes and Society in the British Greater Caribbean, 1624–1783* (Baltimore, MD: Johns Hopkins University Press, 2008).

Mulich, Jeppe. *In a Sea of Empires: Networks and Crossings in the Revolutionary Caribbean* (Cambridge: Cambridge University Press, 2020).

Palmié, Stephan and Francisco Scarano (eds). *The Caribbean: A History of the Region and its Peoples* (Chicago: University of Chicago Press, 2013).

Periodical Accounts Relating to the Missions of the Church of the United Brethren Established Among the Heathen, Vol. 1 (London: W. M'Cowall for the Brethren's Society for the Furtherance of the Gospel among the Heathen, 1790).

Pons, Frank. *History of the Caribbean* (Princeton, NJ: Markus Wiener Publishers, 2012).

Pressly, Paul. *On the Rim of the Caribbean: Colonial Georgia and the British Atlantic World* (Athens: University of Georgia Press, 2013).

Putnam, Lara. 'Borderlands and Border Crossers: Migrants and Boundaries in the Greater Caribbean, 1840–1940', *Small Axe*, 18.1 (2014), pp. 7–21.

Rupert, Linda Maguerite. *Creolization and Contraband: Curaçao in the Early Modern Atlantic World* (Athens: University of Georgia Press, 2012).

Schwartz, Stuart. *Sea of Storms: A History of Hurricanes in the Greater Caribbean from Columbus to Katrina* (Princeton, NJ: Princeton University Press, 2016).

Scott, Julius Sherrard III. *The Common Wind: Afro-American Currents in the Age of the Haitian Revolution* (London: Verso, 2020).

'Secretary's Office', *Demerary and Essequebo Royal Gazette*, 15 August 1815.

Vidal, Cécile. *Caribbean New Orleans: Empire, Race, and the Making of a Slave Society* (Chapel Hill, NC: University of North Carolina Press, 2020).

Wagley, Charles. 'Plantation America: A Culture Sphere', in Vera Rubin and Verne Ray (eds), *Caribbean Studies: A Symposium* (Seattle: University of Washington Press, 1960), pp. 3–13.

Weaver, Jace. *The Red Atlantic: American Indigenes and the Making of the Modern World, 1000–1927* (Chapel Hill, NC: University of North Carolina Press, 2014).

Weber, David J. *Bárbaros: Spaniards and Their Savages in the Age of Enlightenment* (New Haven, CT: Yale University Press, 2005).

Williams, Eric. *Capitalism and Slavery* (Chapel Hill, NC: University of North Carolina Press, 1944).

Williams, Eric. *From Columbus to Castro: The History of the Caribbean, 1492–1969* (New York: Vintage Books, 1970).

Two

Mobility as a Lens for Reading the History of Opera in the Colonial Caribbean

Charlotte Bentley

'Mobility', Tim Cresswell has argued, 'is fundamental to what it means to be human'.[1] Put in these terms, it is perhaps little wonder that various academic disciplines have undergone what we might think of as a 'mobile turn' in the last few years: our scholarly foci and preoccupations have shifted—again to borrow from Cresswell—from 'roots' to 'routes', from a vision of culture as fixed in place to one that attempts to capture the messy and fascinating entanglements that drive processes of hybridity and exchange.[2]

Historical studies, theatre studies and musicology have all been influenced by such a turn. Opera scholarship, in particular, has seen a flowering of interest in opera on the move. In studies ranging from explorations of opera's reception beyond Europe's largest cultural centres and the peripatetic careers of individual singers,[3] to recent work that has focussed on opera itself as a mobile subject,[4] scholars have started to tackle the ways in which mobilities can reshape our understanding of opera's roles in the world, past and present. The methodological nationalism that for so long shaped opera studies has begun to give way to an approach that emphasizes the mobility of

---

[1] Tim Cresswell, *On the Move: Mobility in the Western World* (New York and London: Routledge, 2006), p. 1.
[2] Cresswell, *On the Move*, 1.
[3] For two examples, see Jens Hesselager (ed.), *Grand Opera outside Paris: Opera on the Move in Nineteenth-Century Europe* (London: Routledge, 2018) and Katherine K. Preston, *Opera for the People: English-Language Opera and Women Managers in Late 19th-Century America* (New York: Oxford University Press, 2017).
[4] Francesca Vella takes this perspective in *Networking Operatic Italy* (Chicago, IL: University of Chicago Press, 2021).

people, materials and ideas, and their entanglements with colonialism and globalization.[5]

Indeed, looking at mobility, as Stephen Greenblatt reminds us, means addressing

> colonization, exile, emigration, wandering, contamination, and unintended consequences, along with the fierce compulsions of greed, longing, and restlessness, for it is these disruptive forces that principally shape the history and diffusion of identity and language, and not a rooted sense of cultural legitimacy.[6]

In other words, mobility is never neutral, but is instead shaped by power dynamics between individuals and between individuals and institutions, nations and empires, man and nature, scholar and subject, and in other ways besides. Along these lines, Cresswell has suggested an important distinction between movement and mobility: mobility is movement that is invested with meaning and by turns valued, contested and reinterpreted.[7]

This link between mobility and power is doubly meaningful for studies of the colonial Caribbean, which as a territory and cultural imaginary was subject to the forces of competing imperial powers, globalizing commercial interests and the exoticist fantasies that accompanied them. Indeed, Tessa Murphy has recently demonstrated that a mobility-focussed approach to the Caribbean can help challenge existing understandings of the hegemony of colonial rule in the region during the early modern period.[8] Focussing on what she calls the 'Creole archipelago'—the Lesser Antilles—she demonstrates how indigenous people established patterns of movement between the islands that crossed the contested and closely defended boundaries between European empires. She goes on to show how people on the margins of these empires—free and enslaved, and of European and African ancestry—drew on those routes established by the indigenous Kalinago people; their stories, she argues, highlight not just the oppressive nature

---

[5] For calls to move beyond methodological nationalism in opera studies, see Axel Körner, 'Beyond *Nationaloper*: For a Critique of Methodological Nationalism in Reading Nineteenth-Century Italian and German Opera', *Journal of Modern Italian Studies*, 25.4 (2020), pp. 402–19.

[6] Stephen Greenblatt (ed.), *Cultural Mobility: A Manifesto* (Cambridge: Cambridge University Press, 2010), p. 2.

[7] Cresswell, *On the Move*, 2.

[8] Tessa Murphy, *The Creole Archipelago: Race and Borders in the Colonial Caribbean* (Philadelphia: University of Pennsylvania Press, 2021).

of European colonialism in the region, but also the limits of its power. This focus on mobility, then, nuances not just our existing histories of power relations, but also conceptions of Caribbean geographies.

Opera, theatre and music in the region, however, have not yet received such nuanced attention through the lens of mobility. My aim in this chapter, then, is to take the first steps towards a mobility-focussed approach to the operatic life of the colonial Caribbean, asking what it might involve and how it might reshape our existing understandings of cultural activity and its relationship with the broader history of the region. First, I will lay out a few introductory points on operatic mobility in the colonial Caribbean and some suggestions for studying it. Then, I will tackle the issue of operatic circuits, arguing that the idea of operatic 'circulation' is both promising and problematic for understanding mobility within the Caribbean context. Rather than insisting on the notion of circuitry, I suggest instead a shift of scholarly focus to the ways in which musicians' journeys helped to define or conceptualize the colonial Caribbean as a space for mobility. Finally, I examine how individuals conceived of themselves as moving subjects, in how they presented their own movements and how they characterized their relationships with the people they met on their travels. Their words, I argue, reveal frictions that serve both to reinforce and to subtly challenge present-day understandings of opera's relationship with colonial power in the Caribbean.

Operatic mobility in the colonial Caribbean

When approaching operatic mobility in the context of the colonial Caribbean, the most obvious place to start is with the physical movement of performers through the region. Many cities and towns had a theatre (or a public building that could double as a theatre), in which operatic activity could take place if a suitable opportunity presented itself, as it did with varying degrees of frequency across the islands and surrounding coastlines. It is not possible here to give a comprehensive overview of operatic activity in the Caribbean during the whole colonial period, but I wish to highlight a few different 'types' of operatic activities, which relied to varying degrees on physical mobility.

The first involved troupes of performers who were recruited for a particular theatre, as was common in colonial Saint-Domingue, Martinique and Guadeloupe, as well as Havana's Teatro Tacón and other theatres at various points. Another kind of operatic activity, and one which dominated most parts of the Caribbean, consisted of touring troupes who would spend anything from a couple of weeks to a few months in a particular place before moving on.[9] Local singers and instrumentalists frequently performed with both resident and visiting troupes.[10] Just as these different kinds of physical mobilities overlapped and interlinked (the presence of a resident troupe of imported singers did not mean that a town could not also host touring troupes or that locals never mounted works), so too did individual performers' careers move between and beyond these different kinds of operatic activities.

Traces of this mobility have principally been preserved in the press. While immigration and other official records can be patchy in the information they contain, the sheer volume of information found in the press—however short-lived individual publications were—and the major digitization drives of recent years make it most scholars' first port of call. Local theatrical reports sometimes commented on where a visiting troupe had previously been engaged or where it was going after leaving a particular town, or mentioned the recruiting process for a resident troupe. Similarly, the daily press and specialized musical and theatrical periodicals published in Paris, Milan, London and other major European cultural centres soaked up news, including theatrical news, from around the world and summarized it in easily digestible chunks, leaving readers (at the time and since) in possession of something akin to global (operatic) trivia. Some preserve fascinating if fleeting insights into individual performers' movements. French music magazines like *La France théâtrale* often contained lists of performers seeking work, which listed their last place of employment and from which it is possible to identify individuals returning to Europe after an engagement in a Caribbean theatre.[11] Similarly, Italian magazines such as *Teatri, arti e letteratura* contained references to individual performers and troupes travelling in the Caribbean region.[12]

---

[9] Lauren R. Clay, for instance, mentions the colonial tours of French theatre troupes in *Stagestruck: The Business of Theater in Eighteenth-Century France and Its Colonies* (Ithaca, NY: Cornell University Press, 2013), pp. 203–05, 212.

[10] Julia Prest has discussed the performing career in Saint-Domingue of a locally born woman of colour, 'Minette', in 'Parisian Palimpsests and Creole Creations: Mme Marsan and Dlle Minette play Nina on the Caribbean Stage', *Early Modern French Studies*, 41.2 (2019), pp. 170–88.

[11] Examples of lists of singers seeking work in Paris can be found in *La France théâtrale* (12 September 1844) and in most other issues until the end of that year.

[12] For one example, see 'Polemica', *Teatri, arti e letteratura* (1 September 1824), p. 12.

The picture these sources create is a fragmented one, built up of snippets of operatic activity in an array of different places. Although individuals' names crop up in different accounts and the mobility of those individuals is frequently signalled, these publications do not present a 'joined-up' account of Caribbean operatic mobility. Rather, they create a kaleidoscopic image of an operatic world in which movement was key; they present a neutralized, flattened impression of that movement, in which the power dynamics of mobility have often been sidelined or ironed out.

In this chapter, I take as case studies two individuals from the mid-nineteenth century whose lives and careers allow for greater nuance in the notion of mobility than my brief sketches above. The first, Max Maretzek (1821–97), was an opera manager, born in Moravia, who arrived in the United States in 1848 (after working in Germany, France and England); he toured the country extensively with his own Italian Opera Company in the following decades, and several of those tours extended to parts of the Caribbean. The second is Louis Moreau Gottschalk (1829–69), a New Orleans-born virtuoso pianist, who spent many years touring the Caribbean region during the late 1850s. While Maretzek was a total outsider, who travelled to the Caribbean purely for business, Gottschalk had a certain emotional attachment to the region as his maternal grandmother's family were colonists in Saint-Domingue, before the revolution caused them to flee to New Orleans.[13]

Although Gottschalk was not an opera singer or manager himself, he did compose a one-act opera (now lost) during his stay in Havana in 1857, and he was accompanied on his travels between December 1856 and the summer of 1858 by the young soprano Adelina Patti and her family.[14] Concert programmes from St Thomas and other Caribbean islands show that they shared the stage, with Patti's performances of favourite arias from Verdi's *La Traviata* and Rossini's *Il Barbiere di Siviglia* being interleaved with Gottschalk's virtuoso performances of piano fantasias based on operas such as Donizetti's *La Favorite* and Verdi's *Macbeth*.[15] These piano fantasias hint at another kind of mobility: cultural mobility,

---

[13] For an extensive biography of Gottschalk, see S. Frederick Starr, *Bamboula! The Life and Times of Louis Moreau Gottschalk* (New York and Oxford: Oxford University Press, 1995).

[14] Starr mentions Patti's departure in *Bamboula!*, 270.

[15] For an example of an opera-filled concert programme that Gottschalk and Patti presented in St Thomas, see Donald Thompson, 'Gottschalk in the Virgin Islands', *Anuario Interamericano de Investigacion Musical*, 6 (1970), pp. 95–104. An image of the programme is inserted between pages 96 and 97.

which Stephen Greenblatt has described as the 'continual metamorphosis' of works and genres through 'reinterpretation', 'refashioning' and, in some cross-cultural contexts, 'misunderstanding' (accidental or deliberate).[16] While I do not have space here to consider this kind of mobility more fully, it offers another potential avenue for future work.

Maretzek and Gottschalk are exceptional case studies in the sense that they offer ways of bypassing some of the issues I highlighted above concerning fragmentary pictures of mobility generated from the press. Both left records of their own travel experiences: Maretzek published two volumes of memoirs (*Crotchets and Quavers* (1855) and *Sharps and Flats* (1890)) in the United States, while Gottschalk left notes and diary entries from his time in the Caribbean, which his sister later prepared for posthumous publication under the title *Notes of a Pianist* (1881). Gottschalk also sent articles about his travels for publication in *La France théâtrale*.[17] These, of course, do not replace the need for other, non-autobiographical materials, but they do assist considerably in understanding the musicians' trajectories and experiences, and they open up ways of understanding mobility beyond the simple piecing together of who was where and when.[18]

Circuits

The notion of 'circuits' of operatic movement is one of the most influential ways in which operatic and theatrical mobility has been theorized in the existing literature. John Rosselli, for instance, has argued that 'within the Americas the circuits along which singers and musicians moved were fairly distinct', and he outlines three different examples of common routes taken by troupes and sets of places they

---

[16] Greenblatt (ed.), *Cultural Mobility*, 77 and 91–95.
[17] Max Maretzek, *Crotchets and Quavers: Or, Revelations of an Opera Manager in America* (New York: S. French, 1855); Max Maretzek, *Sharps and Flats: A Sequel to* Crotchets and Quavers (New York: American Musician Publishing Co., 1890); Louis Moreau Gottschalk, *Notes of a Pianist*, ed. Clara Gottschalk and trans. Robert E. Peterson (Philadelphia, PA: J.B. Lippincott and Co., 1881).
[18] Nonetheless, they still adopt a certain fragmentary style: Maretzek's accounts are not linear, but jump between different points in his career, while Gottschalk's frequently lack detail about how and when he travelled between places. In both cases, however, their accounts provide enough of the bigger picture for researchers to be able to fill in many of the gaps using press and other sources. Gottschalk's movements, in particular, have been painstakingly assembled by Starr.

visited.[19] One covers Brazil and the upriver areas of Argentina; a second covers the Caribbean, including coastal mainland areas; and the third encompasses the western coasts of Panama, Costa Rica, Guatemala and Mexico.[20] The latter two circuits, he argues, overlapped with a fourth, which operated in North America, and Katherine Preston has supported this, mentioning various troupes that travelled from Havana up into the United States.[21]

Rosselli's evocation of circuits is useful for approaching mobility in the sense that he hints at some of the factors that controlled or directed troupes' travels, thereby acknowledging that their movements were shaped by power dynamics of various kinds. In particular, he highlights how existing transport infrastructures—within and between nations and imperial spaces—enabled troupes' movements, as their routes relied on the availability of water transport.[22] This was the case not only within the Caribbean, but in areas of the continental mainland too, where it was often easier to travel by sea or river than to cross difficult terrain or areas lacking infrastructure. In the 1840s and 1850s, for instance, it was still common for troupes moving from New York to New Orleans to take a steamer around the coast rather than travel by land.[23]

The notion of circuitry has implications that are worth unpicking: first, it suggests a kind of closed system with set inputs and outputs (if we assume the metaphor is based on electrical circuitry or similar); second, it suggests a kind of stability or repeatability (a circuit implies more than a single instance of movement); finally, it suggests how people conceive of or map space, as a circuit presents a version of a region through which people follow established routes. All these elements were evident in theatre circuits from the late nineteenth and early twentieth centuries, on which theatre historians have carried out extensive work, although none to my knowledge have focussed exclusively on the Caribbean.

---

[19] John Rosselli, 'The Opera Business and the Italian Immigrant Community in Latin America 1820–1930: The Example of Buenos Aires', *Past and Present*, 127.1 (1990), pp. 165–66.

[20] Rosselli, 'The Opera Business', 165–66.

[21] Katherine K. Preston, *Opera on the Road: Traveling Opera Troupes in the United States, 1825–60* (Urbana: University of Illinois Press, 1993), 113–22.

[22] Rosselli, 'The Opera Business', 165.

[23] The French troupe from the Théâtre d'Orléans in New Orleans did this on their tours of the north-east in 1843 and 1845: see Mary Grace Swift, 'The Northern Tours of the Théâtre d'Orléans, 1843 and 1845', *Louisiana History: The Journal of the Louisiana Historical Association*, 26.2 (1985), pp. 155–93 (167).

Christopher Balme's work on the Bandmann circuit, for instance, has highlighted how companies followed pre-arranged routes between a network of theatres (which were often owned by a single impresario or syndicate), thereby establishing a specific pattern of movement.[24] Similar patterns emerged in the United States in the second half of the nineteenth century, as Katherine Preston has shown.[25] While, for Preston, such circuits developed through the solidification of specifically national theatrical infrastructures, Balme concludes in the case of the Bandmann troupes that the circuit is evidence of 'globalized theatre' in the years around 1900.[26] The notion of circuitry, then, has had different resonances in different contexts.

I suggest that it is worth thinking more deeply about whether 'circuit' is the best term for understanding earlier mobilities and those in the Caribbean in particular. As yet, I have found little evidence of circuits similar to those described above in the region in the late eighteenth and first three-quarters of the nineteenth century. There is evidence of paired connections between places (for instance, troupes moved between Havana and New Orleans at various times), but such dyadic connections hardly justify the label 'circuit'.[27] Looking at my two case-study musicians, then, I will highlight how their mobility captures some of the characteristics of circuitry but in other respects challenges how broadly the concept may be applied in the colonial Caribbean.

Maretzek's account hints at the notion of an operatic circuit between the United States and the Caribbean. Already an experienced opera impresario in the United States (if not always financially successful), he decided in February 1852 to try to expand his profits by looking further afield.[28] In *Crotchets and Quavers*, Maretzek explains that his Italian opera troupe and a competitor company had just finished a season in New York and were unoccupied and looking for their next engagement:

---

[24] Christopher B. Balme, 'The Bandmann Circuit: Theatrical Networks in the First Age of Globalization', *Theatre Research International*, 40.1 (2015), pp. 19–36. See also Christopher B. Balme, *The Globalization of Theatre 1870–1930: The Theatrical Networks of Maurice E. Bandmann* (Cambridge: Cambridge University Press, 2020).

[25] Preston, *Opera for the People*, 239–310 and 495–560.

[26] Balme, 'The Bandmann Circuit', 19.

[27] For troupes moving between New Orleans and Havana, see Charlotte Bentley, 'Southern Exchanges: Italian Opera in New Orleans, 1836–1842', in Axel Körner and Paulo Kühl (eds), *Italian Opera in Global and Transnational Perspective: Reimagining* Italianità *in the Long Nineteenth Century* (Cambridge: Cambridge University Press, 2021), pp. 113–32.

[28] He states this himself in *Crotchets and Quavers*, 220–21.

Both were still actuated by a purely Italian jealousy of each other; while either party feared the engagement of the opposing one by Don Francisco Marty y Torrens [impresario of the Teatro Tacón in Havana], for the purpose of sending it to New Orleans, Mexico and Havana. Now, a precisely, or very nearly similar project, had been running for several months in my own brain—for I believe it is admitted that we all carry some portion of this article in the interior of our skulls.[29]

Maretzek, then, outlines something that he presents as a kind of existing operatic circuit covering New Orleans, Havana and Mexico, and he suggests that there was competition to travel on it, at least between the companies hoping to be engaged by Marty y Torrens. In Maretzek's vision, the point of input to the circuit was the United States, through New Orleans and the Gulf of Mexico. In this, Maretzek and Gottschalk align, as Gottschalk also began his tour of the Caribbean region from the United States, via New Orleans.

But it is worth pointing out that, important though this northern point of entry to the Caribbean became in the mid-nineteenth century, it was far from being the only or oldest point of entry. One of the potential pitfalls of viewing operatic mobility in the Caribbean through the lens of circuits is that it becomes tempting to assume too much consistency or stability. Indeed, impresarios in Havana such as Francis Brichta and Marty y Torrens had previously recruited troupes directly from Italy, which did not pass through the United States,[30] and French troupes for Martinique and Guadeloupe (and, earlier, Saint-Domingue) came directly from France.[31] Meanwhile, in December 1856 the Havana-based *Diario de la Marina* noted that audiences in the town of Matanzas, Cuba, were eagerly expecting the arrival of an opera troupe travelling from the French town of Le Havre, while the people of Havana waited for Maretzek's troupe from the United States.[32] The dominance of certain entry points to the Caribbean system was not fixed but rather, as Ditlev Rindom has recently illustrated, reflected changing operatic tastes and political relationships beyond the region itself.[33]

---

[29] Maretzek, *Crotchets and Quavers*, 221.
[30] Benjamin Walton, 'Italian Operatic Fantasies in Latin America', *Journal of Modern Italian Studies*, 17.4 (2012), pp. 460–71 (460–61).
[31] Daniel Mendoza de Arce, *Music in North America and the West Indies from the Discovery to 1850: A Historical Survey* (Lanham, MD and Oxford: Scarecrow Press, 2006), pp. 115–18 and 214–15.
[32] 'Cronica', *Diario de la Marina* (16 December 1856).
[33] Ditlev Rindom, 'Arcadia Undone: Teresa Carreño's 1887 Italian Opera Company in Caracas', in Axel Körner and Paulo Kühl (eds), *Italian Opera*, pp. 192–213.

Furthermore, the notion of circuitry, with its implications of repeatability and closure, potentially obscures the diversity of both the distance and the direction of performers' movements, and also suggests a kind of regularity that belies the complex mix of contingency and design that underpinned troupes' and individuals' mobility at the mid-nineteenth century. Indeed, many of Gottschalk's movements in the Caribbean in the late 1850s were determined by his attempts to reach Caracas, as his acquaintance in New York, General José Antonio Páez (a driving force of Venezuelan independence, who was in exile in the United States between 1850 and 1858), had provided him with letters of introduction to a number of important musical and high-society people there.[34] However, the outbreak of war in New Granada (where Páez himself returned to fight, becoming president and dictator in 1861) delayed Gottschalk's plans, leading to his wandering around the Caribbean. He travelled to many of the places in which he performed, not with the aim of giving concerts, but in the hope of being able to get a ship to New Granada: he tried St Thomas first, then Puerto Rico, before then attempting to find passage from Barbados (via Trinidad).

Gottschalk was not alone in having his movements shaped by contingency. While in the town of St Pierre, Martinique, still in the hope of eventually being able to reach Caracas, he encountered a family of singers—the Busattis—who had come to the island from New Granada, fleeing the war. In Caracas, Busatti had been impresario of an opera company in which his wife and daughter had been singers. He had worked in the Caribbean over a number of years, with apparently little pattern to his movements: he was mentioned as part of a troupe, consisting largely of Italians, who performed in Santiago de Cuba in 1841,[35] and again as leader of an opera troupe in Puerto Rico in 1842 and later in the 1840s,[36] and in New York in the early 1850s.[37] In Martinique the Busattis gave concerts of opera excerpts to make ends meet, and Gottschalk speculated that they would make good money if they were able to make up a full troupe as, in spite of the subsidy offered by the French colonial government for the provision of opera, there

[34] See Starr, *Bamboula!*, 261.
[35] In 'Nachrichten', *Allgemeine musikalische Zeitung*, 37 (1841), p. 749.
[36] For sources see Malena Kuss, 'Puerto Rico', in Malena Kuss (ed.), *Music in Latin America and the Caribbean: An Encyclopedic History* (Austin: University of Texas Press, 2004), pp. 151–88 (178).
[37] For mention of his activities in New York, see Heléna Tóth, *An Exiled Generation: German and Hungarian Refugees of Revolution, 1848–1871* (Cambridge: Cambridge University Press, 2014), p. 132.

was apparently no resident troupe at that moment in the late 1850s.[38] Whether the Busattis did indeed stay in Martinique I have not yet been able to discover, but their path to the island illustrates well that operatic mobility was shaped by geopolitical circumstances that intruded upon any artistic or business plans they may have had.

Beyond circuits: mapping the colonial Caribbean through operatic journeys

The notion of circuitry does not fully capture all the nuances of operatic mobility in the colonial Caribbean. I now want to develop the idea of mapping, to suggest that rather than simply illustrating existing operatic circuits, Gottschalk and Maretzek's accounts of their journeys create visions of the Caribbean region that are quite different from each other, both spatially and in terms of their power dynamics. They were hardly exceptional in mapping the space differently: the geographical boundaries of what defines the Caribbean have proved to be particularly mobile, historiographically speaking, as discussed in Chapter One of this volume.[39] In *Creole Archipelago*, Murphy suggests the possibility of dividing the islands of the Caribbean Sea into subregions—distinguishing the Lesser Antilles from the Greater Antilles—while other scholars have included not just the islands, but also the coastal areas of Central and South America that border the Caribbean Sea.[40] To the north, New Orleans has been positioned within the colonial Caribbean both during its period as a French colony (1718–63) and while it was a Spanish protectorate (1763–1800 officially, but 1803 in popular perception), and again in the few years after 1809 when it was deluged with a wave of refugees from the earlier revolution in Saint-Domingue, who had settled in eastern Cuba before being expelled by the Spanish.[41] Others, too, have

---

[38] Gottschalk, *Notes of a Pianist*, 114.
[39] See also Anton Allahar's review article 'Identity and Erasure: Finding the Elusive Caribbean', in *Revista Europea de Estudios Latinoamericanos y del Caribe*, 79 (2005), pp. 125–34.
[40] Murphy, *Creole Archipelago*; L.H. Roper's edited collection *The Torrid Zone: Caribbean Colonization and Cultural Interaction in the Long Seventeenth Century* (Columbia: University of South Carolina Press, 2018), presents a much-expanded vision of the colonial Caribbean, including a chapter on South Carolina.
[41] See, for instance, Cécile Vidal, *Caribbean New Orleans: Empire, Race, and the Making of a Slave Society* (Chapel Hill: University of North Carolina Press, 2019) and *The Road to Louisiana: The Saint-Domingue Refugees, 1792–1809*,

argued the case for understanding the city of Veracruz, on the shores of the Gulf of Mexico, within the greater Caribbean region.[42] Both Veracruz and New Orleans have maintained Caribbean connections as part of their cultural image, even as tangible economic and demographic links with the region have waned. The present volume includes discussion of New Orleans and Paramaribo (in Suriname) as well as several of the Caribbean islands.

A focus on Gottschalk and Maretzek's operatic mobility can help us define the colonial Caribbean not as a fixed geographical or cultural entity, but as a place in flux that was shaped and reshaped by the competing needs of the people who lived there and travelled through it. Maretzek himself presents an extremely limited vision of the geographical extent of the Caribbean (confined to the Gulf of Mexico), while Gottschalk travelled far more widely. Gottschalk reflected on his journeys, saying 'I have successively visited the Spanish, English, French, Dutch, Swedish, and Danish Antilles, the Guyanes, and the shores of Para'.[43] In early 1854, he left the United States from New Orleans, travelling to Cuba, where he spent several months, before returning to New Orleans. In late 1856, he returned to Havana with the Patti family, before travelling on to the island of St Thomas, which was at the time a Danish colony (today it is one of the US Virgin Islands), with a brief stop at Port-au-Prince in Haiti. From there, the group travelled to Puerto Rico because Gottschalk's intended destination, Caracas, was consumed by civil war. The Pattis left Gottschalk in Puerto Rico, but he continued his journey, going to Kingston, Jamaica in the hope of being able to take a ship from there to Caracas, but the ongoing war once again foiled his plans. He therefore headed to Barbados, intending to travel from there to the island of Trinidad and enter New Granada from the east. With still no hope of getting to Caracas, Gottschalk moved on to British Guiana and then Dutch Guiana, and eventually to Martinique and Guadeloupe, where he spent over a year, before returning to Havana in 1860.[44]

Gottschalk's travels, then, saw him creeping west to east along the island chain, not, of course, in the way that Murphy describes the Kalinago and later marginalized people voyaging, but in a way that is nonetheless determined by the physical geography of the region rather

ed. Carl A. Brasseaux and Glenn R. Conrad (Lafayette: The Center for Louisiana Studies, University of Southwestern Louisiana, 1992).

[42] See, for one example, Joseph M.H. Clark, *Veracruz and the Caribbean in the Seventeenth Century* (Cambridge: Cambridge University Press, 2023).

[43] Gottschalk, *Notes of a Pianist*, 118.

[44] Starr has painstakingly pieced together most of the details of Gottschalk's movements in *Bamboula!*, 256–309.

than any sense of needing to abide by imperial borders. In those first three years of his Caribbean travels, Gottschalk repeatedly crossed between Spanish, Dutch, French and British imperial spaces, also stopping briefly in places—notably Haiti—that had become independent from colonial rule through bloody conflict.

Unlike Maretzek, who concerned himself primarily with large cities that might have the infrastructure to host his opera company and the interest and resources among its public to make performances profitable, Gottschalk stopped more frequently and in places of varied sizes. While in Cuba in 1854, for instance, he did not confine himself to Havana but travelled to Matanzas, Cárdenas, Cienfuegos, Santiago de Cuba, Puerto Príncipe and Remedios (where he presented concerts), and the town of Trinidad (where he did not).[45] While Maretzek took a single city to represent a whole island or nation, Gottschalk's perceptions were based on much more extensive experiences in the places to which he travelled.

The geography of the Caribbean presented in Maretzek's and Gottschalk's accounts, then, is conceptually quite different, although in practical terms they reveal many of the same preoccupations. Maretzek obsesses over the officially drawn boundaries of the colonial or postcolonial state, focussing on the workings of governance in Havana and Veracruz (as with the other places he visited) and their impact on him as an opera manager. His recollections of his stay in Havana in early 1857 involve a detailed account of his interactions with the colonial captain-general regarding the attendance figures for, and audience behaviour at, opera performances.[46] Yael Bitrán Goren has rightly observed that Maretzek's attitudes towards Mexico were those of a 'modern colonizer':[47] in explaining his rationale for touring beyond the United States, Maretzek describes Mexico as 'literally untrodden ground. In fact, Mexico was an almost purely virgin soil for Opera.'[48] To drive home this characterization of Mexico as fresh territory for operatic business, he unashamedly draws parallels between himself and Spanish conquistador Hernán Cortés.[49]

He does not necessarily seem to have understood New Orleans, Havana and Veracruz as part of a greater Caribbean region, although

---

[45] See Starr, *Bamboula!*, 170–94.
[46] Maretzek, *Sharps and Flats*, 28–32.
[47] Yael Bitrán Goren, 'Musical Women and Identity-Building in Early Independent Mexico (1821–1854)' (PhD thesis, Royal Holloway, University of London, 2012), p. 148.
[48] Maretzek, *Crotchets and Quavers*, 221.
[49] Maretzek, *Crotchets and Quavers*, 222.

there is plenty of evidence that those places were well connected with each other and with other areas of the Caribbean. Instead, he conceptualizes Havana and Veracruz through the lens of Spanish imperial power, making little effort to distinguish between the Spanish colonial government in Cuba and the independent government of Mexico; he also positions them as part of a cultural imperialist future for the United States, seeing both as ripe for financial and cultural exploitation by opera troupes from the United States.

Conversely, imperial boundaries featured little in Gottschalk's mapping of the Caribbean: he made his way between the islands, using his facility with languages to his advantage, and he largely ignored the imperial politics of the region. As S. Frederick Starr has pointed out, Gottschalk arrived in Havana in 1854 during a time of great political tension between the Spanish colonial government in Cuba and the United States, and he was initially prevented from performing in the city's major concert venues as a result, but showed 'a remarkable indifference, if not obtuseness toward political realities' in persisting with his Cuban visit.[50] While Gottschalk undoubtedly benefitted from the attention and support of colonial elites in the other places that he visited on his tour, his account only references geopolitics in so far as it had an impact on his freedom to move between places.

Rather than just focussing on the direction and repeatability of 'circuits' of operatic movement within the Caribbean, then, musicians' journeys and their accounts of them can instead provide a more nuanced insight into the power dynamics of mobility. Their 'mind-mapping' of the region (to borrow Desley Deacon's term), which both preceded and resulted from their physical movements across it, creates a window onto their own status as travellers and their sense of their own identity.[51] To highlight this, I want to turn to one element that is inevitably present in travellers' accounts of the Caribbean: water. As noted earlier, Rosselli's claims about operatic circuits highlight the importance of water transport to mobility, and both Maretzek and Gottschalk mention travelling by sea in their memoirs. Maretzek has a moment of triumph when his singers, who he complains have been causing him trouble by spending his money excessively, are struck down with terrible sea sickness in the Gulf of Mexico.[52] While his triumph is short-lived, and

---

[50] Starr, *Bamboula!*, 172.
[51] See Desley Deacon, 'Location! Location! Location! Mind Maps and Theatrical Circuits in Australian Transnational History', *History Australia*, 5.3 (2008), pp. 81.1–81.16.
[52] Maretzek, *Crotchets and Quavers*, 229.

later in the journey he too suffers with sea sickness, in that moment the sea adopts a kind of disciplinary function, putting the singers in their place while maintaining his position of authority and superiority as manager. In other words, when his troupe is in a space beyond the immediate control of any of the governments with which Maretzek was so fascinated, the sea plays a surrogate regulatory role.

Meanwhile, for Gottschalk, the sea serves as a space for reflection: when sailing past the coast of Haiti he recalls memories of his childhood, of his grandmother in New Orleans recounting his family's flight from the violence of the Haitian Revolution. At other times on his travels, too, the sea provokes daydreams, such as when he describes 'the phosphorescence of the sea in these tropical latitudes, where it seems to roll in waves of living silver' off the coast of Costa Rica.[53] The tropical sea, for Gottschalk, is a space of illusion, of shifting identities, and it calls to his mind's eye 'the scenes of the theatre, where behind a veil of silver gauze is displayed, amid the bluish light of the bengal fires, the splendour of the enchanted palace of the final apotheosis'.[54] Indeed, there is a sense from Gottschalk's account that the sea facilitates his restless movement, allowing him to slip away from places as the urge took him.

There are similarities in the men's accounts of sea travel in the Caribbean region, however, that mark them out as privileged travellers, shaped by and sharing in European colonial attitudes to mobility. For both Maretzek and Gottschalk, the sea is fundamentally a boundary to be traversed, a space that separates the lands that are their goals. Even Gottschalk the wanderer, who lacked Maretzek's fixation on financial exploitation, demonstrates how his wanderings were essentially terrestrial in their aim, saying 'when I became tired of the same horizon, I crossed an arm of the sea, and landed on a neighbouring island, or on the Spanish Main'.[55] The sea, then, emerges from their accounts as something that must be crossed in order for them to engage in their land-based creative activities, rather than a particularly meaningful space in and of itself.

This, then, suggests that both men to a degree (Gottschalk perhaps less than Maretzek) adopt a landlocked way of thinking about culture and its expression. This contrasts strongly with the value Kevin Dawson has suggested people of the African diaspora tended to afford to bodies of water, viewing them 'as social and as social and cultural spaces, not

---

[53] Gottschalk, *Notes of a Pianist*, 396.
[54] Gottschalk, *Notes of a Pianist*, 396.
[55] Gottschalk, *Notes of a Pianist*, 118.

as intervals between places'.[56] Murphy, too, highlights how 'watery geography' was fundamental to the Kalinagos, and that the sea 'did not present the frightening prospect [to them] that it did to the Europeans who authored the archives on which historians largely rely'.[57] In this way, then, Maretzek and Gottschalk's status as representatives of hegemonic power becomes clear: while neither of them was involved with the governance or direct maintenance of colonial power in the Caribbean region, they framed their mobility in ways that were land-centred.

Maretzek and Gottschalk on mobility

Enlightening though it can be to tell 'moving stories', to borrow John-Paul Ghobrial's term for mobility-focussed historical narratives, it is important not to overstate historical mobility.[58] Not everyone was equally mobile, and not everyone had the same degree of freedom to determine their own movements. In this final section, I shall examine how Maretzek and Gottschalk considered the mobility of other people they met during their travels in the Caribbean and how they understood their own mobility in comparison.

When Maretzek recalled his visits to Veracruz in 1852, he wrote on various occasions of the difficulty of engaging suitable local orchestral and choral musicians to supplement his troupe. He eventually recruited a group of 12 'mulatto' men to augment his orchestra, whose playing he described in the following unfavourable terms: '[c]ould I have imagined a group of tom-cats giving vent to their amorous feelings on the roof of my dwelling, at one o'clock in the morning, it would scarcely have been worse'.[59] Perceptions of racial difference formed a large part of Maretzek's judgement of these local musicians, and he doubtless played upon these differences to appeal to the assumed tastes of readers in the United States, where he published the first volume of his memoirs in 1855. For instance, in berating them for their playing, he referred to the leader of the ensemble variously as a 'black scoundrel' and a

---

[56] Kevin Dawson, *Undercurrents of Power: Aquatic Culture in the African Diaspora* (Philadelphia: University of Pennsylvania Press, 2018), p. 2.

[57] Murphy, *The Creole Archipelago*, 4.

[58] John-Paul Ghobrial, 'Moving Stories and What They Tell Us: Early Modern Mobility Between Microhistory and Global History', *Global History and Microhistory: A Supplement Volume of* Past and Present, ed. John-Paul Ghobrial, *Past and Present*, 242.14(S) (2019), pp. 243–80.

[59] Maretzek, *Crotchets and Quavers*, 293.

'black rascal', thus emphasizing racial difference at every opportunity.[60] Maretzek eventually decided that the ensemble should only play the final eight bars of the first act of the unspecified opera, but *pretend* to play for the rest of the performance. With their pretending, Maretzek was enchanted:

> I am also happy to say, that they never played anything nearly as well as they acted playing. Nothing could well have been more glorious than to see the French horn's cheeks distended with his imaginary efforts, or to note the way in which the bows simulated the scraping of the strings of the violins. Nothing could have more admirably shammed the reality.[61]

Thus, Maretzek does not simply invite—but actively compels—his black musicians into a kind of colonial mimicry, where they imitate their white counterparts within the orchestra, but silently. Maretzek writes from the position of a man who cannot envisage any challenges to his authority. His account of how he simultaneously forced the musicians' mimicry and silenced them is nonetheless open to reinterpretation using postcolonial theories about the 'menace' and the potentially threatening aspects of mimicry as part of the ambivalence of colonial discourse.[62] It is possible, then, that these musicians were mocking 'white performance'.

In contrast to his disappointment with his orchestra, Maretzek spoke of his chorus in Veracruz with great pride. Worried that he did not have time to recruit a chorus locally and train them, he enlisted all the (white) servants who were travelling with the troupe as chorus members, since they had heard the operas many times, both in the theatre and during their employers' private practice sessions. Maretzek recalls that his plan worked brilliantly, as '[e]ven the ladies' maids, men-servants, and theatrical tailors knew the old Operas by heart, and were inspired by the contact of their voices with those of these artists'.[63]

The twin characterizations of the chorus and the orchestra, one made immediately after the other, suggest an interesting perspective on Maretzek's view of mobility. He and his troupe are presented as a mobile group, the white servants who travel with them included. Indeed, the servants are

---

[60] Maretzek, *Crotchets and Quavers*, 294.
[61] Maretzek, *Crotchets and Quavers*, 295.
[62] Homi Bhabha, 'Of Mimicry and Man: The Ambivalence of Colonial Discourse', *October*, 28 (1984), pp. 125–33.
[63] Maretzek, *Crotchets and Quavers*, 291.

portrayed not only as physically mobile, but as socially mobile too, at least within the context of the tour: Maretzek recounts how the public celebrated the chorus members loudly, calling them 'by name', throwing bouquets to the ladies and sending them champagne between acts.[64] In this sense, then, the physical mobility of the tour is characterized as empowering servants to become temporary celebrities in their own right.

Meanwhile, the black orchestral musicians, whose race Maretzek always points out, are presented as being rooted in place and permitted only to pretend to play, rather than giving actual performances. They are silenced and rendered powerless, even as Maretzek admits that he needs their services to make his orchestra appear more numerous. Nonetheless, Maretzek characterizes mobility as something to which the black musicians he encountered aspired: on another occasion he describes the flattery he used to manipulate a violinist into doing his bidding, asking the musician why he had 'never yet visited the United States' and lying to him, saying that he had heard the man's name mentioned in New York and Paris.[65] The flattery works, and the violinist visibly swells with pride, but he then confides in Maretzek that he feels 'frightened, lest they might take it into their heads to *sell* me'.[66] While Maretzek reports all this as a supposedly humorous anecdote, the reference to the violinist's fears of being sold into slavery suggest that his mobility is prevented by societal attitudes to his race; ultimately, his fears reflect less on the Caribbean itself and more on his perceptions of racial prejudice and inequality in the United States. However embellished or imagined Maretzek's recounting of this anecdote might be, he nonetheless thematizes mobility—not just his own, but other people's—in his paired reflections on the chorus and the orchestra, and in doing so gives his impressions on social and racial dynamics as they could be expressed through operatic performance.

Gottschalk in many respects expressed quite a different attitude to his own position as a traveller. Maretzek's accounts are full of references (not always particularly positive ones) to the people with whom he travelled: he recounts anecdotes about things that happened to members of his opera troupe on their voyages, the irritation they caused him by bringing an entourage with them and the general difficulties that travelling en masse created. Gottschalk, however, rarely mentions travelling companions in his memoirs, although he spent the first 18 months of his Caribbean trip accompanied by Adelina Patti

---

[64] Maretzek, *Crotchets and Quavers*, 291.
[65] Maretzek, *Crotchets and Quavers*, 241.
[66] Maretzek, *Crotchets and Quavers*, 241.

and her family. He narrates his movements in the first person singular, presenting himself as a solo traveller. While Maretzek's account evokes a sense of collective mobility (which he, as the impresario responsible, directed), Gottschalk's evokes a sense of the Romantic wanderer, whose experiences were unique to him rather than shared.

The notion of 'vagabondry'—a term Gottschalk uses to describe his movements—finds useful counterpart in his account in two other concepts: 'torpor', which is a term he uses to describe the islands of the Caribbean, and technology, which only occasionally comes into his reminiscences of his time in the region.[67] 'Torpor' suggests stasis, but it links closely to Gottschalk's romanticized image both of himself as a traveller and of the places he visits, while the evocation of technology serves at times to temporarily puncture that image. He often characterizes his own movements as a constant, restless wandering, but in search of what, exactly, he never makes clear. He frequently expresses his intention to leave 'immediately' for a new place,[68] and writes often of the need to '[begin] again my vagabond course'.[69] However, he appears to value deeply the times when circumstances—either his own ill-health or external events—compel him to stay still. It is in these moments that he juxtaposes his own propensity to move with the ways in which the natural environment impels him to stay still. He writes: 'the country of the Antilles imparts a voluptuous languor which is contagious; it is a poison which slowly infiltrates all the senses, and benumbs the soul with a species of ecstatic torpor'.[70] Accordingly, he describes his stay on various Caribbean islands as an initial struggle between his will to lead 'a healthy and active life' and what he perceived to be the seductive, almost dangerous stasis of island life, surrounded by parrots, guava trees, crickets and all manner of exotic wildlife.[71]

Tempting though Gottschalk found the tropical environs and the pace of life they offered him (and indeed, he did embrace it for extended periods, staying in some places for several months before finally resolving to move on), he also associated them with what he described as a sense both of the 'primitive' and of the 'immoral', and he wrote of how 'in the depths of [his] conscience' something willed him to move on.[72] While such characterizations of tropical regions as primitive or

---

[67] Gottschalk uses the term 'vagabond' in *Notes of a Pianist*, 118 and 120, and for 'torpor' see note 70, below.
[68] See, for example, Gottschalk, *Notes of a Pianist*, 107.
[69] Gottschalk, *Notes of a Pianist*, 118.
[70] Gottschalk, *Notes of a Pianist*, 99.
[71] Gottschalk, *Notes of a Pianist*, 120.
[72] Gottschalk, *Notes of a Pianist*, 120.

morally lacking were both frequent Romantic tropes and significant to the development of notions of the Global South, they can also be read through the lens of mobility: Gottschalk's mobility was temporarily eroded by his own conflicting desires for the lush natural environment and slower pace of life he experienced on the islands where he stayed.

Technology only occasionally features in Gottschalk's account of his Caribbean travels but, when it does, he presents it and the mobility it affords as a stark contrast to the 'voluptuous' stasis he attributes to the natural beauty of the islands. In one notable instance, he writes of a train journey from Cárdenas to Havana during his tour of Cuba in 1853.[73] Gottschalk describes the uncomfortable 'jerks' of the train's movements and its 'groans', before eventually personifying the locomotive and holding an imaginary dialogue with it about the torments of travelling. In contrast to the allure of the mountains, volcanoes, exotic vegetation, wildlife and, indeed, people by which Gottschalk felt himself being seduced during his Caribbean sojourn, the train ride he experiences in Cuba comes across as an unwelcome intrusion of the industrialized world into his romanticized exotic fantasy.

This chapter has offered some potential starting points from which to approach operatic mobility in the colonial Caribbean, while also highlighting some of the challenges of studying mobility in this context. Although I was only able to explore Maretzek's and Gottschalk's accounts relatively briefly, they both offer ways into exploring mobility that go beyond simply charting who travelled where and when. This is in no way to dismiss the work of piecing together performers' movements: Starr and others have done much to bring clarity to the details of Gottschalk's travels. Nonetheless, considerable work remains to be done on other performers' movements in the region and this, I anticipate, will allow us to re-evaluate the notion of circuitry. Given the large number of individuals involved and the scope of their journeys, as well as the fact that many archival traces of those journeys remain compartmentalized by reference to historical empires, modern nations and also language (the subject of Chapter Three), the task of piecing them together perhaps needs to be a collaborative one, echoing recent calls for 'group scholarship' within the broader field of global music history—and the one made in Chapter Three of this volume.[74]

[73] Gottschalk, *Notes of a Pianist*, 98–99.
[74] See 'Editorial: Rethinking the West' in *IMS Musicological Brainfood*, 3.1 (2019), pp. 6–10.

What I have offered here is perhaps a further step, or at least one to be taken alongside the nuts and bolts of piecing together performers' movements. I have set out some of the ways in which we might shift the focus from movement to mobility, to follow Cresswell's definitions of the terms, and to look at the power relations—both in the geopolitics of the region and in individuals' careers—that underpin those movements. While it was beyond the scope of this chapter to consider it in detail, mobility extends beyond physical movement in space to encompass transformations—of genres, ideas and meanings—that in turn develop from that spatial movement. The colonial Caribbean shaped and was shaped by mobilities of many kinds. In this context, a focus on operatic mobility specifically comes to show not just the ways in which the region and its complex history shaped the history of opera, but how opera and those who performed it played a role in mapping and defining the region in ways that could at some times subtly challenge more familiar formulations of power relations, and at other times reinforce or reinscribe them.

Bibliography

Allahar, Anton. 'Identity and Erasure: Finding the Elusive Caribbean', *Revista Europea de Estudios Latinoamericanos y del Caribe*, 79 (2005), pp. 125–34.

Anon. 'Editorial: Rethinking the West', in *IMS Musicological Brainfood*, 3.1 (2019), pp. 6–10.

Balme, Christopher B. 'The Bandmann Circuit: Theatrical Networks in the First Age of Globalization', *Theatre Research International*, 40.1 (2015), pp. 19–36.

Balme, Christopher B. *The Globalization of Theatre 1870–1930: The Theatrical Networks of Maurice E. Bandmann* (Cambridge: Cambridge University Press, 2020).

Bentley, Charlotte. 'Southern Exchanges: Italian Opera in New Orleans, 1836–1842', in Axel Körner and Paulo Kühl (eds), *Italian Opera in Global and Transnational Perspective: Reimagining* Italianità *in the Long Nineteenth Century* (Cambridge: Cambridge University Press, 2021), pp. 113–32.

Bhabha, Homi. 'Of Mimicry and Man: The Ambivalence of Colonial Discourse', *October*, 28 (1984), pp. 125–33.

Bitrán Goren, Yael. 'Musical Women and Identity-Building in Early Independent Mexico (1821–1854)' (PhD thesis, Royal Holloway, University of London, 2012).

Brasseaux, Carl A. and Glenn R. Conrad (eds). *The Road to Louisiana: The Saint-Domingue Refugees, 1792–1809* (Lafayette: The Center for Louisiana Studies, University of Southwestern Louisiana, 1992).

Clark, Joseph M.H. *Veracruz and the Caribbean in the Seventeenth Century* (Cambridge: Cambridge University Press, 2023).

Clay, Lauren R. *Stagestruck: The Business of Theater in Eighteenth-Century France and Its Colonies* (Ithaca, NY: Cornell University Press, 2013).

Cresswell, Tim. *On the Move: Mobility in the Western World* (New York and London: Routledge, 2006).

Dawson, Kevin. *Undercurrents of Power: Aquatic Culture in the African Diaspora* (Philadelphia: University of Pennsylvania Press, 2018).

Deacon, Desley. 'Location! Location! Location! Mind Maps and Theatrical Circuits in Australian Transnational History', *History Australia*, 5.3 (2008), pp. 81.1–81.16.

Ghobrial, John-Paul. 'Moving Stories and What They Tell Us: Early Modern Mobility Between Microhistory and Global History', *Global History and Microhistory: A Supplement Volume of* Past and Present, ed. John-Paul Ghobrial, *Past and Present*, 242.14(S) (2019), pp. 243–80.

Gottschalk, Louis Moreau. *Notes of a Pianist,* ed. Clara Gottschalk and trans. Robert E. Peterson (Philadelphia, PA: J.B. Lippincott and Co., 1881).

Greenblatt, Stephen (ed.). *Cultural Mobility: A Manifesto* (Cambridge: Cambridge University Press, 2010).

Hesselager, Jens (ed.). *Grand Opera outside Paris: Opera on the Move in Nineteenth-Century Europe* (London: Routledge, 2018).

Körner, Axel. 'Beyond *Nationaloper*: For a Critique of Methodological Nationalism in Reading Nineteenth-Century Italian and German Opera', *Journal of Modern Italian Studies*, 25.4 (2020), pp. 402–19.

Kuss, Malena. 'Puerto Rico', in Malena Kuss (ed.), *Music in Latin America and the Caribbean: An Encyclopedic History* (Austin: University of Texas Press, 2004), pp. 151–88.

Maretzek, Max. *Crotchets and Quavers: Or, Revelations of an Opera Manager in America* (New York: S. French, 1855).

Maretzek, Max. *Sharps and Flats: A Sequel to* Crotchets and Quavers (New York: American Musician Publishing Co., 1890).

Mendoza de Arce, Daniel. *Music in North America and the West Indies from the Discovery to 1850: A Historical Survey* (Lanham, MD and Oxford: Scarecrow Press, 2006).

Murphy, Tessa. *The Creole Archipelago: Race and Borders in the Colonial Caribbean* (Philadelphia: University of Pennsylvania Press, 2021).

Prest, Julia. 'Parisian Palimpsests and Creole Creations: Mme Marsan and Dlle Minette play Nina on the Caribbean Stage', *Early Modern French Studies*, 41.2 (2019), pp. 170–88.

Preston, Katherine K. *Opera for the People: English-Language Opera and Women Managers in Late 19th-Century America* (New York: Oxford University Press, 2017).

Preston, Katherine K. *Opera on the Road: Traveling Opera Troupes in the United States, 1825–60* (Urbana: University of Illinois Press, 1993).

Rindom, Ditlev. 'Arcadia Undone: Teresa Carreño's 1887 Italian Opera Company in Caracas', in Axel Körner and Paulo Kühl (eds), *Italian Opera in Global and Transnational Perspective: Reimagining* Italianità *in the Long Nineteenth Century* (Cambridge: Cambridge University Press, 2021), pp. 192–213.

Roper, L.H. (ed.). *The Torrid Zone: Caribbean Colonization and Cultural Interaction in the Long Seventeenth Century* (Columbia: University of South Carolina Press, 2018).

Rosselli, John. 'The Opera Business and the Italian Immigrant Community in Latin America 1820–1930: The Example of Buenos Aires', *Past and Present*, 127.1 (1990), pp. 155–82.

Starr, S. Frederick. *Bamboula! The Life and Times of Louis Moreau Gottschalk* (New York and Oxford: Oxford University Press, 1995).

Swift, Mary Grace. 'The Northern Tours of the Théâtre d'Orléans, 1843 and 1845', *Louisiana History: The Journal of the Louisiana Historical Association*, 26.2 (1985), pp. 155–93.

Thompson, Donald. 'Gottschalk in the Virgin Islands', *Anuario Interamericano de Investigacion Musical*, 6 (1970), pp. 95–104.

Tóth, Heléna. *An Exiled Generation: German and Hungarian Refugees of Revolution, 1848–1871* (Cambridge: Cambridge University Press, 2014).

Vella, Francesca. *Networking Operatic Italy* (Chicago, IL: University of Chicago Press, 2021).

Vidal, Cécile. *Caribbean New Orleans: Empire, Race, and the Making of a Slave Society* (Chapel Hill: University of North Carolina Press, 2019).

Walton, Benjamin. 'Italian Operatic Fantasies in Latin America', *Journal of Modern Italian Studies*, 17.4 (2012), pp. 460–71.

ID
Three

Multilingual Approaches to Colonial-Era Caribbean Theatre Research: Challenges and Interventions

Susan Thomas

This chapter problematizes the hegemony of monolingualism in colonial-era Caribbean theatre research. It considers monolingualism as linguistic ability, as a discursive and historical framework and as part of the structures governing canon creation, publishing and reception. As a region, the Caribbean shares a history of imperialism, colonization and occupation; forced and coerced labour; trans-regional migration and constant (re)negotiations of power and identity relations between centre and periphery. However, those shared characteristics—strengthened by inter-island migration and commerce—are often overlooked in favour of narratives that divide territories in the Caribbean basin by nation or colony or, more broadly, by European language group. Beginning by considering the impacts of this linguistic division on Caribbean theatre and history research, I explore the ways in which this monolingual parsing of the region's cultural history continues, in Bethany Wiggin's words, to 'haunt our critical practices'.[1]

In a 2003 article in *Profession*, Mary Louise Pratt issued a call for a new public awareness of—and commitment to—multilingualism.[2] Her influential essay was structured around four misconceptions about language, language learning and multilingualism, and four proposals for shifting public ideas through scholarship, education and policy. This chapter borrows and adapts this structure from Pratt, changing her 'misconceptions' about multilingualism to 'challenges' for recognizing multilingualism in Caribbean history and adapting our research and writing to a multilingual reality. I begin with an epistemological challenge that has led to a false understanding of the Caribbean and

---

[1] Bethany Wiggin, 'Monolingualism, World Literature, and the Return of History', *German Studies Review*, 41.3 (2018), pp. 487–503 (488).
[2] Mary Louise Pratt, 'Building a New Public Idea about Language', *Profession* (2003), pp. 110–19.

its history as a fragmented assortment of monolingual islands, colonies or nations. In this section, I consider how this misconception plays out in our disciplinary training generally and in Caribbean studies specifically, especially when dealing with the colonial era. The next section focusses on the navigational challenges that we face in changing from a monolingual to a multilingual framework, including obstacles to language learning and linguistic competencies and the presence and impact of archival silences. I then propose strategies for how a shift towards an epistemology of multilingualism might be carried out, with a particular emphasis on collaboration and interdisciplinarity. In the final section of the chapter, I propose a heightened awareness of the role and practice of translation in our work.

The 'fallacy of monolingualism'

The Caribbean is—and has always been—a multilingual space where colonizing languages such as English, French, Spanish and Dutch, as well as multiple west and central African languages, were imposed atop seven different indigenous language groups.[3] The languages existed alongside a variety of locale-specific Creoles, and smaller communities of immigrants and workers spoke other languages such as Yiddish, Ladino or—in the later period—Cantonese and Hindi. Indeed, an overarching commonality within Caribbean culture since the earliest days of European colonization has been its polyglot soundscape and experience. Yet in spite of this, humanities scholars operating in the region tend to employ an epistemological framework that stems from an ideological supposition that Bethany Wiggin has described as the 'monolingual fallacy'.[4] The supposition of a monolingual nation (or a monolingual colony), Wiggin writes, is actually a very modern practice and is based on nineteenth-century premises tied to the rise of the nation state and corresponding constructions of ethno-nationalism.[5] For those of us in music, theatre and performance studies, this monolingual framework has implications for multiple levels of our work, including discursive frameworks, archival practice, archival

---

[3] Julian Granberry, 'Indigenous Languages of the Caribbean', in William F. Keegan, Corinne L. Hofman and Reniel Rodríguez Ramos (eds), *The Oxford Handbook of Caribbean Archeology* (London and New York: Oxford University Press, 2013).

[4] Bethany Wiggin (ed.), *Babel of the Atlantic* (University Park, PA: Pennsylvania State University Press, 2019), p. 8.

[5] Wiggin, 'Monolingualism', 488–89.

interpretation, textual interpretation and translation, semiotic analysis and scholarly dissemination.

The division of the research field by language is further compounded by a tendency to downplay linguistic diversity even within specific Caribbean sites, where the polyglot environment in which theatre was produced, performed and received is often unheard in the primary sources through which we access this history.[6] This presumptive pairing of monolingualism and colony/empire hinders our understanding of the Caribbean as an interconnected and fluid space, and obstructs our understanding of the ways in which theatrical traditions and performers circulated throughout the region, shaping both local and regional economies of entertainment. Reconsidering Caribbean opera and theatre as operating within a constantly shifting, multilingual environment allows us to re-evaluate the ways in which the scripts, libretti, payment records and legal proceedings that we find preserved in archives, or the critiques and descriptions that we read about in diaries or travelogues, resounded in their own time and place.[7]

All of the authors included in this volume have thus found ourselves, at one time or another, in conferences and publications on 'the Anglophone Caribbean', 'the Hispanic/Spanish Caribbean', the 'Francophone Caribbean' or, in isolation, 'Haitian Studies' since, as Jean Jonassaint has poignantly shown, there is a robust dissociation between

---

[6] Recent scholarship is beginning to address the multilingual nature of Caribbean cultures. Juliane Braun's work on Francophone drama in New Orleans under Spanish and US control, for example, offers an important corrective in thinking about the Louisiana port city as a resiliently polyglot space. See Juliane Braun, *Creole Drama: Theatre and Society in Antebellum New Orleans* (Charlottesville, VA and London: University of Virginia Press, 2019).

[7] In asking readers to consider the ways that silenced or unheard voices resound in Caribbean theatrical history, I refer not only to performative utterances that are lost to the historical record (the improvisations of actors, the shouts of audiences), but also to the effort to locate and hear historical voices that have not been materially present in traditional archival sources—a theoretical stance that requires broad interdisciplinary engagement. The potential decolonial praxis offered by the merger of sound studies and history, and the broad reconceptualization of archives of knowledge, is perhaps most successfully apparent in the field of indigenous studies. See, for example, Jessica Bissett Perea, *Sound Relations: Native Ways of Doing Music History in Alaska* (New York and London: Oxford University Press, 2021) and Dylan Robinson, *Hungry Listening: Resonant Theory for Indigenous Sound Studies* (Minneapolis, MN: University of Minnesota Press, 2020).

studies of postcolonial Haiti and studies of the rest of the French Antilles.[8] Julia Prest, Logan J. Connors and other scholars of theatre and opera in Saint-Domingue thus find themselves working in a liminal historical space, one that does not quite fit with the history of the rest of the colonial Francophone Caribbean and remains as a palimpsest, but also apart from that of Haiti, the free nation that superseded it.

These monolingual designations and fragmentations have significant impacts on our understanding of the region in which we work and the way our scholarship is produced and disseminated, making each of us contributors to the mosaic-like epistemological framework that has resulted in what Derek Walcott famously referred to as the region's 'shattered histories'.[9] In Chapter One of this volume, Dexnell Peters calls for a reunification of these historical fragments in order to create a regional colonial-era Caribbean history that embraces fluidity, movement and interconnectivity. Such an understanding of the Caribbean has multiple precursors. For example, Antonio Benítez-Rojo famously conceived of a 'meta-archipelago', in which instances of insular difference echo and resound, 'repeating' and installing their aesthetics, values, linguistic practice and ways of knowing in other islands (real or symbolic) far beyond their original borders. This performative connection between the Caribbean and its many iterations, Michel-Rolph Trouillot notes, has resulted in the borders between centre and periphery becoming 'notoriously fuzzy'.[10] From the mainland, Walter D. Mignolo offers the fluid model of 'border thinking';[11] a practice that embraces porosity, migration and cultural flows. As promising as these models are for allowing a trans-territorial understanding of movement, migration and identity, it is rare to see scholars cross the linguistic divide to apply them. Thus, we see Benítez-Rojo most frequently applied to the work of Cubanists, while the work of Trouillot and other theorists from the Francophone Caribbean is most often applied to that of scholars writing about the same

[8] Jean Jonassaint, 'Literatures in the Francophone Caribbean', *Yale French Studies*, 103 (2003), pp. 55–63.
[9] Derek Walcott, 'The Antilles: Fragments of Epic Memory', Nobel Prize in Literature Lecture (1992) <https://www.nobelprize.org/prizes/literature/1992/walcott/lecture/>.
[10] Michel-Rolph Trouillot, 'The Caribbean Region: An Open Frontier in Anthropological Theory', *Annual Review of Anthropology*, 21.1 (1992), pp. 19–42 (19).
[11] Walter D. Mignolo, *Local Histories/Global Designs: Coloniality, Subaltern Knowledges, and Border Thinking* (Princeton, NJ: Princeton University Press, 2000), p. 45.

islands or colonies. Furthermore, to truly capture Caribbean difference requires a fluid understanding of both the temporality of historical experiences and the geographic and linguistic logics that envoiced them and gave them meaning. In other words, the conceptual metaphors that have been used to model Caribbean histories and realities *require* an awareness of the region's historical—and present—multilingualism for those models to do their intended conceptual work.

'The sea', Derek Walcott tells us, 'is history'.[12] The ocean has long been a preferred metaphor for archipelago theorists, literary scholars, poets and cultural critics who have sought to create a regional understanding of the Caribbean basin and its transatlantic connections. The metaphor serves for its obvious geographical specificity as well as its unstoppable tidal power and, while critics have attempted to employ other metaphors to capture the importance of movement and multiplicity,[13] the sea's constancy in shaping Caribbean narratives is remarkable. Perhaps it is the sea's seeming indifference to the lands that it shapes, the *flotas* (fleets) that traverse it,[14] the sounds that seem to fly across its surface, that draw historians, poets and critics back to it, again and again. Yet there is another forceful fluidity at work in the construction and realization of Caribbean history and experience, one that is perhaps less tangible but no less impactful, and that is the sound and mobility of language and linguistic practice. As an unseen expressive and syntactical force, linguistic flows throughout the Caribbean were hardly disinterested in their application. Language is an active and agentic force. It invades ears, reorders minds, shapes expression, identifies individuals and names and orders the things and experiences we encounter in the world around us. Language voices song and shapes the technique of those who sing it. The linguistic competencies and preferences of audiences help to determine

---

[12] Derek Walcott, *The Star-Apple Kingdom* (New York: Farrar, Straus and Giroux, 1979), p. 25.

[13] Consider, for example Deleuze and Guattari's concept of the rhizome and its Caribbeanization in the form of the mangrove, and Laëtitia Saint-Loubert's gloss on Gerard Genette's idea of the threshold. See Gilles Deleuze and Felix Guattari, *A Thousand Plateaus*, trans. Brian Massuni (London: Athlone Press, 1988), p. 7; Richard Burton, '"KI MON NOU YE": The Idea of Difference in Contemporary French West Indian Thought', *New West Indian Guide*, 67.1 and 2 (1993), pp. 5–32. Cited in Richard L.W. Clarke, 'Root Versus Rhizome: An "Epistemological Break" in Francophone Caribbean Thought', *Journal of West Indian Literature*, 9.1 (2000), pp. 12–41 (12); and Laëticia Saint-Loubert, *The Caribbean in Translation: Remapping Thresholds of Dislocation* (Oxford: Peter Lang, 2020), pp. 22–23.

[14] Antonio Benítez-Rojo, *The Repeating Island: The Caribbean and the Postmodern Perspective* (Durham, NC: Duke University Press, 1997), p. 7.

the selection of theatrical content and the librettists and playwrights that produce it.

Language, like a tide, can also wash away difference and can erase the inconvenient. For example, speaking of the 'colonial era' in the Caribbean highlights shared traits and experiences at the same time that it creates a viscous temporal ambiguity, potentially causing discrepancies, contrasts or disparities to sink out of sight. Yet those discrepancies, whether they are submerged at the bottom of our consciousness or not, persist. After all, the 'colonial era' in some locations was experienced as deeply nationalist in others. Consider, for example, the distinctly different ends to colonial rule in Haiti (1804), New Orleans (1803), Cuba (1898) and Jamaica (1962). The 'colonial era' designation can thus serve to wash out and obscure the experiences of places that decolonized themselves early (Haiti) or late (Jamaica, the Bahamas, etc.), or that underwent multiple colonizations by different European powers (Trinidad, Jamaica, New Orleans and others). 'Colonial-era' used as an adjective is more supple. But the inability of any terminology to fully encompass the complex messiness of history (much less a multilingual one) is an important qualifier that we would all do well to remember, especially when considering how that multilingual history is presented through translation to readers, as will be discussed below.

Navigational challenges

For those of us working on the musical and theatrical history of sites within the Caribbean basin, the supposition of monolingualism can impact the archives we visit, the texts we choose to study, the critical models we select to analyse them and even our conceptions of the very geographies that produced those texts and resulting cultural practices. Exorcizing the monolingual fallacy from our worldview and replacing it with a scholarly practice that centres the musico-dramatic practices that we study within a multilingual context is not a simple process, however, and requires a re-envisioning not only of the field in which we research but also of our own disciplinary fields themselves and of our relationship to them. In this section, I recognize two specific methodological challenges that we face as scholars, the first being issues with linguistic competency and language learning and the second concerning the need to recognize and address archival silences regarding multilingualism.

For English-speaking historians working in the Caribbean, those of us who work on French-, Spanish- or Dutch-speaking islands have competencies in the language of our specialization, but often lack linguistic competencies in other 'Caribbean' languages. This lack of multilingual capacity impacts directly upon our ability to negotiate archives and research bureaucracies in different locations and colonial contexts as well as our ability to read and interpret historical, theatrical and musical sources. For example, in conversations leading up to the publication of this volume, Jill Lane recounted that while she was in the archives researching nineteenth-century theatre in Havana, she came across papers written in Chinese that appeared to document the financial records and paperwork for a Chinese-owned theatre in Centro Habana's nascent Chinatown.[15] Such a discovery is striking in an archival context that presumes near-total Spanish-language hegemony, and it represents an opportunity for silenced voices to resound—in their own words. Yet Lane is not alone among historians working in Cuban archives (whether Cuban or visiting international scholars) in not being able to read such a document. Thus, at least temporarily, those newly discovered voices remained unheard by the majority of scholars. Yet the presence of such documents begs tantalizing questions. How might our understanding of late colonial Cuban popular theatre (a genre in which caricature of newly arrived Chinese immigrants was increasingly common) be shaped if we better understood how Chinese immigrants to Cuba self-represented in their own theatrical productions as well as how they adapted and changed existing Cuban theatrical tropes?

An additional challenge for us as opera and theatre historians is that the archives in which we work, as Eric Ketelaar has noted, are both temples and prisons,[16] sites that simultaneously venerate and privilege particular pasts while containing and controlling access to that knowledge. As sites that were invested in preserving colonial and neocolonial power, our archives, whether in the Caribbean, Madrid, Aix-en-Provence or New Orleans, often present us with a monolingual curation of the past in which the voices of the privileged were notated and preserved and the lived, multilingual and multivernacular context in which their works were performed, heard and understood is obscured or missing. Indeed, there is no searchable index for which state, institutional or religious archives contain musical or theatrical sources in languages other than the dominant colonial tongue and those that exist, like the Chinese theatre records discovered by Lane, may languish in silence precisely due to their

---

[15] Jill Lane, discussions during CECTON conference workshop, August 2021.
[16] Eric Ketelaar, 'Archival Temples, Archival Prisons: Modes of Power and Protection', *Archival Science*, 2 (2022), pp. 221–38.

difference from 'expected' monolingual records. Archival materials may thus present researchers with silence about the region's polyglot past and even in cases where evidence of multilingualism does appear, its exceptionalism in the archival record can hinder our understanding of its role and its impact.

'Silences only exist,' Michael Moss and David Thomas write, 'when researchers in the archives notice them.'[17] Archival silences can be metaphoric—gaps in curation—but those gaps can also point to literal silences. As researchers we should be attuned to both. 'Silence,' writes Edwin C. Hill Jr, 'functions in tandem with the profusion of confused sounds, commotion, and disorder within the imperial mapping of soundscapes.'[18] Theatrical production is, after all, a noisy business and not just in making spoken words or sung dialogue audible to audiences. What, for example, was the linguistic soundscape of the costume shop or the wigmaker's studio? If we read in a diary that a particular performance was not well received, how do we imagine the audience's sonic response? Did they jeer and, if so, in what language?

How, as historians, can we make multilingual voices resound if they are absent from our archival sources? Juliane Braun notes that the monolingualism present in archival sources has a grounding in theatrical practice that may not shed much light on linguistic conditions on the ground. 'From their inception to the 1760s,' she writes, 'the theatres in the French Caribbean colonies looked towards the metropole', bringing touring actors and singers from France who performed French productions.[19] How did these visiting actors and singers interact with locals and did they (like good actors anywhere) change elements of the scripts to match linguistic and cultural characteristics of the colony? Braun notes that while less common than the performance of imported plays and operas, adaptations of pre-existing works into new Creole-language compositions that addressed the Caribbean context, or even writing new works in Creole, were not uncommon. *Papa Simon ou les Amours de Thérèse et Janot* (Papa Simon or the Loves of Thérèse and Janot), for example, was an adaptation of Rousseau's 1752 opera *Le Devin du village* (The Village Fortune Teller) that was performed in Saint-Domingue in the 1770s and 1780s (and possibly as early as 1758)

---

[17] Michael Moss and David Thomas, *Archival Silences: Missing, Lost and Uncreated Archives* (London and New York: Routledge, 2021), p. 11.
[18] Edwin C. Hill Jr, *Black Soundscapes White Stages: The Meaning of Francophone Sound in the Black Atlantic* (Baltimore, MD: Johns Hopkins University Press, 2013), p. 7.
[19] Braun, *Creole Drama*, 16.

under the title *Jeannot et Thérèse*, and is attributed to a writer named Clément.[20] While the Creole dialogue of *Jeannot et Thérèse* represents an exception to the majority of archival findings related to late eighteenth- and early nineteenth-century theatrical production in the Francophone Caribbean, what might it suggest to us about the archival silences we encounter? If, as Marie-Christine Hazaël-Massieux suggests, the Creole voiced in *Jeannot et Thérèse* represented the speech of the eighteenth-century elite in the town of Le Cap,[21] what might this tell us about the multilinguistic fabric of colonial Francophone Caribbean life? How was such a locale-specific Creole understood in New Orleans—did it call up its island and social class of origin? Did actors change it in performance to match local dialect(s)?

Responding to another kind of erasure, Julia Prest considers the white imitation of black dance that was part of the performance of Clément's *Jeannot et Thérèse* in Saint-Domingue. Comparing this performance practice to enslaved people's mimicry and mockery of colonial dance traditions such as the minuet, Prest finds that the white colonial elite imitated black dance culture as a 'temporary theatrical inoculation' against the presumed threat of black dance and ritual.[22] Her analysis not only addresses the embodied, moving and sounded histories that are so difficult for archives to preserve, but her article can also be read as a response to an 'archival silence' and to Ricardo Roque's call for more research on colonial imitators.[23]

Even in cases where multilingual markers are preserved in archival documents or dramatic texts, they are often read through a monolingual lens. For example, nineteenth-century Cuban popular theatre frequently showcased linguistic markers of African-ness in the black stage dialect known as *bozal* as well as presenting European or Asian immigrants speaking marked Spanish and regional Spanish

---

[20] For more on *Jeannot et Thérèse*, see Marie-Christine Hazaël-Massieux, '*Jeannot et Thérèse*: Les deux versions', in *Textes anciens en créole français de la Caraïbe. Histoire et analyse* (Paris: Éditions Publibook, 2008), pp. 127–83; Bernard Camier and Marie-Christine Hazaël-Massieux, '*Jeannot et Thérèse*: un ópera comique en créole au milieu du XVIIIe siècle', *Revue de la société haïtienne d'histoire et de géographie*, 215 (2003), pp. 135–66; and Julia Prest, 'Pale Imitations: White Performances of Slave Dance in the Public Theatres of Pre-revolutionary Saint-Domingue', *Atlantic Studies*, 16.4 (2019), pp. 502–20.
[21] Hazaël-Massieux, '*Jeannot et Thérèse*', 131.
[22] Prest, 'Pale Imitations', 515.
[23] Ricardo Roque, 'Mimesis and Colonialism: Emerging Perspectives on a Shared History', *History Compass*, 13.4 (2015), pp. 201–11 (206).

dialects. This performance of linguistic diversity could simultaneously do decolonial and oppressive work. Linguistic difference—and its accompanying musical settings—could serve as a way to mark Cuba's essential difference from Spain in both sonic and lexical terms. At the same time, the presentation of linguistic diversity was a signifying tool for identifying social, racial and ethnic difference not only through the contrast of Spanishness and Otherness, but also through an identification of the multilingual nature of Spanish Iberia itself, with Galician, Catalonian, Ladino or Canarian speech identifiers indexing particular social and class characteristics.

Bozal, or the theatrical performance of black speech, was especially freighted, as Jill Lane has shown in her study of *bufo* theatre.[24] It has been described by Kristina Wirtz as a 'speech register' or a 'speech genre' in which characters are marked by associations of African-ness within a monolingual Spanish context. Tracing a history of parodied African speech, she breaks down how the reproduction or the 'enregisterment' of *bozal* speech contributed to the idea of a timeless and traceable African-ness through which, borrowing from Bahktin, 'social orders are not merely reflected, but actually constructed'.[25] Like the performance of black dance genres by white imitators described by Prest, *bozal* thus represented a rhetorical riposte to the perceived omnipresent threat of Cuba's enslaved population. It is clear, however, that *bozal* was not entirely a white invention and that it drew heavily from Afro-Cuban vernacular idiom. While Wirtz pushes back against the efforts by some scholars to use the written record of theatrical or literary *bozal* as a doorway to reconstruct a lost record of Spanish Creole speech in Cuba, she does consider the ways in which *bozal* practice adapted idioms from black vernacular speech at particular moments in Cuban history—such as during the Independence wars in the late nineteenth century—as a way to undercut Afro-Cuban political claims.

On the white Cuban stage, the performance of *bozal* could thus be considered a defence of monolingualism as it was the speech register's difference from standard Spanish that constituted the heart of the parody. At the same time, the voicing of *bozal* was a performative acknowledgement of Cuba's inherent linguistic diversity, not only in its

---

[24] Jill Lane, *Blackface Cuba, 1840–1895* (Philadelphia, PA: University of Pennsylvania Press, 2005) and Chapter Five of this volume.

[25] Christina Wirtz, 'The "Brutology" of *Bozal*: Tracing a Discourse Genealogy from Nineteenth-Century Blackface Theater to Twentieth-Century Spirit Possession in Cuba', *Comparative Studies in History and Society*, 55.4 (2013), pp. 800–33.

attempts to exert control over black vernacular speech, but also in its implicit recognition of unheard and unarticulated African languages. *Bozal* parody thus opened up a space between the performed speech register—actual vernacular speech—and silenced, lost or protected African languages that challenges us to reconsider the strictly monolingual construction of Cuban culture that has dominated the literature.

Strategic interventions

An initial and obvious corrective to the monolingual fallacy in Caribbean studies would be to encourage additional language training in the official languages of the Caribbean, including Haitian Kreyòl, Jamaican and other island-specific Creoles. In the United States, language requirements for graduate students in musicology generally require some level of reading knowledge in one Romance language as well as German, while theatre studies degrees generally require reading knowledge in at least one foreign language. In the UK, such study is not generally part of the formal degree requirements, but linguistic competency is expected of scholars who require it for their research. As academics who are directly involved in creating the pipeline for the next generation of scholars, we should stress to our students with research interests in the Caribbean that linguistic competency is not just desirable but, in fact, essential. We should not only encourage our students to gain competency in the primary colonial language that they may encounter in archival sources and in published scholarship, but also to study at least one other language with relevance to their area of interest. For example, a Cubanist with interest in the first wave of migration from Saint-Domingue from 1791–1804 might choose to study French, while a scholar of seventeenth-century Jamaican theatre might study Jamaican Creole as well as Spanish.

However, this recommendation comes at a time when language study in higher education is under threat. The time required to learn a language is in conflict with the need to reduce costs as well as the time necessary to complete graduate study. As a result, degree programmes in the USA have reduced language requirements dramatically, and colleges and universities are increasingly shuttering language programmes as a result. David Gramling has noted the economic policies and institutional practices that enforce and defend what he terms 'late mono/lingualism'—a syntactic formation intended to show that monolingualism is a 'changing, historically sedimented, though not necessarily declining system'.[26] He also notes a neoliberal tendency to employ the idea and terminology of multilingualism in such a way as to actually defend a monolingual status quo. Gramling suggests, for example, that the ubiquity and facility of language and translation apps devalue and disincentivize the labour necessary to learn and master an additional language.[27]

Neither these institutional problems nor the lack of linguistic competencies in other languages can be quickly or easily resolved. Rather than setting for ourselves the likely unreachable goal of individualized polyglot scholarship, where the focus is on individual attainment and linguistic control, I suggest that we instead aim for truly multilingual scholarship, with an emphasis on dialogue, relationality and collaboration. How might our understanding of the performance traditions of the colonial Caribbean change if music and theatre scholars from 'Francophone', 'Anglophone' and Spanish-speaking colonies worked together? What might we discover about the movements of musicians, the sharing of styles and the reworkings of storylines? How might our scholarship and analysis change if we bring scholars from Creole studies and linguistics into the mix? Such multilingual collaboration and expertise would allow us to gain a better understanding of the Caribbean as a multilingual and interconnected region at the same time as gaining increased insight at the textual level into how the works that we study generated meaning in their own specific contexts or how that meaning changed over time or in different locations.

This call for multilingual collaborative research is not a new concept. Gramling notes that Mary Louise Pratt, in the 2003 essay that I mentioned earlier, proposed addressing the lack of multilingual expertise in the United States by creating a 'broad coalition of scholars, learners, teachers, and policy-makers who would commit long-term to the civic work of creating a new public idea about "language, language learning, multilingualism, and citizenship"'.[28] He comments that, although Pratt's observations have stood up over the past two decades, including her critique that the 'linguistically unequipped' status of the United States (to which one might add the United Kingdom, especially after Brexit) presented challenges to its own democracy, the simple

---

[26] David Gramling, *The Invention of Multilingualism* (Cambridge: Cambridge University Press, 2021), p. 13.
[27] Gramling, *The Invention of Multilingualism*, 4–8.
[28] Pratt, 'Building a New Public Idea', 112, cited in Gramling, *The Invention of Multilingualism*, 2.

proposals that she laid out for better equipping scholars and institutions have largely gone unheeded.[29]

Collaboration between multilingual scholars working in a wider swath of locations and archives is one solution to the access issues caused by language, location and the finite nature of individual finances. Carrying out and supporting collaborative, multilingual work requires that we consider the institutional boundaries that stand in its way. Some interventions, such as the creation of conference panels that work across linguistic and territorial lines or edited volumes (like this one) that take a broad view of the multilingual Caribbean as a cultural region, are relatively simple and can be handled by academics themselves. While the diverse perspectives that can be gathered in an edited volume are useful and important, however, as noted in the introduction to the present one edited volumes cannot achieve the same goals as coordinated research, although they definitely move us in the right direction.

Such coordinated, collaborative research requires different resources and funding structures from the individualized humanities projects that are more typical of our respective disciplines, and it will require pressure on academic institutions and funding agencies to create additional opportunities for collaborative work.[30] This collaborative work should ideally include collaborations with *scholars in the locations in which we work*, creating not only a team of scholars who not only have different linguistic competencies but also different positionalities and cultural responses to linguistic cues. Édouard Glissant wrote that at times the only choices available for those speaking languages deemed at risk of disappearing under linguistic hegemonic pressure seemed to be to 'live in seclusion or open up to the other'.[31] As scholars, however, we face a similar choice: to continue the intellectual insularity of

---

[29] Gramling, *The Invention of Multilingualism*, 3–4.
[30] It appears that the UK has been doing slightly better at funding collaborative research than the USA, where the 'Collaborative Research Grants' offered by the National Endowment of the Humanities represent only a drop in the ocean in terms of funding research in the humanities. Recently funded collaborative projects in the UK appear to demonstrate a promising recognition of multilingualism as well as interdisciplinarity. These projects include the interdisciplinary project 'The Phantom on Film', funded by the Leverhulme Trust International Network Grant, and a UK Research and Innovation grant for the collaborative and multilingual project 'Doctrine, Devotion, and Cultural Expression in the Cults of Medieval Iberian Saints'.
[31] Édouard Glissant, *Poetics of Relation*, trans. Betsy Wing (Ann Arbor, MI: University of Michigan Press, 2009), p. 103.

monolingualism or to expand our conceptual, evidentiary and critical work—as well as its impact—through multilingual and trans-territorial collaboration.

Scholars of the colonial-era Caribbean could also gain much by incorporating the work and wisdom of scholars, writers, playwrights, poets and literary critics who have conceptualized the Caribbean in very different historical moments from the ones in which we work. Borrowing theoretical models developed for different historical contexts or geographic locations can admittedly be a tricky business. Yet it is in the work of twentieth- and twenty-first-century writers reflecting on contemporary Caribbean culture that we find the most comprehensive efforts to recentre the multilingualism of daily Caribbean life. This literature offers us tangible conceptual tools, including a growing body of decolonial literature and theatrical works, a corresponding body of literary analysis and a wholly independent realm of critical theory. It also offers us compelling arguments and tools through which to (re) consider Caribbean history through a multilingual lens.

How might Martinican writer Édouard Glissant's 'poetics of relation', for example, forged in the twentieth-century context of the *négritude* movement, open our eyes to consider different ways of framing the historical past and our ability to perceive the Caribbean's 'Roar [sic], in which we could still hear intoned every language of the world'?[32] James Reay Williams, writing about the twentieth-century novel, also establishes a polyglot soundscape as the norm, noting that monolingualism is the exception in Caribbean life, rather than the rule.[33] Indeed, the heterogeneous nature of Caribbean language is so prevalent that literary scholars such as Kamau Brathwaite, Jean Bernabé, Patrick Chamoiseau and Raphaël Confiant have suggested that *créolité* (Creoleness) should be at the centre of scholarly engagement with Caribbean texts, including those ostensibly written in 'standard' European languages. Furthermore, they reject the notion of Creole language as derivative of specific colonial tongues. 'La créolité n'est pas monolingue' (*creoleness is not monolingual*) they declare. 'Elle n'est pas non plus d'un multilinguisme à compartiments étanches. Son domaine c'est le langage. Son appétit: toutes les langues du monde.'[34] (*Nor is its*

---

[32] Glissant, *Poetics of Relation*, 125.

[33] James Reay Williams, *Multilingualism and the Twentieth-Century Novel: Polyglot Passages* (Basingstoke: Palgrave Macmillan, 2019).

[34] Jean Bernabé, Patrick Chamoiseau and Raphaël Confiant, *Éloge de la créolité: In Praise of Creoleness*, trans. M.B. Taleb-Khyar (Baltimore, MD: Johns Hopkins University Press, 1990), pp. 48 and 108. It is something of an irony

multilingualism divided into isolated compartments. Its field is language. Its appetite: all the languages of the world.)

While these authors are speaking specifically of twentieth-century Caribbean literature, their work offers important implications for those of us working in colonial contexts as well as in other linguistic environments. As scholars of music, theatre and performance, we tend to reach for the critical theory produced for the linguistic environment in which we work. It is rare, for example, for a Cubanist to cite Anglophone critics Derek Walcott (St Lucia) or Kamau Brathwaite (Barbados), or Francophone writers such as Jean Jonassaint (Haiti) or Édouard Glissant (Martinique). Similarly, while we do see increasing amounts of trans-territorial connection in emerging fields such as archipelago studies, it is still quite uncommon for a music or theatre historian who works on colonial Trinidad or Martinique to extend their inquiry to Cuban writers such as Fernando Ortiz, Antonio Benítez-Rojo or Nicolás Guillén. A wider utilization of critical theory on Caribbean linguistic and cultural flows drawn from across the entire region could offer music and theatre scholars new frameworks for considering multilingual impacts on performance practice, reception history, theatrical production and dissemination.

Additionally, to understand the signifying and decolonial potential of the space between languages or between speech registers, a greater understanding of Creole languages as well as other non-hegemonic languages referenced on the stage or in the archives is also necessary. What would it look like to centre *créolité* in our reception studies? Could such a framework aid us in better understanding how the scripts and libretti we find preserved in archives resounded in their time and how they indexed ideas about coloniality and power relations in their multilingual contexts? What might we gain, if we centred *créolité*, rather than metropolitan views, in our analysis of *Jeannot et Thérèse*? There are important movements happening in this direction. Bernard Camier, for example has explored how Clément's play can be seen as both a marker of colonial Creole society and also an agent for its creation, noting that in its production and performance colonists go from being 'Creole in themselves' to 'Creole for themselves'.[35] Might the views of Bernabé,

---

that the authors' homage to *créolité* was written in French (rather than Martinican Creole) and translated into English.

[35] Bernard Camier, '*Jeannot et Thérèse* (Clément, Cap-Français, 1758): A Question of Creole Identity', in Jeffrey M. Leichman and Karine Bénac-Giroux (eds), *Colonialism and Slavery in Performance: Theatre and the Eighteenth-Century French Caribbean*, Oxford University Studies in the Enlightenment (Liverpool: Liverpool University Press, 2021), p. 89–109 (109).

Chamoiseau and Confiant open our eyes not only to the political work accomplished by Francophone Creole languages in their own historical contexts, but also to the politics of linguistic representation on the nineteenth-century Cuban stage, even though Cuba never developed or maintained its own Creole language?

The case study of Chinese theatre in Havana mentioned previously calls into question how, as historians of performance, we deal with non-hegemonic languages that are often written out of the cultural histories of the places in which we work. The coolie labour system brought Chinese migrant workers to islands across the Caribbean, with the first wave of colonial-era immigration bringing primarily Cantonese-speaking immigrants to Cuba, British Guiana, Jamaica and Trinidad. These waves of immigration impacted not only hegemonic representation of colonial underclasses, but also created emerging markets for new theatrical entertainment, as Jill Lane's anecdote illustrates. Yet so much work remains to be done. Where, for example, are the Jamaican theatre historians with competencies in Chinese language, and how could those linguistic competencies enrich our understanding of popular theatre practices in the last century of British colonialism?[36] How might a centring of other non-hegemonic languages, such as Hindi, Ladino or Yiddish, shape our understanding of musical and theatrical practice and reception across the region?

Reparative translation

In *The Caribbean in Translation: Remapping Thresholds of Dislocation*, Laëtitia Saint-Loubert calls for a Caribbean studies that explores the region through an 'explicitly comparative lens', and that 'aims to echo Caribbean linguistic diversity and resist a monolinguistic reading and artificial mapping of the region's literary output'.[37] Describing the

---

[36] The role and impact of Chinese immigrants across the Caribbean has been gaining increased attention. See for example, the special issue on 'The Chinese in the Caribbean' published in the *Caribbean Quarterly*, 50.2 (June 2004); Elliott Young, *Alien Nation: Chinese Immigration in the Americas from the Coolie Era through World War II* (Chapel Hill, NC: University of North Carolina Press, 2014); and Anne-Marie Lee-Loy, 'Chinese Characters in Anglo-Caribbean Literature', in Michael A. Bucknor and Allison Donnell (eds), *The Routledge Companion to Anglophone Caribbean Literature* (Abingdon and New York: Routledge, 2011), pp. 375–82.

[37] Saint-Loubert, *The Caribbean in Translation*, 2.

Caribbean as a 'region fundamentally concerned by translation', she notes that:

> each island and territory of the region could [...] be said to perform continuous acts of translation through their internal exchanges, be it within the boundaries of a single island, territory or with immediate neighbours, but also externally, with more distant interlocutors and partners that also often coincide with former or neocolonial powers. Those exchanges might entail bridging linguistic and cultural differences engendered by centuries of multilingual encounters that have varied in scope and nature, as well as over time and space, but that nevertheless keep on exposing the region's original sense of fragmentation.[38]

Ottmar Ette considers the Caribbean's historical, experiential and discursive fragmentation as something rich in epistemic, semiotic and creative potential, but also sees this potential existing in tension with a need for repair.[39] That repair, he suggests, might most productively be located in a full engagement with the region's multilingual reality. Following this logic, Ette cites Walter Benjamin's call for a reparative restoration of language, a restoration that Benjamin delegates to the translator to carry out:

> Wie nämlich Scherben eines Gefäßes, um sich zusammenfügen zu lassen, in den kleinsten Einzelheiten einander zu folgen, doch nicht so zu gleichen haben, so muß, anstatt dem Sinn des Originals sich ähnlich zu machen, die Übersetzung liebend vielmehr und bis ins Einzelne hinein dessen Art des Meinens in der eigenen Sprache sich anbilden, um so beide wie Scherben als Bruchstück eines Gefäßes, als Bruchstück einer größeren Sprache erkennbar zu machen.[40]

> *As fragments of a vessel, in order to be reassembled, to fit in even the smallest detail, must match one another, although they need not be like one another, so too must the translation, instead of making*

---

[38] Saint-Loubert, *The Caribbean in Translation*, 1.
[39] Ottmar Ette, 'Islands, Borders and Vectors: The Fractal World of the Caribbean', in Lieven D'hulst, Jean-Marc Moura, Liesbeth De Bleeker and Nadia Lie (eds), *Caribbean Interfaces* (Amsterdam and New York: Rodopi, 2007), pp. 109–53.
[40] Walter Benjamin, 'Die Aufgabe des Übersetzers', in Tillman Rexroth (ed.), *Gesammelte Schriften*, Vol. 4 (Frankfurt am Main: Suhrkamp, 1980), p. 18.

> *the original similar to its own sense of things, rather lovingly and in detail adapt itself to the original's mode of signification in its own language, thus making both, like the fragments of a vessel, recognizable as a fragment of a larger language.*[41]

Benjamin calls for a recognition of the translator as both a skilled artisan (capable of repair) and as an artist in their own right who is able to recognize, re-envision and recreate the artistic aim of the original text which, he notes, is not to instruct, entertain or edify the reader.[42] It is worth noting that Derek Walcott in his Nobel Lecture famously called up Benjamin's fragmented vase, its relationship to an original, and the 'shards' of multilingual vocabularies. 'Break a vase', he wrote, 'and the love that reassembles the fragments is stronger than that love which took its symmetry for granted when it was whole'. Like Benjamin, Walcott ties a praxis of repair to personal emotional commitment, to *love*. He continues: 'Antillean art is this restoration of our shattered histories, our shards of vocabulary, our archipelago becoming a synonym for pieces broken off from the original continent'.[43]

In 1998, Susan Bassnett and André Lefevere argued for cultural studies to take the 'translation turn' and move translation to centre stage.[44] Edwin Gentzler writes that, although initially regarded as unrealistic, Bassnett and Lefevere's call has begun to be answered: 'Once cultural studies began studying concepts of linguistic and cultural pluralism, the fragmentation of the literary or cultural artifact, and the multiple histories behind the emergence of artistic objects, the turn to language and translation trajectories was inevitable.'[45] For Caribbeanists, these same characteristics shape our understanding of—and access to—colonial histories, and we would do well to turn our focussed attention to language and translation as well.

For scholars residing in English-speaking countries working and writing within the multilingual context of the Caribbean, translation looms large, conceptually, metaphorically (as Saint-Loubert describes) and pragmatically. We work in a scholarly and publishing ecosystem

---

[41] English translation taken from Ette, 'Islands, Borders and Vectors', p. 124. It is worth noting that in Ette's essay, only his translation—and not Benjamin's original—is included.
[42] Benjamin, 'Die Aufgabe des Übersetzers', 9.
[43] Walcott, 'The Antilles'.
[44] Susan Bassnett and André Lefevere, *Constructing Cultures: Essays on Literary Translation* (Philadelphia, PA: Clevedon, 1998), p. 123.
[45] Edwin Gentzler, *Translation and Identity in the Americas: New Directions in Translation Theory* (New York: Routledge, 2008), p. 1.

that privileges English and works to maintain its hegemony, a situation that has led Philip G. Altbach to describe English as the 'imperial tongue' dominating academic scholarship.[46] This reality requires us to build a stronger awareness of how our own writing translates and reshapes the multilingual Caribbean texts and contexts we study and write about for Anglophone readers, especially in cases where we directly translate the source texts we work with into English.

Musicologists, especially, have historically taken a rather pedestrian and uncritical approach to the role and the impact of translation in our own work, particularly those of us who work in non-hegemonic contexts such as the Caribbean. As mentioned above, once a certain level of linguistic competency is achieved (perhaps by passing a rudimentary translation exam), a student's understanding of source material in the other language is assumed, and translation of words and quotations from source texts in scholarly writing is regarded as somewhat of a rote activity. It is very rare for musicologists to receive any specific training in translation at all. The only two texts on music and translation, Helen Julia Minors's edited volume *Music, Text and Translation* and Lucile Desblache's *Music and Translation* sit apart from the methodological texts generally given to graduate students.[47]

Like the need for scholars to recognize and actively address archival silences, repairing our relationship to translation first requires an awareness of our role as translators. Translation from a source language into English occurs in our work in ways large and small. We might, for example, engage in what I would call 'focussed translation', the purposeful translation of an entire work or an embedded song or text. Or we might practise more 'passing translation', where we quickly cite a term or a few lines within our own prose, or even summarize a passage. Passing translation, in particular, may be done so smoothly and with such authority by the writer that it obscures or effaces the fact that translation has even taken place. In either situation, however, the translator wields enormous power to shape meaning and interpretation, making translation a 'dangerous act, potentially subversive and always significant'.[48] Addressing this reality, Susan Bassnett describes

---

[46] Philip G. Altbach, 'The Imperial Tongue: English as the Dominating Academic Language', *Economic and Political Weekly*, 42.36 (8–14 September 2007), pp. 3608–11.

[47] Helen Julia Minors, *Music, Text and Translation* (London, New Delhi, New York and Sydney: Bloomsbury, 2013); Lucile Desblache, *Music and Translation: New Mediations in the Digital Age* (London: Palgrave Macmillan, 2019).

[48] Susan Bassnett, *Translation Studies*, Fourth edition (London and New York: Routledge, 2014), p. 9.

the changes that have taken place in translation studies over the past three decades, noting that the 'cultural turn' that translation studies underwent in the 1990s has caused greater awareness of the fact that 'translation involves much more than the transfer of texts produced in one language into another. Translation is acknowledged as a textual process that always involved a dual context—the source and the target', with the translator and their process occupying a site in between, of ongoing and unresolved meaning-formation.[49]

Whether directly translating source texts or synthesizing the meaning in a document that is not quoted in its entirety, however, we must recognize the power we wield and the choices that we make. Lawrence Venuti changed the field of translation studies when he recognized two styles of translation that he saw as doing particular cultural and political work. The first, 'domestication', seeks to translate seamlessly the source text into the cultural and linguistic preferences of the receiving language.[50] The nuances of multilingual syntax in the source text would thus be rendered invisible in a domesticated translation or, perhaps even more problematically, replaced by cultural markers understood within the receiving context but which might index meanings from significantly different historical and cultural contexts, for example the replacing of *bozal* Spanish with minstrel-derived English. Such domesticating strategies, Venuti believes, enact a kind of epistemic violence as they erase the values inherent in the source text and the culture that created it, and instead convert it into a text that follows the cultural norms of the target language and the presumed reader. In contrast to this approach, he proposes the concept of 'foreignization', which strategically seeks to retain structural or stylistic elements of the source text with the goal of making the translation visible. In addition, this approach attempts to acknowledge and retain the affective and signifying nuances that resist translation.[51] Thus, rather than rendering invisible the translator's role with the goal of creating a translation that reads fluently, Venuti stresses that a good translation should bear the signs of its intervention. 'Fluency masks a domestication of the foreign text that is appropriative and potentially imperialistic [...] It can be countered by a *foreignising* translation that registers the irreducible differences of the foreign text.'[52]

[49] Bassnett, *Translation Studies*, 11.
[50] Lawrence Venuti, *The Translator's Invisibility: A History of Translation* (London and New York: Routledge, 1995; 2018), pp. 5–6 and 16–17.
[51] Venuti, *The Translator's Invisibility*, 13–14.
[52] Lawrence Venuti, *The Translation Studies Reader*, Second edition (London and New York: Routledge, 2004), p. 341.

Foreignizing strategies might include retaining the syntax of the original language, keeping some words that do not have a clear equivalent in the source language and making translational choices that draw a reader's attention to the fact that they are reading a translation.

Considering *which* texts to translate at all can also be a foreignizing strategy. What do we do, for example, with terms that appear frequently in colonial-era research that are now widely recognized as dehumanizing or offensive? In contemporary English-language writing, for example, we tend to avoid using the word 'slave', due to its objectifying nature, and use the more humanizing 'enslaved person' instead. What do we do, then, when translating colonial-era texts that refer to *esclaves* or *esclavos*? Awareness of this type of choice actually pits Venuti's decolonial politics of translation against a separate decolonial politics of naming. Do we domesticate the source text and change *esclavos* to 'enslaved people' in order to adapt to contemporary sensitivities? Or do we translate the source text literally? Doing so must come with the understanding that there may not be a foreignizing impact on the reader since the contemporary shift in usage from 'slave' to 'enslaved person' is quite new and English-language readers might simply see 'slave' as normalized language. A different foreignizing strategy might be applied to outdated, derogatory racializations such as the use of *nègre* in the Francophone Caribbean. Here, choosing not to translate the term at all allows its presence—and the particular kind of casual violence it exerts—to be recognized in the translation and sidesteps the risk of normalization through domestication. Similarly, we need to consider how to handle the translation of texts with multilingual markers (a Spanish source text, for example, with words or phrases in French or Yoruba). A fully domesticated text would put the lexical understanding of the reader first and would flatten the multilingual variety entirely into English. Instead, I would recommend leaving the multilingual markers in place and providing translational signposts for readers, where necessary, either in parentheses or footnotes. In all of these instances, the translator can have a greater impact by making themselves and their role visible and acknowledging and explaining the choices that they make.

In his piece 'Against Monolingualism' John Gallagher challenges us to see that 'a history that takes language seriously can be genuinely radical'.[53] For writers, historians and performers of colonial-era Caribbean theatre

---

[53] John Gallagher, 'Against Monolingualism', *History Workshop* (1 April 2020) <https://www.historyworkshop.org.uk/against-monolingualism/>.

and opera, language—written, spoken, sung or spontaneously uttered as a jeer or a cheer—is at the centre of our work. We only need to listen, and then to engage. Reconceiving of our research sites as multilingual spaces; creating networks of scholars whose strengths and knowledge will allow us to make linkages between various fragmented histories; being willing to cross boundaries of discipline and historical era to benefit from other theoretical concepts and models; questioning the epistemological structures of our institutions and pressing for changes, both large and small, where we can—these are all steps that turn us towards a collaborative praxis that will hopefully lead to a fuller understanding of the theatrical cultures and histories of the colonial-era Caribbean as well as the cultures and histories that came afterwards.

Bibliography

Altbach, Philip G. 'The Imperial Tongue: English as the Dominating Academic Language', *Economic and Political Weekly*, 42.36 (8–14 September 2007), pp. 3608–11.

Bassnett, Susan. *Translation Studies*, Fourth edition (London and New York: Routledge, 2014).

Bassnett Susan and André Lefevere. *Constructing Cultures: Essays on Literary Translation* (Philadelphia, PA: Clevedon, 1998).

Benítez-Rojo, Antonio. *The Repeating Island: The Caribbean and the Postmodern Perspective* (Durham, NC: Duke University Press, 1997).

Benjamin, Walter. 'Die Aufgabe des Übersetzers', in Tillman Rexroth (ed.), *Gesammelte Schriften*, Vol. 4 (Frankfurt am Main: Suhrkamp, 1980).

Bernabé, Jean, Patrick Chamoiseau and Raphaël Confiant. *Éloge de la créolité: In Praise of Creoleness*, trans. M.B. Taleb-Khyar (Baltimore, MD: Johns Hopkins University Press, 1990).

Braun, Juliane. *Creole Drama: Theatre and Society in Antebellum New Orleans* (Charlottesville, VA and London: University of Virginia Press, 2019).

Burton, Richard. '"KI MON NOU YE": The Idea of Difference in Contemporary French West Indian Thought', *New West Indian Guide*, 67.1 and 2 (1993), pp. 5–32.

Camier, Bernard. *'Jeannot et Thérèse* (Clément, Cap-Français, 1758): A Question of Creole Identity', in Jeffrey M. Leichman and Karine Bénac-Giroux (eds), *Colonialism and Slavery in Performance: Theatre and the Eighteenth-Century French Caribbean*, Oxford University Studies in the Enlightenment (Liverpool: Liverpool University Press, 2021), pp. 89–112.

Camier, Bernard and Marie-Christine Hazaël-Massieux. '*Jeannot et Thérèse*: un ópera comique en créole au milieu du XVIIIe siècle', *Revue de la société haïtienne d'histoire et de géographie*, 215 (2003), pp. 135–66.

Clarke, Richard L.W. 'Root Versus Rhizome: An "Epistemological Break" in Francophone Caribbean Thought', *Journal of West Indian Literature*, 9.1 (2000), pp. 12–41.

Daniel, Yvonne. *Caribbean and Atlantic Diaspora Dance: Igniting Citizenship* (Urbana, Chicago and Springfield, IL: University of Illinois Press, 2011).

Deleuze, Gilles and Felix Guattari. *A Thousand Plateaus*, trans. Brian Massuni (London: Athlone Press, 1988).

Desblache, Lucile. *Music and Translation: New Mediations in the Digital Age* (London: Palgrave Macmillan, 2019).

Ette, Ottmar. 'Islands, Borders and Vectors: The Fractal World of the Caribbean', in Lieven D'hulst, Jean-Marc Moura, Liesbeth De Bleeker and Nadia Lie (eds), *Caribbean Interfaces* (Amsterdam and New York: Rodopi, 2007), pp. 109–53.

Gallagher, John. 'Against Monolingualism', *History Workshop* (1 April 2020) <https://www.historyworkshop.org.uk/against-monolingualism>.

Gentzler, Edwin. *Translation and Identity in the Americas: New Directions in Translation Theory* (New York: Routledge, 2008).

Glissant, Édouard. *Poetics of Relation*, trans. Betsy Wing (Ann Arbor, MI: University of Michigan Press, 2009).

Gramling, David. *The Invention of Multilingualism* (Cambridge: Cambridge University Press, 2021).

Granberry, Julian. 'Indigenous Languages of the Caribbean', in William F. Keegan, Corinne L. Hofman and Reniel Rodríguez Ramos (eds), *The Oxford Handbook of Caribbean Archeology* (London and New York: Oxford University Press, 2013).

Hazaël-Massieux, Marie-Christine. *Textes anciens en créole français de la Caraïbe. Histoire et analyse* (Paris: Éditions Publibook, 2008).

Hill, Edwin C. Jr. *Black Soundscapes White Stages: The Meaning of Francophone Sound in the Black Atlantic* (Baltimore, MD: Johns Hopkins University Press, 2013).

Jonassaint, Jean. 'Literatures in the Francophone Caribbean', *Yale French Studies*, 103 (2003), pp. 55–63.

Ketelaar, Eric. 'Archival Temples, Archival Prisons: Modes of Power and Protection', *Archival Science*, 2 (2022), pp. 221–38.

Lane, Jill. *Blackface Cuba, 1840–1895* (Philadelphia, PA: University of Pennsylvania Press, 2005).

Lee-Loy, Anne-Marie. 'Chinese Characters in Anglo-Caribbean Literature', in Michael A. Bucknor and Allison Donnell (eds), *The Routledge Companion to Anglophone Caribbean Literature* (Abingdon and New York: Routledge, 2011), pp. 375–82.

Manuel, Peter (ed.). *Creolizing Contradance in the Caribbean* (Philadelphia, PA: Temple University Press, 2009).

Mignolo, Walter D. *Local Histories/Global Designs: Coloniality, Subaltern Knowledges, and Border Thinking* (Princeton, NJ: Princeton University Press, 2000).

Minors, Helen Julia. *Music, Text and Translation* (London, New Delhi, New York and Sydney: Bloomsbury, 2013).

Moss, Michael and David Thomas. *Archival Silences: Missing, Lost and Uncreated Archives* (London and New York: Routledge, 2021).

Perea, Jessica Bissett. *Sound Relations: Native Ways of Doing Music History in Alaska* (New York and London: Oxford University Press, 2021).

Pratt, Mary Louise. 'Building a New Public Idea about Language', *Profession* (2003), pp. 110–19.

Prest, Julia. 'Pale Imitations: White Performances of Slave Dance in the Public Theatres of Pre-revolutionary Saint-Domingue', *Atlantic Studies*, 16.4 (2019), pp. 502–20.

Robinson, Dylan. *Hungry Listening: Resonant Theory for Indigenous Sound Studies* (Minneapolis, MN: University of Minnesota Press, 2020).

Roque, Ricardo. 'Mimesis and Colonialism: Emerging Perspectives on a Shared History', *History Compass*, 13.4 (2015), pp. 201–11.

Saint-Loubert, Laëticia. *The Caribbean in Translation: Remapping Thresholds of Dislocation* (Oxford: Peter Lang, 2020).

Trouillot, Michel-Rolph. 'The Caribbean Region: An Open Frontier in Anthropological Theory', *Annual Review of Anthropology*, 21.1 (1992), pp. 19–42.

Venuti, Lawrence. *The Translation Studies Reader*, Second edition (London and New York: Routledge, 2004).

Venuti, Lawrence. *The Translator's Invisibility: A History of Translation* (London and New York: Routledge, 1995; 2018).

Walcott, Derek. 'The Antilles: Fragments of Epic Memory', Nobel Prize in Literature Lecture (1992) <https://www.nobelprize.org/prizes/literature/1992/walcott/lecture/>.

Walcott, Derek. *The Star-Apple Kingdom* (New York: Farrar, Straus and Giroux, 1979).

Wiggin, Bethany. 'Monolingualism, World Literature, and the Return of History', *German Studies Review*, 41.3 (2018), pp. 487–503.

Wiggin, Bethany (ed.). *Babel of the Atlantic* (University Park, PA: Pennsylvania State University Press, 2019).

Wirtz, Christina. 'The "Brutology" of Bozal: Tracing a Discourse Geneology from Nineteenth-Century Blackface Theater to Twentieth-Century Spirit Possession in Cuba', *Comparative Studies in History and Society*, 55.4 (2013), pp. 800–33.

Williams, James Reay. *Multilingualism and the Twentieth-Century Novel: Polyglot Passages* (Basingstoke: Palgrave Macmillan, 2019).

Young, Elliott. *Alien Nation: Chinese Immigration in the Americas from the Coolie Era through World War II* (Chapel Hill, NC: University of North Carolina Press, 2014).

Part II

Approaches

Four

Connecting Metropole and Colony? Harlequin Travels to Suriname

Sarah J. Adams

In her ground-breaking book, *White Innocence*, Afro-Surinamese Dutch anthropologist Gloria Wekker points out that scholarship still overwhelmingly discusses metropolitan and colonial cultures 'as separate worlds [...] that did not impinge upon each other'.[1] This isolated treatment of cultural formations in either the Netherlands or its colonies neglects the constant movement and interaction of bodies, goods and knowledge that impacted and shaped those two orbits. Taking Wekker's complaint seriously, this chapter will seek to study the cultures of the Netherlands and the Dutch Caribbean together in a single field of analysis.[2] More specifically, it will turn to the popular Harlequin figure, originally from the Italian commedia dell'arte tradition, and evaluate his relation to the principles and practices of colonial power at the time when he travelled across the Atlantic and started populating the Paramaribo stages in the decades around 1800.

Harlequin is a particularly intriguing figure because he embodies exclusion and empowerment simultaneously. In a period marked by the expansion of slavery and increased imperialist fervour, Anglo-American scholars have argued, Harlequin's black mask could be easily interpreted

---

[1] Gloria Wekker, *White Innocence: Paradoxes of Colonialism and Race* (Durham, NC: Duke University Press, 2016), p. 25. The research for this article informs my bigger project, 'Blackface Burlesques', which is supported by the Research Foundation of Flanders (FWO). I would like to thank Michiel van Kempen for making available to me his unpublished survey of theatre performances in Suriname (1770–1999), and for drawing my attention to Harlequin's similarity to the Afro-Suriname trickster, Anansi.

[2] This is also the approach recommended by Ann Laura Stoler and Frederick Cooper in 'Between Metropole and Colony: Rethinking a Research Agenda', in Stoler and Cooper (eds), *Tensions of Empire: Colonial Cultures in a Bourgeois World* (Berkeley: University of California Press, 1997), p. 4.

as a reference to Afro-Atlantic identities.[3] Many aesthetic and dramaturgical elements of the 'harlequinade' (a pantomime featuring Harlequin), whose black-masked protagonist was often connected to idiocy, lust and subjection, were later moulded into the racist fare of minstrel performers (which are discussed in Chapter Five of this volume).[4] However, experts in the commedia dell'arte tradition also stress that we should not underestimate the subversive nature of Harlequin.[5] He has been a pure outsider since his sixteenth-century origins in Italy and was positioned as critical of stories that were managed by those in power. As one of the traditional *zanni* or servants, Harlequin broke all conventions and was able—often with the help of supernatural forces—to transform himself into anything, thus embodying sociopolitical change and celebrating the relativity of orders.

As a consequence, the harlequinade seems to simultaneously carry out and challenge the dichotomies between metropole and colony, and between sentiments of the colonizer and the colonized. Such binaries were strategically produced and reproduced by colonials, but as Ann Laura Stoler and Frederick Cooper remind us, they have also been etched deeply in our historiographies.[6] While these categoric conceptions have proven enduring, they were entirely out of sync with the centrality of colonialism in metropolitan wealth and with the quotidian experiences in the overseas colonies. This paradox recalls what Elizabeth Maddock Dillon has referred to as the 'intimate distance' of colonial relations. In the metropole, Dillon asserts in *New World Drama*, white people distanced themselves from racialized exploitation by taking recourse to geographical distance and representational strategies of erasure whereas, in the colonies, colonists dissociated themselves in juridical and biological terms from black people—enslaved or otherwise

---

[3] These include John O'Brien, *Harlequin Britain: Pantomime and Entertainment, 1690–1760* (Baltimore, MD: Johns Hopkins University Press, 2004), pp. 117–37; Robert Hornback, *Racism and Early Blackface Comic Traditions: From the Old World to the New* (Cham: Palgrave Macmillan, 2018).

[4] For a trans-European study of Africanized Harlequins and their relation to minstrel culture, see Hornback, *Racism and Early Blackface*. Eric Lott, too, pays some attention to Harlequin's roots in the commedia dell'arte in *Love and Theft: Blackface Minstrelsy and the American Working Class* (New York: Oxford University Press, 1993; 2013), p. 21.

[5] One text that captures Harlequin's subversive character quite brilliantly is Michele Bottini, 'You Must Have Heard of Harlequin...', trans. Samuel Angus McGehee and Michael J. Grady, in Judith Chaffee and Olly Crick (eds), *The Routledge Companion to Commedia dell'Arte* (New York: Routledge, 2017), pp. 55–56.

[6] Stoler and Cooper, 'Between Metropole and Colony', 8.

subjected—with whom they lived in profound communion in spatial terms.[7]

Attempting to connect Dutch metropolitan discourses to those of the colony, this chapter will think of Harlequin as a hybrid figure who materializes the connection between the zones. I here employ the term 'hybridity' as proposed by Mikhail Bakhtin and fleshed out by Homi K. Bhabha. Bakhtin has used the concept primarily in a linguistic context, referring to the idea that one utterance can be double-voiced. This happens quite evidently in Creole languages but, as Robert C. Young asserts, Bakhtin also uses hybridization to describe 'the ability of one voice to ironize and unmask the other within the same utterance'.[8] Such politicized hybridity emerges in society through a 'carnivalesque aesthetics', in which transgressive behaviour thrives beneath the surface of social order, constantly threatening to overturn the status quo.[9] In *The Location of Culture*, Bhabha shifts this undermining of authority through hybridization to 'the dialogical situation of colonialism'.[10] Hybridity, for Bhabha, rises as an active moment of resistance when colonial power loses its supposed purity and finds itself open to criticism. Harlequin was a nimble and gaudy type who, wearing a black mask, subscribed to the boundaries that (white) authority had drawn up, but at the same time his small-scale revolutions could destabilize those boundaries.

The harlequinade has received little scholarly attention in relation to the Netherlands and Suriname, even though it became a staple of the theatrical culture on both sides of the Dutch Atlantic. Harlequin emerged in the late-seventeenth and early-eighteenth-century Low Countries as a part of fully fledged comedies, entr'actes or short slapstick episodes. In the closing decades of the eighteenth century then, the harlequinade made its entrance into Amsterdam pantomime and dance productions with high-tech stages, special effects and large orchestras. These new musical productions focussed primarily on exotic fantasy, grandeur and magic.[11] In the Netherlands, Harlequin also

---

[7] Elizabeth Maddock Dillon, *New World Drama: The Performative Commons in the Atlantic World, 1649–1849* (Durham, NC and London: Duke University Press, 2014), pp. 131–32.

[8] Robert J.C. Young, *Colonial Desire: Hybridity in Theory, Culture and Race* (London and New York: Routledge, 1995), p. 19.

[9] See Mikhail Bakhtin, *Rabelais and His World*, trans. Hélène Iswolsky (Bloomington: Indiana University Press, 1984).

[10] Young, *Colonial Desire*, 21; Homi K. Bhabha, *The Location of Culture* (London and New York: Routledge, 1994), pp. 102–22.

[11] Jacob Adolf Worp, 'Arlekijns en Krispijns op ons tooneel', *Noord en Zuid* (1896), pp. 35–43; Robert Erenstein, 'De invloed van de commedia dell'arte in

appeared regularly as a trickster figure in carnivals and youth culture. He first entered the Suriname stage in 1789 in a pantomime production by one S. Azor, titled *De Chineese Schim, genaamd Arlequin de Tovenaar* (The Chinese Silhouette, also known as Harlequin the Magician). Many more pantomimes and harlequinades were programmed in the years and decades that followed, but these productions have remained unstudied until today. The limited studies on Suriname's theatrical culture focus on the overwhelming presence of canonical Amsterdam box-office successes in the Paramaribo repertoire list, including the tragedies and comedies of Voltaire, Lucretia W. van Merken and, most prominently, August von Kotzebue. This has led researchers to assume that the Suriname stage largely mirrored that of the Netherlands.[12] However, we need to be careful not to treat colonial-era Caribbean theatre as a mere copy of the metropolitan model—nor should we assume that the metropole offered any kind of model at all.[13] According to Dillon and Peter Reed, it was precisely the often-neglected burlesque genres that were open to local revisions.[14] Pantomimes, dance acts and masquerades were, by their nature, ephemeral. They relied heavily on the situation in which they were staged and were not always tethered to a written script—something that severely complicates our understanding of these productions today.

As my case study, I will analyse the Dutch farce *Arlequin, tovenaar en barbier* (Harlequin, magician and barber) in the fraught context in which it was produced as it cruised the ocean and took to the Suriname stage in April 1813 and August 1814. Written in 1730 by the Dutch comic

Nederland tot 1800', *Scenarium: Nederlandse reeks voor theaterwetenschap*, 5 (1981), pp. 91–106.

[12] Michiel van Kempen, *Een geschiedenis van de Surinaamse literatuur*, Vol. 1 (Breda: De Geus, 2003), pp. 95–101; Merel van Leeuwen, 'Kotzebue en de ondergang of redding van het Nederlandse Theater: De import- en exportroute van *De kruisvaarders van August* von Kotzebue naar en van de Amsterdamse Schouwburg in de negentiende eeuw' (MA dissertation, University of Amsterdam, 2019), pp. 70–75.

[13] Stoler and Cooper, 'Between Metropole and Colony', 3. Scholars have made this point in relation to theatre in France and Saint Domingue, too. See various chapters in Jeffrey Leichman and Karine Bénac-Giroux (eds), *Colonialism and Slavery in Performance: Theatre and the Eighteenth-Century French Caribbean*, Oxford University Studies in the Enlightenment (Liverpool: Liverpool University Press, 2021).

[14] Dillon, *New World Drama*, 156; Peter Reed, *Rogue Performances: Staging the Underclasses in Early American Performances* (New York: Palgrave Macmillan, 2009), p. 19.

playwright Willem van der Hoeven, the farce stages the tricks Harlequin played on (and tribulations he suffered at the hands of) some of the well-known *vecchi*—here Pantaloon, Capitano and Doctor Belloardo. At first sight, *Arlequin, tovenaar en barbier* is completely detached from any explicit colonialist themes and patterns. However, it does produce scenes and dramaturgies that bring to the fore the complex dynamic between colony and metropole, and between colonizer and colonized. It can teach us about the opportunities and obstacles that arise when studying those fields in reference to each other.

Coding Harlequin's mask

Before travelling to Suriname, *Arlequin, tovenaar en barbier* had proved extremely popular in playhouses across the Netherlands.[15] Although van der Hoeven wrote down the harlequinade in 1730, its Amsterdam premiere took place in 1698 and it had been staged dozens of times in the following years. It is thus very likely that some of the aesthetics and arrangements had changed drastically by 1730. The farce was a favourite with the public in the Amsterdam Theatre until the 1780s, and it was programmed long after in other playhouses across the Netherlands. Indeed, it was so popular that Cornelis Troost, one of the most famous Dutch artists of the eighteenth century, dedicated one of his works to *Arlequin, tovenaar en barbier* in 1737 (see Figure 1 below).

Van der Hoeven's farce never became this popular in Suriname, but it did have two healthy runs at the Jewish Theatre in April 1813 and August 1814. There were two main theatre buildings in Paramaribo. The Holland Theatre, also termed the Christian Theatre, was constructed in 1775 and its main residing troupe Pro Excolenda Eloquentia, containing both professional actors and amateurs, presented up to eight new productions a year.[16] As in the metropole, Jewish people were not welcome in the Holland Theatre. Given that at least one-third of the white population in Suriname was Jewish, this policy was remarkable. The local Jewish people, however, built their own playhouse in Saramaccastraat in 1776. Their main theatre company, De Verreezene Phoenix (The Resurrected Phoenix), was known for its professionalism, and created some twelve new productions every year, in addition to burlesque shows and circus

---

[15] For a list of performances in the Amsterdam Theatre, see the Onstage database of the University of Amsterdam: <https://www.vondel.humanities.uva.nl/onstage/plays/837>.
[16] Van Kempen, *Een geschiedenis* 1, 96.

performances.[17] Nothing is known about their production of van der Hoeven's farce, except that it was paired with C.G. de Falbaire's *De school der zeeden* (The School of Morals) in 1813 and with Kotzebue's *De papegaai* (The Parrot) in 1814.

The plot of *Arlequin, tovenaar en barbier* is quite simple. Harlequin is the mischievous and witty servant of Anthonio, who is in love with Pantaloon's daughter Sofy. The latter, however, is fated to marry either Capitano or Doctor Belloardo. In keeping with the commedia tradition, Capitano and Belloardo represent physical and intellectual haughtiness: the former constantly brags about his military bravery yet flees as soon as action is needed, while the latter is an arrogant type who uses Latin phrases in and out of season. The farce mainly shows the schemes of Harlequin to trick Pantaloon into believing that Anthonio, whose financial means are apparently insufficient, is in fact the best match for his daughter. By making himself invisible, for instance, Harlequin is able to repeatedly hit Capitano and Belloardo with his trademark stick and create confusion.

Traditionally, Harlequin's presence on stage was socially coded. His creative gimmicks challenged existing orders and made those in power look like incompetent fools.[18] In van der Hoeven's farce, it is Harlequin's goal to prevent a marriage based on capital and prestige and to advance an affectionate relationship that transcends socioeconomic divides. But could audiences understand Harlequin's mask as racially coded too? Before looking at Paramaribo, let us examine how Harlequin was perceived in the metropole. It is not clear when exactly an Afro-diasporic identity became available as a referent for Harlequin's mask in the Netherlands. The first production to unambiguously present Harlequin as black was Jean Rochefort's 1803 pantomimic ballet, *Pantalon, Oost-Indisch planter, of Arlequin uit slaverny door toverkunst* (Pantaloon East Indian planter, or Harlequin magically liberated from slavery), in which a wood nymph magically transforms a plantation slave into the black-masked Harlequin and gives him supernatural powers to rebel against his former masters. Evidence suggests, however, that Harlequin may have already been racialized decades earlier. A Dutch carnival cartoon of 1742, for

[17] Van Kempen, *Een geschiedenis* 1, 97–98; 192–95. For a contemporary discussion of the Jewish Theatre, see David Nassy, *Geschiedenis der kolonie van Suriname* (1791) (Amsterdam: S. Emmering, 1974), pp. 181–82.
[18] Scott McGehee, 'The Pre-Eminence of the Actor in Renaissance Context: Subverting the Social Order', in Judith Chaffee and Oliver Crick (eds), *The Routledge Companion to Commedia dell'Arte* (New York: Routledge, 2015), pp. 9–16.

Figure 1: Cornelis Troost, *Arlequin, tovenaar en barbier: De bedrogen rivalen*, 1738. The Hague: Mauritshuis. Inventory number 183. Retrieved through Wikimedia Commons.

instance, openly referred to him as a 'Blackie' ('Swartkop')—a racist slur that was commonly used for people of African descent.[19] Troost's painting, mentioned earlier, seems to indicate that van der Hoeven's Harlequin, too, may have been understood by Dutch audiences as a black individual. In it, Harlequin does not wear his conventional black half-mask with a red knob to symbolize diabolism, but a deep-brown, full-face mask with dark eyebrows and a beard. Since actors of the Amsterdam Theatre did usually wear the half-masks of the commedia dell'arte, it is intriguing that Troost, consciously or unconsciously, put forward a mask that more closely resembled a black man's face than a stock commedia mask.

At the same time, it is unsurprising that Troost seemed to have in mind an Africanized character for Antonio's servant in *Arlequin, tovenaar en barbier*. Servitude in the metropole could be linked to blackness quite evidently. From the mid-seventeenth century onwards, an Afro-Atlantic community had started to settle in the Jewish quarter of Amsterdam, and it swelled steadily through the next century. Most members of this community had travelled from Suriname with their (former) masters and were employed as servants in wealthy families.[20] As Karwan Fatah-Black and Matthias van Rossum have shown, some of these people would even have been enslaved (there is a persistent idea among historians that enslaved Africans and Asians who set foot ashore in the Dutch Republic were liberated all at once, but slavery existed there until well into the nineteenth century).[21]

Racialized and forced labour conditions are the undeniable backgrounds against which we need to read the Suriname productions of van der Hoeven's farce. Although 1814 marked the year in which the

---

[19] It is an allegorical cartoon in which Pulcinella and Harlequin represent two opposing sides in the Austrian War of Succession, Germany and France respectively. The cartoon is held at the Amsterdam Rijksmuseum and is available at <https://www.rijksmuseum.nl/nl/collectie/RP-P-OB-83.772>.

[20] For the black community in early-modern Amsterdam, see Mark Ponte, '"Al de swarten die hier ter stede comen:" Een Afro-Atlantische gemeenschap in zeventiende-eeuws Amsterdam', *TSEG / Low Countries Journal of Social and Economic History*, 15.4 (2019), pp. 33–62; Carl Haarnack and Dienke Hondius, '"Swart" in Nederland: Afrikanen en Creolen in de noordelijke Nederlanden vanaf de Middeleeuwen tot de twintigste eeuw', in Esther Schreuder and Elmer Kolfin (eds), *Black is Beautiful: Rubens tot Dumas* (Zwolle: Waanders, 2008), pp. 88–107.

[21] Karwan Fatah-Black and Matthias van Rossum, 'Slavery in a "Slave Free Enclave?" Historical Links between the Dutch Republic, Empire and Slavery, 1580s–1860s', *Werkstatt Geschichte*, 66/67 (2014), pp. 55–74.

King of the Netherlands—for reasons more strategic than idealistic—abolished the Dutch slave trade, concrete measures were not taken until 1819. Moreover, many plantations were booming in this period. The economic crisis of the 1770s (provoked by an insatiable demand for capital in the colonies, which led to a rash of speculation and, ultimately, a credit crisis) had resulted in a temporary reduction in sugar, coffee, cotton and mixed crop plantations in Suriname, from 406 in 1770 to 383 in 1812, only to mount back to 416 in 1820 and 564 in 1829.[22] In the same decades, Suriname witnessed a rapidly shifting demography. By the time De Verreezene Phoenix produced *Arlequin, tovenaar en barbier*, more than half of the free population in Paramaribo was non-white. One reason for this development is the wave of white emigration in the 1770s, which gave free men of colour the opportunity to fill positions that had long been held exclusively by white people.[23] Most importantly, however, it was domestic relations that closed the gap between white people, people of colour (*kleurlingen*) and black people. The dearth of white women in Suriname, as in Indonesia, had turned concubinage into an established and accepted phenomenon in Dutch colonial sites. Women of colour who, willingly or unwillingly, entered into sexual relationships with white plantation managers could obtain freedom for themselves or, more frequently and successfully, lobby to have their children manumitted.[24]

The question is how colonial theatre audiences made sense of Harlequin, his mask and his position as a servant in these charged circumstances of slavery and 'miscegenation'. Even though there is no confirmation that actors of De Verreezene Phoenix, like other troupes in Paramaribo, had black masks at their disposal, it is plausible that they did. First, the Jewish theatre company was known for its aesthetic skill. Second, and more importantly, advertisements for slave auctions indicate that Harlequin had become a common name for enslaved people in Suriname.[25] This means that plantation

---

[22] Kwame Nimako and Glenn F.W. Willemsen, *The Dutch Atlantic: Slavery, Abolition and Emancipation* (London: Pluto Press, 2011), p. 68.
[23] Rosemarijn Hoefte and Jean Jacques Vrij, 'Free Black and Colored Women in Early-Nineteenth-Century Paramaribo', in David Barry Gaspar and Darlene Clark Hine (eds), *Beyond Bondage: Free Women of Color in the Americas* (Urbana: University of Illinois Press, 2004), pp. 145–68 (152).
[24] Hoefte and Vrij, 'Free Black and Colored Women', 153–56.
[25] These appear in *Surinaamsche Courant* 20 (11 March 1830), *Surinaamsche Courant* 63 (7 August 1832) and *Nieuwe Surinaamsche Courant* 74 (16 September 1835), to name but a few examples. As outlined in Chapter Nine of this volume, enslaved people named Arlequin, or Scapin or especially

managers and owners must have recalled the popular commedia figure as they purchased their new captives at the slave markets and gave them new names. The Holland and Jewish Theatres were indeed primarily oriented towards elite audiences and the largest share of the spectators—but not all of them, as we shall see below—would have been slave owners.[26] All this suggests that the black-masked Harlequin was perceived as a black individual. His servile status, in a society defined by and depending on the slavery-based plantation economy, will have supported this idea.

Marking Anthonio's servant as black also made sense in the light of the growing number of black people and people of colour who found a way to skirt the social, gendered and racial divisions along which colonial society was organized. More specifically, Harlequin's supposedly fixed racial and social identity may have been a reflection of the fear and anxiety which this new pattern provoked among white colonials.[27] Operating the logic of 'intimate distance', colonials insisted on a cultural, social and political dissociation from the free black people, *kleurlingen* and captives—people with whom they lived in close spatial intimacy. In an attempt to prevent social boundaries between white people and black people from collapsing, in 1804 the Court of Policy and Criminal Justice, for instance, raised taxes on manumissions from 50–100 to 250–500 guilders.[28] Numerous other regulations were proposed to maintain legal and socioeconomic distance, and all of them had the same professed objective: openly signalling that black people's inferior status was unalterable.[29] The correlation between blackness and servitude was presented as immutable and was crystallized in the figure of Harlequin, who possibly confirmed and perhaps reinforced the strict boundaries which colonials so nervously cemented in their new regulations and laws.

Figaro—all potentially subversive servant figures—were present in colonial Saint-Domingue (and elsewhere).
[26] Van Kempen, *Een geschiedenis* 1, 98.
[27] For more on concubinage in the Dutch East Indies and the implications of these sexual bonds for white, male, colonial identity, see Ann Laura Stoler, 'Making Empire Respectable: The Politics of Race and Sexual Morality in 20th-Century Colonial Cultures', *American Ethnologist*, 16.4 (1989), pp. 634–60 (638).
[28] Hoefte and Vrij, 'Free Black and Colored Women', 149.
[29] Hoefte and Vrij, 'Free Black and Colored Women', 152.

The politics of blackface ridicule

Harlequin's black mask, however, was not solely a symbol of racialized subjection. As I have argued elsewhere for the Amsterdam stage, Harlequin also was a ready-made figure for racialized comic appropriation.[30] Mediated through generic conventions, he was a nimble, infantile and lusty black type who conjured a subtle mix of fascination and aversion, of laughing with and laughing at. Throughout the farce, Harlequin's bold jokes and ventures towards Capitano and Belloardo meet with reprimands from Pantaloon, who repeatedly attacks Harlequin both verbally and physically. Ignoring these demurrals and assaults, Harlequin is always energized to take his opponents for a further ride. He is pre-eminently a figure who brings together sentiments of terror and pleasure. It is perhaps no coincidence then, that the harlequinade as a genre seems to subtly disappear from the Amsterdam stage in tandem with the arrival of minstrelsy. In Paramaribo, too, the final recorded harlequinade, *Pantalon Bakker of De drie bedrogen minnaars* (Pantaloon Baker, or The three deceived lovers), was scheduled some years after the first minstrel troupe, the 'American Ethiopian Minstrels', took to the stage in 1854.[31]

Harlequin's ultimate prank in *Arlequin, tovenaar en barbier* is particularly interesting in this respect, because it includes an episode of explicit blackface ridicule. Wearing a blond toupée and a barber's apron, Harlequin pretends to be a hairdresser who could transform the ugliest and oldest men into attractive suitors. Capitano and Belloardo, wanting to seduce the young Sofy, are lured into paying him a visit. Troost's painting shows this scene and depicts the men tied to the chairs in Harlequin's improvised shop. They both wear sailcloth around their necks and one wears an oversized bowl used as a shaving mug. Seeing all those *bric-à-brac* materials, Capitano and Belloardo become suspicious. As Harlequin heavy-handedly treats their hair with a currycomb, they bellow with pain: 'Ben jy een Barbier! Ik geloof eer dat je een Barbaar zult weezen' (*Are you a Barber! You are more like a Barbarian*).[32] Harlequin, however, continues to work towards the supreme moment of his joke: painting their faces black!

---

[30] Sarah J. Adams, *Repertoires of Slavery: Dutch Theater Between Abolitionism and Colonial Subjection, 1770–1810* (Amsterdam: Amsterdam University Press, 2023), pp. 126–33.

[31] Michiel van Kempen's inventory lists the first minstrel show in the summer of 1854 and the last recorded harlequinade in the summer of 1859.

[32] [Willem van der Hoeven], *Arlequin, tovenaar en barbier* (Amsterdam: David Ruarus, 1730), 40.

Preparing for this antic, Harlequin must have thought that Pantaloon, who kept defending Capitano and Belloardo despite their stupidity, would never consent to black men, or men painted in black, marrying his daughter. When the two men finally leave the barber shop, their appearance provokes laughter among bystanders:

MIZO	Wat schepsels benne dit! Dit zyn twee kluchtige dingen!
PIEROT	Twee mooye vastelavond gekken, om mé in de bocht te springen.
MIZO	Zoet, jongens, trek zo niet, laat ons de menschen eerst bezien. Heeden! 't Lyken wel twee Moorze keuningen.[33]

MIZO	*What kind of creatures are those? They are two farcical things!*
PIEROT	*Two lovely carnival fools, ready to go on a spree.*
MIZO	*Now, boys, easy, let us have a look at these men more closely. Dear! They look like two Moorish kings.*

Even though Capitano and Belloardo make haste to wash off their faces in the nearest creek, they are rebuffed and rejected by Pantaloon, who now admits that perhaps Anthonio is a better match for Sofy after all. Harlequin's comic carousel had proved successful.

Using blackface as an emblem of sexuality and folly was a trope in Dutch theatre long before van der Hoeven's harlequinade. As far back as the fourteenth-century Dutch farce *De Buskenblaser* (The Box Blower), for instance, blackface was used for such purposes. Attempting to look more handsome, the old white protagonist of the farce is tricked into blowing into a box, thus blackening his own countenance. As he shows himself lustily before his much younger wife, she mocks him for being 'swert al een moriaen' (I.120) (*black as a Moor*) and claims that she 'sach noit leliker creature' (I.125) (*never saw an uglier creature*).[34] Crafting Harlequin's barber scene, van der Hoeven replayed a longstanding association between stage blackness, laughter, sexuality and, as the reactions of Mizo and Pierot reveal, racial alterity. He also capitalized on the common sentiments of white metropolitans regarding the Dutch

---

[33] [van der Hoeven], *Arlequin, tovenaar en barbier*, 44.
[34] The Dutch quotations are taken from (anonymous) 'Buskenblazer, Sotternieën', in Pieter Leendertz Jr (ed.), *CD-ROM Middelnederlands* (The Hague and Antwerp: Sdu Uitgevers/Standaard Uitgeverij). English translations are cited in Hornback, *Racism and Early Blackface*, 43.

Afro-Atlantic community, whose members were generally held in low esteem, ridiculed and feared.[35]

It is intriguing how part of the humour in this barber scene seems to consist in the fact that the bystanders immediately recognize that these two 'creatures' are not actually black people—they merely *look* like Africans. The ironic distance installed between white actors and their comic, racialized impersonations was one of the central ingredients for minstrelsy and a key strategy for white metropolitan audiences to give vent to their fascination with blackness while also oppressing it through ridicule.[36] To a certain extent, the same rationale may have been appropriate in Paramaribo, where the scene allowed white actors and spectators to degrade Afro-diasporic people by mocking them, thus hoping to reassert white dominance in the light of the increased and, in the eyes of colonists, worrisome social mobility of non-white people in the colony.

However, as Jill Lane has illustrated with regard to the mid-nineteenth-century Cuban context, the performative pattern of stage blackness—realized through black masks or make up—was a highly complex and charged sign in the colonial theatre.[37] The simultaneous drawing up and traversing of racial boundaries may have had a much more powerful potential in the context of Suriname than in the Dutch metropole. The idea that skin colour could be painted on one's face and subsequently washed off implied that blackness and whiteness were indeed unstable and, more problematically for white colonists, negotiable categories. Harlequin comes to the fore as a hybrid figure that testified to the desires of the colonizer while simultaneously satirizing and subverting them.

Magic rebellions and spider Anansi

Harlequin thus possibly succeeded in unmasking binaries and presenting them as constructed and artificial. In a colonial context, his rebellion had the potential to be more radical still. The reason for this lies in

[35] Miriam Claude Meijer, *Race and Aesthetics in the Anthropology of Petrus Camper, 1722–1789* (Amsterdam: Atlanta, 1999), p. 59.
[36] Lott, *Love and Theft*, 6.
[37] Jill Lane, 'Blackface Nationalism, Cuba 1840–1868', *Theatre Journal*, 50.1 (1998), pp. 21–38. See also Julia Prest's essay on the complex and charged uses of blackface in Saint Domingue, 'The Familiar Other: Blackface Performance in Creole Works from 1780s Saint-Domingue', in Leichman and Bénac-Giroux, *Colonialism and Slavery*, pp. 41–63.

the supernatural powers that Harlequin uses to enact his protest. Magical resolutions had been a fundamental feature of the Italian commedia dell'arte, and Dutch metropolitan playwrights and ballet masters underscored the centrality of supernaturalism in the titles of their creations: *Fleur d'Epine, of de Triomf van Arlequin door Toverkunst* (1799) (Fleur d'Epine, or the Triumph of Harlequin by Magic), Rochefort's *Pantalon, Oost-Indisch planter, of Arlequin uit slaverny door toverkunst* (mentioned earlier) and *Arlequin op het toovereiland* (1839) (Harlequin on the magical island), to name but a few examples.[38] In all these productions, Harlequin is aided by supernatural forces to overcome his more powerful opponents.

If Harlequin's claim to magic was a mere convention in the Dutch metropole—and a very popular one—I believe it would have had a strikingly different undertone in Suriname, where Harlequin's magical tricks and enterprises may have reminded white planters in the audience of the traditions, belief systems and rituals that were taken to the Caribbean by African captives. Colonial accounts of the cultures of black people and *kleurlingen* in Suriname reveal sentiments of contempt, fear and fascination alike. The divine-healers, or *loekoemannen*, and their plantation ceremonies as part of *winti* in particular, receive much attention in these publications. A *loekoeman* possessed the power to cure all kinds of problems, from bad luck to physical maladies, and had the gift of prophecy.[39] In his description of Guyana and Suriname (1770), Jan Jacob Hartsinck, former president of the shareholders of the West Indian Company, admits that little is known about the 'Plegtigheden van Toveryën' (*Magic Ceremonies*) of these healers, as black people keep them 'voor de Blanken zeer bedekt; en niet dan door geheime navorschingen kan men daar iets van te weeten krygen' (*well-hidden from the whites; and only by secret inquiry can one get access*).[40] Nonetheless, white authors had clear prejudices about the *loekoemannen*. Hartsinck called them false 'Tovenaars' (*sorcerers*) and 'vervleeschte Duivels' (*incarnations of the devil*). David Nassy, in his *Geschiedenis der kolonie van Suriname* (1791), wrote concerning the 'bovennatuurlyke' (supernatural) actions of Quassy, the most famous *loekoeman* of eighteenth-century Suriname, that they were nothing

---

[38] Richard Stocton Rande, 'The Young Lovers', in Chaffee and Crick (eds), *The Routledge Companion to Commedia dell'Arte*, 70–81 (75).

[39] Natalie Zemon Davis, 'Judges, Masters, Diviners: Slaves' Experience of Criminal Justice in Colonial Suriname', *Law and History Review*, 29.4 (2011), pp. 925–84.

[40] Jan Jacob Hartsinck, *Beschryving van Guiana, of de wilde kust in Zuid-America* (Amsterdam: Gerrit Tielenburg, 1770), p. 904.

more than 'lapzalvery' (*quackery*) and the special symbol of 'het bedrog der Negers' (*the delusion of black people*).[41]

Importantly, in a description of a *winti* ceremony with a *loekoeman*, captain John Gabriel Stedman pointed to the potential dangers of such gatherings. He noted that:

> these meetings [are] exceedingly dangerous among the slaves, who are often told to murder their masters or desert to the woods, and on which account the excessiveness of this piece of fanaticism is forbidden in the Colony of Surinam[e], on pain of the most rigorous punishment. Yet it is often put in execution in private places.[42]

Ceremonial gatherings, like collective dancing and singing, indeed worried colonials because they could be a vehicle for criticism and protest.[43] Hartsinck remarked that some individuals went to those gatherings with the intention of starting riots and to 'kwaade oogmerken smeeden, en dezelve ook aan de zulke, die daar van anders geen denkbeeld of gedachten hadden, inboezemden' (*forge evil purposes, and inspire those who otherwise had no idea or thoughts of* [*protesting*]).[44] The worst that could happen was indeed that participants would be excited to revolt against their masters. In Suriname the threat of rebellion was high. The planter class was well aware that black people outnumbered them many times over and they witnessed an incessant surge of rebellions.[45] Between 1750 and 1759, no fewer than fifteen uprisings took place in Suriname. Some years later, in 1763, a major revolt broke out in the neighbouring colony of Berbice and between the 1770s and 1790s the Aluku, in what have become known as the Boni Maroon Wars, successfully ambushed different plantations in the Cottica region.[46]

---

[41] Nassy, *Geschiedenis van de kolonie Suriname*, 55 and 66. For more on Granman Quassy, see Davis, 'Judges, Masters, Diviners'. Stedman's *Narrative* includes an engraving of Quassy, which can be consulted at <http://www.slaveryimages.org/s/slaveryimages/item/1530>.

[42] John Gabriel Stedman, *Stedman's Surinam: Life in an Eighteenth-Century Slave Society*, eds Richard Price and Sally Price (Baltimore, MD and London: Johns Hopkins University Press, 1992), p. 263.

[43] See also Julia Prest's article, 'Pale Imitations: White Performances of Slave Dance in the Public Theatres of Pre-Revolutionary Saint-Domingue', *Atlantic Studies*, 16.4 (2018), pp. 502–20.

[44] Hartsinck, *Beschryving van Guiana*, 908–09.

[45] In 1791 there were 45,000 plantation slaves in Suriname and 1,360 white plantation residents (a ratio of 33:1). For Suriname as a whole, the ratio was 16:1. Hoefte and Vrij, 'Free Black and Colored Women', 164.

[46] For the best discussion of the Boni/Aluku resistance, see Wim Hoogbergen,

Thereafter, the Haitian Revolution engulfed the wider Caribbean orbit with revolutionary sentiment. It inspired portions of the enslaved population in Suriname to escape. One of the measures taken by the Dutch colonial authorities, then, was to issue sharp ordinances to prevent religious and dance meetings, thus accentuating their profound anxiety about slave ceremonies and cultures.[47]

Precisely for this reason, Harlequin's magical rebellions may have struck the theatregoing audiences of Paramaribo as shocking. Reading from a Suriname perspective, van der Hoeven's script seems to capture their anxious sentiments quite explicitly. Pantaloon repeatedly refers to Harlequin as 'een doortrapte Tovenaar' (*a double-dyed Wizard*), 'de Duivel in specie' (*the materialization of the devil*) and 'een bedrieger' (*a fraud*)—thus fearing and slighting Harlequin at the same time, much like Hartsinck and Nassy in their accounts of the *loekoe-mannen*.[48] Capitano and Belloardo fall victim to Harlequin's magical arts repeatedly. The barber scene did not involve any witchcraft, but other scenes did. As noted, Harlequin had the capacity to make himself invisible in order to haunt the place and scare his antagonists to death—allusions to van der Hoeven's Harlequin being a 'spook' (*phantom*) are regularly made, and the title of the *De Chinese Schim* (mentioned earlier) suggests that there, too, Harlequin spooked around other characters.[49] Moreover, Harlequin's ability to transform himself and others into other characters and entities helped him to escape trouble and create new confusion. Belloardo, in scene VII, mutates into a tree:

> BELLOARDO och! och! ik verander in een Eyk. Myn armen zyn al telgen, en myn voeten worden wortelen. Ik voel een Circes toverdrank door all' myn ad'ren bortelen. [...] Daar voel ik myn mond van een harde schors bedekken.[50]

> BELLOARDO *oh! oh! I am transforming into an oak tree. My arms have already changed into branches, and my feet are becoming roots. I feel Circe's potions in all of my veins [...] I feel my mouth being covered with hard bark.*

The Boni Maroon Wars in Suriname (Leiden and Boston, MA: Brill, 1990).
[47] Julien Wolbers, *Geschiedenis van Suriname* (1861) (Amsterdam: S. Emmerling, facsimile 1970), p. 456.
[48] [van der Hoeven], *Arlequin, tovenaar en barbier*, 9–11.
[49] [van der Hoeven], *Arlequin, tovenaar en barbier*, 21 and 31.
[50] [van der Hoeven], *Arlequin, tovenaar en barbier*, 21–22.

Using his creative mind and helped by supernatural forces, Harlequin thus moulded the situation according to his own views and controlled those who normally get to determine the rules. And *Arlequin, tovenaar en barbier* was not the only production in Suriname in which Harlequin triumphed through magic. Titles such as *Het standbeeld van Arlequin, of De magt der tovery* (1813) (Harlequin's Statue, or The power of magic) and *De componist Brombas, of Arlequin hersteld door toverkracht* (1819) (The Composer Brombas, or Harlequin reinstated by magic) suggest that the Paramaribo repertoire was saturated in Harlequin's magic and metamorphoses.

In her analysis of the harlequinade in Charleston, Dillon argues that burlesque shows created much political potential for black people in the colonies—both the harlequinade and slave-led revolution embody disorder, radicalism and subaltern knowledge.[51] But did non-white people in Suriname get to see Harlequin's magical onstage rebellions? According to traditional historiography they did not. As I indicated earlier, most Suriname theatregoers would have been members of the white elite. Officially, only white people or those who passed as white—people born from a white father and a *gekleurde* mother, for instance—could enter the theatre buildings. People of colour, and captives in particular, were not allowed in the theatres of Suriname until the late nineteenth century. The *Surinaamsche Courant* of 1 April 1814, for instance, mentions that 'niemand zal barrevoets worden toegelaten' (*no barefooted individuals will be allowed*). Announcing the performance of 'een aantal buiten gewoone Experimenten' (*some extraordinary experiments*) at the theatre of the Masonic lodge Concordia, the newspaper of 9 August 1822 reminded visitors that 'geen slaven worden toegelaten' (*no enslaved people will be admitted*).[52] Taking such official announcements and accounts at face value, historians have concluded that enslaved people were indeed for a long time excluded from theatre attendance.[53] However, the very existence of such announcements gives us the impression that enslaved people did find their way into the theatres, at least from 1814. Why else would such reminders be necessary? From the 1830s onwards, then, messages trickle through that captives were sometimes admitted to some theatrical occasions,

---

[51] Dillon, *New World Drama*, 164.
[52] Both examples are cited in Van Kempen's unpublished repertoire list. Translations are mine.
[53] Van Kempen, *Een geschiedenis* 1, 98–99; 2, 205–07.

albeit in low-ranking seats and on producing a furlough letter from their masters.[54]

Let us assume that enslaved people and *kleurlingen* were able to enter the theatre buildings of Paramaribo, if only sporadically. What would they have made of the black-masked Harlequin and his subversions of reality? Was his undermining of authority understood as a metaphor for opposition by the colonized? Did such performances hold powerful potential, as Dillon suggests? Unfortunately, sources are lacking to answer such questions. What is certain, though, is that, for many members of the Afro-Surinamese population, Harlequin would not have been the first fictional figure onto whom they could project antislavery sentiments. Their own cultures, too, had narratives and beliefs in which enthralling personalities challenged the status quo and stamped out evil, often using spirit incarnations and metamorphoses.[55] One figure that instinctively comes to mind when thinking about Harlequin is Anansi. *Anansitori* or Anansi stories originated in the Asante culture and were brought to the Caribbean via the transatlantic voyage by enslaved Africans. Anansi is a trickster, most often assuming the form of a black spider, who uses his acute wit to outsmart stronger beings and to triumph in nearly every situation. The choice of a spider rather than another animal has been explained by the creativity, flexibility and adaptability of these arthropods, as well as their capacity to design their own realities—they can set up a new habitat wherever and whenever required.[56]

During colonial times, Anansi was an empowering hero with whom enslaved people, black people and *kleurlingen* could identify. He was a very popular figure, and his influence—right up to the Anansi stories of the present day—should not be underestimated.[57] As burlesque genres often drew from vernacular offstage cultures and appeared as a colourful blend of influences, we might wonder whether these

---

[54] For a circus production by a Demerarian troupe in the spring of 1831, enslaved people were allowed to sit in the fourth tier, next to the children, for 1.5 guilder. In the Spring of 1836, again for a circus production, they were allowed in on condition that they had a letter from their masters giving permission. Examples are taken from Van Kempen's repertoire list.

[55] Hartsinck, *Beschryving van Guiana*, 903.

[56] Much has been written on Anansi. For an essay that excels in clarity, see Verona Spence-Adofo, 'Anansi the Spider: Trickster or Teacher?', Folklore Thursday online (25 June 2020) <https://folklorethursday.com/regional-folklore/anansi-the-spider-trickster-or-teacher/>. For Anansi in a specific Suriname context, see Van Kempen, *Een geschiedenis* 2, 238–50.

[57] Van Kempen, *Een geschiedenis* 2, 242.

stories could have affected the colonial Harlequin whom I have mainly analysed with recourse to van der Hoeven's script. As an African and Afro-diasporic figure Anansi was well known among colonials. The spider was mentioned in Hartsinck's account of Suriname and Guyana as the creator of humankind.[58] However, Hartsinck was not the first Dutchman to report on Anansi. As early as 1704, Willem Bosman had noted in his work on the Guinea coast about Africans' belief in Anansi:

> Sy gelooven dat de eerste menschen van den zelven gemaekt zyn; en niet tegenstaende eenige door ommegang met de Blanken anders geleerd hebbende, so zijn' er niet weinig, die by dat Geloof blyven, en welke waen haer niet uit 't hoofd is te praaten. Dit is voorwaer noch de grootste slegtigeid en onnooselheid, welke ik in de negers bespeurd heb.[59]

> *They believe that the first men were made of [this spider]; and, although some have learned differently as they encountered Whites, there are many individuals who stick to this Faith and we will not be able to talk them out of it. It is indeed not the greatest illness and ignorance which I have seen in African people.*

Bosman's evaluation of Anansi was not only taunting and disrespectful, it also grossly underestimated the subversive powers of this trickster figure. *Anansitori*, like many facets of African culture, were forbidden on Suriname plantations precisely because they represented protest against unrighteous oppression and imagined how seemingly helpless individuals could succeed in overthrowing the yokes imposed by more powerful beings. In Suriname, Anansi gradually became an icon of self-awareness and a hero of resistance to slavery and oppression.[60] The concrete relationship between harlequinades staged in Paramaribo and the vernacular cultures by which they were surrounded is difficult to research, but it is not impossible that there was an interaction between Afro-diasporic narratives and rituals, and theatrical events shaped by the planter class. De Verreezene Phoenix, for instance, certainly did take inspiration from vernacular performance traditions, as one ballet

---

[58] Hartsinck, *Beschryving van Guiana*, 903.
[59] Willem Bosman, *Nauwkeurige beschryving van de Guinese Goud-, Tand- en Slavekust* (Utrecht: Anthony Schouten, 1704), p. 101.
[60] Theo Meder, 'Anansi: een verhaal van migratie. Verslag van het symposium gehouden op 15 juni 2007 op het Meertens Instituut te Amsterdam', *Vertel eens*, 2.3 (2007), pp. 40–59.

production revealingly titled *De tovery der Indianen* (The Magic of the Indians) (1806) illustrates.

I began this chapter with a reference to Gloria Wekker's concern with how scholarship on Dutch imperialism tends to separate the metropole from its colonies and vice versa. Turning to Willem van der Hoeven's popular *Arlequin, tovenaar en barbier* (1730), my contribution subsequently attempted to analyse the dynamics between theatrical culture and colonial power in the contingent but shared spaces of the Netherlands and colonial Suriname. As a method, I have found it useful not only to compare the representation and reception of van der Hoeven's farce in those two different locations, but also to concentrate on the ways in which discourses of metropole and colony, of colonizer and colonized, focussed on its protagonist: the black-masked and rebellious Harlequin. This combined approach to the harlequinade in the metropole and the colony has helped us to understand each separate context better, while also making sense of those two zones as inextricably connected.

In the Netherlands, van der Hoeven's Harlequin could have been easily racialized by the Amsterdam spectators, who witnessed in their city a growing Afro-Atlantic community that testified to the relation of blackness and servitude. The harlequinade's racialized ridicule—in the comic staging of Harlequin himself as much as in the blackface barber scene—capitalized on and magnified white metropolitans' fascination with, and contempt for, black individuals and was a laboratory for the minstrel shows that gradually replaced other colonial burlesque genres. *Arlequin, tovenaar en barbier* may have had similar purviews and effects in Suriname to a certain extent. However, the context in which van der Hoeven's farce took the stage drastically changed. In Suriname, the relation between whiteness, blackness and subjection was more complicated as its plantation society was increasingly confronted with slave-led opposition and (what was understood as) miscegenation. Harlequin's racialized presence and rebellions thus inevitably accumulated meaning when he traversed the Atlantic. The mere convention of wearing a black mask, like the act of putting on and washing off black face paint, could challenge the supposed fixity of complexion and the status and worth that were tied to it. Moreover, Harlequin's opposition to those in power possibly symbolized the social mobility of the growing group of free black people in Paramaribo. Such subversive manoeuvres and interpretations would have been unthinkable in the metropole.

While Harlequin has long been understood as a thoroughly European figure, his presence on the metropolitan and colonial stages was in fact double-voiced: his transgressive performances subscribed to colonial powers and anticolonial resistance alike. Harlequin defended the interests of metropolitans, who depended on a system of dehumanization for their wealth and prowess, but he also expressed critiques of that system. These were established through Harlequin's magical rebellions, which could have been a ghostly reminder of how white colonials failed to get a grip on Afro-Suriname cultures, and an example of how these cultures potentially left a mark on white elite productions.

The oscillating meanings of Harlequin's presence on the stages of the Dutch Atlantic—capturing both pain and pride, abuse and agency—make him a paragon of hybridity. Conceptualizing him as such can help us to make more sense of colonial theatre in general: as a cultural domain that is never univocal or pure. This chapter can be a starting point for researchers to explore the colonial repertoire in a more integrated way that testifies to the complexities of the colonial relation. In addition, and precisely because performance culture is so receptive to 'external' influences, I hope that it stimulates research on Harlequin's meanings and mobility in the Atlantic more generally.[61] To fully grasp his complexity, however, further dialogue is needed.

Bibliography

Adams, Sarah J. *Repertoires of Slavery: Dutch Theater Between Abolitionism and Colonial Subjection, 1770–1810* (Amsterdam: Amsterdam University Press, 2023).

Anon. 'Buskenblazer, Sotternieën', in Pieter Leendertz Jr (ed.), *CD-ROM Middelnederlands* (The Hague/Antwerp: Sdu Uitgevers/Standaard Uitgeverij, 1998).

Bakhtin, Mikhail. *Rabelais and His World*, trans. Hélène Iswolsky (Bloomington: Indiana University Press, 1984).

---

[61] For Harlequin in an Anglo-American context see, among others, Jenna M. Gibbs, *Performing the Temple of Liberty: Slavery, Theater and Popular Culture in London and Philadelphia, 1760–1850* (Baltimore, MD: Johns Hopkins University Press, 2014), pp. 52–86 and Dillon, *New World Drama*, 131–64. For Harlequin (or, rather, Arlequin) in Saint-Domingue, including a locally-produced Arlequin pantomime, see Julia Prest, *Public Theatre and the Enslaved People of Colonial Saint-Domingue* (Cham: Palgrave Macmillan, 2023), 'Mitigated Portrayals' chapter.

Bhabha, Homi K. *The Location of Culture* (London and New York: Routledge, 1994).

Bosman, Willem. *Nauwkeurige beschryving van de Guinese Goud-, Tand- en Slavekust* (Utrecht: Anthony Schouten, 1704).

Bottini, Michele. 'You Must Have Heard of Harlequin...', trans. Samuel Angus McGehee and Michael J. Grady, in Judith Chaffee and Olly Crick (eds), *The Routledge Companion to Commedia dell'Arte* (New York: Routledge, 2015), pp. 55–56.

Brandon, Pepijn and Ulbe Bosma. 'De betekenis van de Atlantische slavernij voor de Nederlandse economie in de tweede helft van de achttiende eeuw', *TSEG / Low Countries Journal of Social and Economic History*, 16.2 (2019), pp. 5–45.

Davis, Natalie Zemon. 'Judges, Masters, Diviners: Slaves' Experience of Criminal Justice in Colonial Suriname', *Law and History Review*, 29.4 (2011), pp. 925–84.

Dillon, Elizabeth Maddock. *New World Drama: The Performative Commons in the Atlantic World, 1649–1849* (Durham, NC and London: Duke University Press, 2014).

Erenstein, Robert. 'De invloed van de commedia dell'arte in Nederland tot 1800', *Scenarium: Nederlandse reeks voor theaterwetenschap*, 5 (1981), pp. 91–106.

Fatah-Black, Karwan and Matthias van Rossum. 'Slavery in a "Slave Free Enclave?" Historical Links between the Dutch Republic, Empire and Slavery, 1580s–1860s', *Werkstatt Geschichte*, 66/67 (2014), pp. 55–74.

Gibbs, Jenna M., *Performing the Temple of Liberty: Slavery, Theater and Popular Culture in London and Philadelphia, 1760–1850* (Baltimore, MD: Johns Hopkins University Press, 2014).

Haarnack, Carl and Dienke Hondius. '"Swart" in Nederland: Afrikanen en Creolen in de noordelijke Nederlanden vanaf de Middeleeuwen tot de twintigste eeuw', in Esther Schreuder and Elmer Kolfin (eds), *Black is Beautiful: Rubens tot Dumas* (Zwolle: Waanders, 2008), pp. 88–107.

Hartsinck, Jan Jacob. *Beschryving van Guiana, of de wilde kust in Zuid-America* (Amsterdam: Gerrit Tielenburg, 1770).

Hoefte, Rosemarijn and Jean Jacques Vrij. 'Free Black and Colored Women in Early-Nineteenth-Century Paramaribo', in David Barry Gaspar and Darlene Clark Hine (eds), *Beyond Bondage: Free Women of Color in the Americas* (Urbana: University of Illinois Press, 2004), pp. 145–68.

Hoogbergen, Wim. *The Boni Maroon Wars in Suriname* (Leiden and Boston, MA: Brill, 1990).

Hornback, Robert. *Racism and Early Blackface Comic Traditions: From the Old World to the New* (Cham: Palgrave Macmillan, 2018).

Jordan, Peter. 'Pantalone and il Dottore: The Old Men of the Commedia', in Judith Chaffee and Oliver Crick (eds), *The Routledge Companion to Commedia dell'Arte* (New York: Routledge, 2015), pp. 62–69.

Lane, Jill. 'Blackface Nationalism, Cuba 1840–1868', *Theatre Journal*, 50.1 (1998), pp. 21–38.
Leichman, Jeffrey and Karine Bénac-Giroux (eds). *Colonialism and Slavery in Performance: Theatre and the Eighteenth-Century French Caribbean*, Oxford University Studies in the Enlightenment (Liverpool: Liverpool University Press, 2021).
Lott, Eric. *Love and Theft: Blackface Minstrelsy and the American Working Class* (New York: Oxford University Press, 1993; 2013).
McGehee, Scott. 'The Pre-Eminence of the Actor in Renaissance Context: Subverting the Social Order', in Judith Chaffee and Oliver Crick (eds), *The Routledge Companion to Commedia dell'Arte* (New York: Routledge, 2015), pp. 9–16.
Meder, Theo. 'Anansi: een verhaal van migratie. Verslag van het symposium gehouden op 15 juni 2007 op het Meertens Instituut te Amsterdam', *Vertel eens*, 2.3 (2007), pp. 40–59.
Meijer, Miriam Claude. *Race and Aesthetics in the Anthropology of Petrus Camper, 1722–1789* (Amsterdam: Atlanta, 1999).
Nassy, David. *Geschiedenis der kolonie van Suriname* (1791) (Amsterdam: S. Emmering, 1974).
Nimako, Kwame and Glenn F.W. Willemsen. *The Dutch Atlantic: Slavery, Abolition and Emancipation* (London: Pluto Press, 2011).
O'Brien, John. *Harlequin Britain: Pantomime and Entertainment, 1690–1760* (Baltimore, MD: Johns Hopkins University Press, 2004).
Ponte, Mark. '"Al de swarten die hier ter stede comen:" Een Afro-Atlantische gemeenschap in zeventiende-eeuws Amsterdam', *TSEG / Low Countries Journal of Social and Economic History*, 15.4 (2019), pp. 33–62.
Prest, Julia. 'The Familiar Other: Blackface Performance in Creole Works from 1780s Saint-Domingue', in Jeffrey Leichman and Karine Bénac-Giroux (eds), *Colonialism and Slavery in Performance: Theatre and the Eighteenth-Century French Caribbean*, Oxford University Studies in the Enlightenment (Liverpool: Liverpool University Press, 2021), pp. 41–63.
Prest, Julia. 'Pale Imitations: White Performances of Slave Dance in the Public Theatres of Pre-Revolutionary Saint-Domingue', *Atlantic Studies*, 16.4 (2018), pp. 502–20.
Prest, Julia. *Public Theatre and the Enslaved People of Colonial Saint-Domingue* (Cham: Palgrave Macmillan, 2023).
Rande, Richard Stocton. 'The Young Lovers', in Judith Chaffee and Oliver Crick (eds), *The Routledge Companion to Commedia dell'Arte* (New York: Routledge, 2015), pp. 70–81.
Reed, Peter. *Rogue Performances: Staging the Underclasses in Early American Performances* (New York: Palgrave Macmillan, 2009).
Spence-Adofo, Verona. 'Anansi the Spider: Trickster or Teacher?', Folklore Thursday online (25 June 2020), <https://folklorethursday.com/regional-folklore/anansi-the-spider-trickster-or-teacher/>.

Stedman, John Gabriel. *Stedman's Surinam: Life in an Eighteenth-Century Slave Society*, eds Richard Price and Sally Price (Baltimore, MD and London: Johns Hopkins University Press, 1992).

Stoler, Ann Laura. 'Making Empire Respectable: The Politics of Race and Sexual Morality in 20th-Century Colonial Cultures', *American Ethnologist*, 16.4 (1989), pp. 634–60.

Stoler, Ann Laura and Frederick Cooper. 'Between Metropole and Colony: Rethinking a Research Agenda', in Ann Laura Stoler and Frederick Cooper (eds), *Tensions of Empire: Colonial Cultures in a Bourgeois World* (Berkeley: University of California Press, 1997).

Surinaamsche Courant 20 (1830), 63 (1832), 74 (1835).

[van der Hoeven, Willem]. *Arlequin, tovenaar en barbier* (Amsterdam: David Ruarus, 1730).

van Kempen, Michiel. *Een geschiedenis van de Surinaamse literatuur*, Vols 1 and 2 (Breda: De Geus, 2003).

van Leeuwen, Merel. 'Kotzebue en de ondergang of redding van het Nederlandse Theater: De import- en exportroute van *De kruisvaarders van August* von Kotzebue naar en van de Amsterdamse Schouwburg in de negentiende eeuw' (MA dissertation, University of Amsterdam, 2019).

Wekker, Gloria. *White Innocence: Paradoxes of Colonialism and Race* (Durham, NC: Duke University Press, 2016).

Wolbers, Julien. *Geschiedenis van Suriname* (1861) (Amsterdam: S. Emmerling, facsimile 1970).

Worp, Jacob Adolf. 'Arlekijns en Krispijns op ons tooneel', *Noord en Zuid* (1896), pp. 35–43.

Young, Robert J.C. *Colonial Desire: Hybridity in Theory, Culture and Race* (London and New York: Routledge, 1995).

Five

Problems of Framing: National or Colonial Approaches to Blackface Performance?

Jill Lane

The colonial history of blackface performance in Cuba coincides with its final—crucial—85 years as a Spanish colony, a period in which the centre of gravity of both Caribbean sugar and slave trades shifted to Cuba in the aftermath and as a direct consequence of the revolution in neighbouring Saint-Domingue, now Haiti. Cuba even inherited Saint-Domingue's moniker the 'pearl of the Antilles'. Saint-Domingue's demise, historian Ada Ferrer tells us, was Spain's and therefore Cuba's opportunity: between 1790 and 1820 more than 325,000 Africans were forcibly disembarked on the island, far more than in the previous three centuries, and the number of *ingenios* (sugar plantations) proliferated, shifting the island's infrastructure definitively to that of a plantation colony. By 1830 'sugar was king' and 'the island of Cuba was producing more of it than any other place on earth'.[1] That project made Cuba 'a colony worth a kingdom' to Spain for the rest of the nineteenth century, especially after the collapse of its empire on the American continent.[2] Historians have marked this as the nineteenth-century rise of 'second slavery', in which the axis produced by the slaveholding southern United States, Cuba and Brazil eclipsed the earlier dominance of the British and French Caribbean sugar islands of the seventeenth and eighteenth centuries.[3] Historians Rafael Marquese, Tâmis Parron and Márcia R. Berbel name this the 'third Atlantic', by which they

---

[1] Ada Ferrer, *Cuba: An American History* (New York: Scribner, 2021), p. 70. See also Ada Ferrer, *Freedom's Mirror: Cuba and Haiti in the Age of Revolution* (Cambridge: Cambridge University Press, 2016), pp. 36–37.

[2] Ferrer, *Freedom's Mirror*, 17–43.

[3] See Dale Tomich, *Through the Prism of Slavery: Labor, Capital, and World Economy* (Lanham, MD: Rowman and Littlefield, 2004) pp. 56–71. Tomich writes 'if slavery was ultimately abolished everywhere in the hemisphere [in the nineteenth century], the "anti-slavery century" was nonetheless the apogee of its development' (57).

mean the economic and political system that replaced both the first Iberian Atlantic system that began in the sixteenth century, and the second, parallel, Atlantic system of north-western Europe that rose in the seventeenth—and dominated the eighteenth—centuries. When both came into crisis following the fall of Saint-Domingue and the subsequent suppression of the slave trade, a 'third Atlantic' system more closely connected the remaining slave economies.[4] Of Cuba and Brazil combined, they write, 'the scale of human suffering generated by the business was unprecedented: between 1831 and 1850, Brazil and Cuba received approximately 10 percent of the total number of enslaved Africans carried to the New World during four centuries'.[5] By one count, another 175,000 were disembarked in Cuba between 1853 and 1864.[6] One particularity of Cuba in this second slavery/third Atlantic is that its colonial plantation regime expanded in an era of both rising international abolitionism (particularly British) and the ascendancy of postcolonial, American national republics, not least the United States, which by the 1850s was Cuba's largest trading partner. Unlike earlier periods of colonialism and slavery, nineteenth-century abolitionism and nationalism provided constant models for ideals of freedom with which Cuba's colonial regime coexisted in tension. (Ferrer writes 'if Haiti became the epicentre of Black Atlantic freedom after 1804, Cuba became its antithesis'.)[7] Indeed, Cuba's own anticolonial struggles later in the century—from the beginning of the first, unsuccessful, war for independence in 1868 to the end of the last in 1898—explicitly linked abolition (and, later, racial equality) to independence. To ask about the representation of race in this context, then, refers us to this complex nexus of late colonial power, slavery and abolition, and burgeoning nationalism.

From the outset, blackface performance in Cuba took place against the backdrop of colonial repression, including censorship of the stage, and the intertwined struggles over slavery and nationhood. In 1812, the year in which authorities suppressed a major antislavery rebellion headed in part by the free black carpenter José Antonio Aponte, we read less portentous but notable news of the early *tonadillas* of *negritos* (satirical songs about 'little blacks') performed by the beloved Cuban

---

[4] Rafael Marquese, Tâmis Parron and Márcia R. Berbel, *Slavery and Politics: Brazil and Cuba, 1790–1850*, trans. Leonardo Marques (Albuquerque, NM: University of New Mexico Press, 2016), pp. 261–66.

[5] Marquese et al., *Slavery and Politics*, 264.

[6] Louis Perez, *Cuba Between Reform and Revolution,* Third edition (New York and Oxford: Oxford University Press, 2006), p. 73.

[7] Ferrer, *Freedom's Mirror*, 338.

gracioso (clown) Francisco Covarrubias, who dominated the Cuban stage until his death in 1850.[8] In 1844, Cuba was rocked by a series of violently repressed slave rebellions and conspiracies that have come to be known as 'La Escalera' (*the ladder*), named after the macabre method of torture to which suspects were subjected, which brutally silenced the voices of black writers and thinkers, like that of the celebrated poet Plácido who lost his life to a firing squad. In their stead we find the blackface voice of the fictional slave 'Creto Gangá', a pseudonym of the writer José Crespo y Borbón, under whose name and heavily distorted 'black' voice Crespo offered satirical social commentary in novels, articles in the press and in the theatre, including the ground-breaking 1847 plantation comedy *Un ajiaco, o la boda de Pancha Jutía y Canuto Raspadura* (A [Cuban] stew, or the wedding of Pancha Jutía and Canuto Raspadura), whose enslaved blackface protagonists set the model for blackface performance thereafter.[9] In 1868 the country witnessed the first salvo in the war of independence, the so-called Grito de Yara (*cry from Yara*), soon followed by the first call for abolition from the rebels; in the same year the island witnessed the explosive emergence of the *teatro bufo*, a vernacular genre that combined popular music and short comic plays in which satirical blackface characters were a signature, with one critic complaining of an island-wide 'bufomania'.[10] The war descended on the capital during—precisely—a *teatro bufo* performance in 1869, in which an actor adapted a line from a play to shout out 'Long live the people who produce the sugar cane!' and be answered by Spanish gunfire.[11] The *teatro bufo*'s elaboration of blackface characters, including variations on the *negrito* and the sexualized *mulata*, reached its apogee in the years following abolition in the 1880s; among its targets for blackface humour was the Afro-Cuban civil rights activist and independence leader Juan Gualberto Gómez.[12] When the United States intervened to end both

---

[8] On Covarrubias, see Rosa Ileana Boudet, *La chimenea encantada: Francisco Covarrubias* (Santa Monica, CA: Ediciones la Flecha, 2017).

[9] On 'Creto Gangá', see Mary Cruz, *Creto Gangá* (Havana: Contemporaneo, 1974); Jill Lane, *Blackface Cuba (1840–1895)* (Philadelphia, PA: University of Pennsylvania Press, 2005), pp. 31–49.

[10] Quoted in Rine Leal, *La selva oscura*, Vol. 2: *De los bufos a la neocolonia, Historia del teatro cubano de 1868 a 1902* (Havana: Arte y Literatura, 1982), p. 27.

[11] On the 'Succesos de la Villanueva', see Leal, *La selva oscura* 2, 53–67 and Lane, *Blackface Cuba*, 96–105.

[12] See Laureano del Monte, *Con don, sin don, ayer y hoy, caricatura trágico-bufa, lírico bailable en un acto y 5 cuadros, y en prosa* (Havana: Imprenta El Aerolito, 1894) and Lane, *Blackface Cuba*, 134–41.

the second war of independence and Spanish colonial rule in Cuba in 1898, the *teatro bufo* marked the arrival of the new neocolonial order with Ignacio Saragacha's *bufo* play *¡Arriba con el himno!* (Up with the anthem!), the central image of which was the American flag replacing what should have been the Cuban one.

Commentators and critics alike have seen in this genealogy of colonial blackface performance a story about the formation of a decidedly national affect, an origin tale for the development of Cuban music, grounded in 'African' rhythmic structures, and of Cuban humour, later known as *choteo*. Essayist and playwright Federico Villoch, remembering the *teatro bufo* of his youth in the 1880s, recalls 'un teatro lleno todas las noches de bote en bote meses y meses' (*a theatre chock-full every night, month after month*) through which 'el alma criollo se expansionaba [...] hasta lo indecible oyendo sus guarachas y sus canciones, y riéndose hasta perder el aliento con sus dicharachos y chistes de sus tipos populares' (*the Creole [island-born] soul expanded beyond description hearing its own guarachas [popular songs] and its songs, and laughing until out of breath with its own word-plays and jokes from its popular characters*). For Villoch, as for others, the *teatro bufo* evokes deep affection because it enabled a feeling of national community: 'se la recuerda con más fijeza y cariño siendo como un adelanto a cuenta de Cuba Libre' (*we remember it with more clarity and affection as an advance credit on Free Cuba*).[13] The theatre creates a palpable experience of the national—but one that is virtual, a 'credit' against an elusive free Cuba to come. For Villoch, as for others, this theatre is the site of enormous nationalist *cariño* (affection)—an emotion that Benedict Anderson elsewhere has called 'political love'.[14] That love story, however, tends to skip and smooth over the palpable presence of blackface as a primary currency in the 'loan' against free Cuba: what indeed does a blackface *negrito* have to do with anticolonial and nationalist sentiment in Cuba's late colonial period?

I suggest some answers to that question in my book *Blackface Cuba (1840–1895)*, which asks for whom, how and why blackface was a vehicle for national imagining in colonial Cuba.[15] Like all scholars of Cuban theatre, I built on the canonical work of Cuban theatre historian Rine

---

[13] Federico Villoch, 'Los Bufos de Salas', *Carteles*, 27.1 (29 September 1946), pp. 22–23 (22).

[14] Benedict Anderson, *Imagined Communities: Reflections on the Origin and Spread of Nationalism* (London: Verso, 1991), p. 143.

[15] Lane, *Blackface Cuba*. See also Jill Lane, 'ImpersoNación', in Inés María Martiatu Terry (ed.), *Bufo y nación: interpelaciones desde el presente* (Havana: Letras Cubanas, 2009), pp. 172–206.

Leal, whose epic two-volume history of Cuban theatre, published in 1975 and 1982, traces—precisely—the development of a distinctly national theatre over three centuries. For Leal, the *bufos* stand in for a long-repressed national theatre: 'impedido el teatro nacional de llegar a la escena, el cubano buscó lo propio a través de una creación menor, que entregó a guaracheros y parodistas' (*with the national theatre denied entry onstage, the Cuban searched for his own through a minor creation, which he delivered to* guaracha-*singers and parodists*).[16] As with Villoch, here this vernacular theatre is a stand-in, a kind of simulacrum, for a 'real' national theatre.

In this chapter, I return to the question of blackface and national meaning as one of historiographic method, and broaden the aperture: rather than assume latent national meaning in colonial blackface performance, as has been the norm, I ask here whether and how colonial blackface helped to shape our understanding of the national in the first place, both in its day and in our present scholarship. To better bring into focus the presumed relation between blackface and national expression, in the pages that follow I consider the *teatro bufo* in relation to US blackface minstrelsy, the better-known blackface genre that reached meteoric popularity during this period and beyond. In both genres we find that blackface was energetically deployed to articulate the particularity of its audiences' social positioning: blackface was peculiarly US 'American', speaking in a precise vernacular to, say, its white, male, working-class audiences of late 1830s New York, as Eric Lott has masterfully shown;[17] or it was peculiarly Cuban, speaking in 1868 to white, Cuban-born, *criollos* on the eve of the first anticolonial war. Tavia Nyong'o's flat assessment applies to both: 'blackface and its heroes became the national Thing'.[18] To understand how blackface made this peculiar claim to national originality in both locales, I believe our study of blackface will benefit from a relational approach that brings into dialogue these different practices, allowing us to appreciate whether blackface was a common coin of the colonial realm, writ large, transcending—but also shaping—its national frames—and if so, why.

I pursue this question alongside Catherine Cole who, writing about Ghanaian and African American performance, provocatively asks 'could

[16] Rine Leal, *Breve historia del teatro Cubano* (Havana: Editorial Letras Cubanas, 1980), p. 75. See also Rine Leal, *La selva oscura*, Vol. 1 (Havana: Arte y Literatura, 1975) and Leal, *La selva oscura* 2.

[17] Eric J. Lott, *Love and Theft: Blackface Minstrelsy and the American Working Class* (New York: Oxford University Press, 1993; 2013).

[18] Tavia Nyong'o, *The Amalgamation Waltz: Race, Performance and the Ruses of Memory* (Minneapolis, MN: University of Minnesota Press, 2009), p. 109.

a transnational appraisal of blackface lead us to conclude that blackface, rather than being a quintessentially American form, is rather a quintessentially colonial one?'[19] She follows Louis Chude-Sokei's evocative analysis of a 'global economy of blackface' which, via a genealogy of the black-on-black performances by Bahamas-born Bert Williams, traces a geography of blackface that connects such sites as Ghana, Jamaica, Trinidad and South Africa.[20] The colonial experience, says Cole, 'is certainly central to any consideration of the global economy of blackface, as the form both traveled and found fertile soil throughout the circuits of empire'.[21] Recent scholarship on US blackface minstrelsy has, indeed, traced blackface across the Anglo-Atlantic world, following the colonial and postcolonial circuits that linked the USA and the UK before and well after US independence. Jenna Gibbs, in *Performing in the Temple of Liberty*, richly compares the theatrical and popular print cultures of London and Philadelphia, demonstrating how these formed a shared, transnational 'lexicon of recognizable meanings and symbols that co-mingled Enlightenment notions of natural rights and antislavery, neoclassical motifs [...] and blackface burlesque'.[22] Robert Nowatzki maps nothing less than the emergence of a 'blackface Atlantic' in his comparative work on representations of African Americans in abolitionist work and in minstrelsy on both sides of the Anglo Atlantic.[23] For Cuba and Spain, in turn, Tànit Fernández demonstrates how the *teatro bufo* negotiated the relation of peninsular Spain to its prized colony through gendered representations of Spanish immigrants, particularly Catalans, and ideas of cross-racial desire.[24] Examining blackface in the Spanish vernacular theatre of this period known as

[19] Catherine Cole, 'American Ghetto Parties and Ghanaian Concert Parties: A Transnational Perspective on Blackface', in Stephen Johnson (ed.), *Burnt Cork: Traditions and Legacies of Blackface Minstrelsy* (Amherst, MA: University of Massachusetts Press, 2012), pp. 223–57 (224).

[20] Louis Chude-Sokei, *The Last 'Darky': Bert Williams, Black-on-Black Minstrelsy and the African Diaspora* (Durham, NC: Duke University Press, 2006), pp. 114–60.

[21] Cole, 'American Ghetto', 225.

[22] Jenna M. Gibbs, *Performing the Temple of Liberty: Slavery, Theater, and Popular Culture in London and Philadelphia, 1760–1850* (Baltimore, MD: Johns Hopkins University Press, 2014), p. 5.

[23] Robert Nowatzki, *Representing African Americans in Transatlantic Abolitionism and Blackface Minstrelsy* (Baton Rouge, LA: Louisiana State University Press, 2010), p. 6.

[24] Tànit Fernández de la Reguera Tayà, *Cuba y Cataluña en la segunda mitad del siglo XIX: Teatro popular e identidades (proto)nacionales* (Madrid: Editorial Pliegos, 2020).

género chico, Mar Soria argues that blackface recreated imperial racial hierarchies and thus 'buttressed the economic foundations of the Spanish empire built upon the slavery system'.[25]

While it presumes a hemispheric frame that cuts across these Anglo- and Iberian-Atlantic perspectives, my aim in juxtaposing the *teatro bufo* and US blackface minstrelsy is to better illuminate the specific work of blackface in relation to race and national structures of feeling in this period, in a reflection that will return us to the space of Cuba's colonial Caribbean theatre. If Cole asks us to imagine blackface as inherently colonial, I aim via a relational analysis to consider how Cuban blackface—and its racial counterfeit—may have functioned as a currency that translated the colonial into the national. How did blackface articulate—how did it function as a site of articulation for— the relation between the colonial and the national, and the overarching weight of race in that equation?

Cuban *teatro bufo* and US blackface minstrelsy

As a technology of representation, blackface was enormously elastic, encompassing both abolitionism and proslavery sentiments in the USA, and anticolonialism and proslavery sentiments in Cuba. But we find it was almost always *localizing*: in its early iterations,[26] both minstrelsy and the *teatro bufo* conjured ways of feeling that helped US and Cuban publics see themselves *as* a particular public, sometimes for the first time. For the USA, scholars have established a vibrant transatlantic genealogy for blackface entertainments, notably crediting the comic impersonations of black Americans by English actor Charles Matthews,

---

[25] Mar Soria, 'Colonial Imaginings on the Stage: Blackface, Gender, and the Economics of Empire in Spanish and Catalan Popular Theater', in N. Michelle Murray and Akiko Tsuchiya (eds), *Unsettling Colonialism: Gender and Race in the Nineteenth-Century Global Hispanic World* (Albany, NY: State University of New York Press, 2019), pp. 135–69 (136).

[26] The two forms reached their apex at different historical moments: scholars usually focus on antebellum blackface minstrelsy as the apogee of that form, from about 1830 to the mid-1850s, before it solidified into a stock formula that characterized minstrelsy for the rest of the century, during and well after the American Civil War. In colonial Cuba, as noted, the form was dominant in the period marked by the anticolonial wars, from 1868 to 1898. Both forms outlived abolition (1865 in the USA, 1886 in Cuba) and continued to develop well into the era of radio, film and even television, and abated only with the success of the civil rights movement of the 1960s in the USA, and with the arrival of the Revolution in Cuba in 1959.

who performed in the early 1820s, as one progenitor. Yet by the time Thomas Dartmouth Rice—the ostensible 'originator' of the form— brought his wildly popular 'Jump Jim Crow' act to London in 1837, it was fully received as a US American import. Contemporary commentators marvelled that Rice and his many imitators might gain the status of national artists. The often-cited James K. Kennard, for one, writing for *Knickerbocker Magazine* in 1845, posed the question 'Who Are Our National Poets?', asking 'in which class of our population must we look for our truly original and American poets? What class is more secluded from foreign influences, receives the narrowest education, travels the shortest distance from home?' He replies, ironically, '[o]ur Negro slaves to be sure!' But in the place of enslaved people, he cites a range of theatrical characters from the repertoire of blackface minstrelsy: '[f]rom that class come the Jim Crows, the Zip Coons, the Dandy Jims, who have electrified the world'. T.D. Rice, he says, 'accordingly learned their poetry, music, and dancing, blacked his face', and was making a fortune with 'his counterfeit presentment of the American national opera'.[27] History sometimes agrees, now without irony: witness W.T. Lhamon's 2009 anthology of songs and plays, titled simply *Jim Crow, American*.[28]

The *bufos* similarly had transatlantic progenitors: the first Cuban company, the Bufos Habaneros, were inspired by a visit from the so-called Bufos Madrileños (the Madrid Bufos) in 1867, led by the dynamic Spanish theatre entrepreneur Franciso Arderíus, from whom they borrowed a basic theatrical formula and a penchant for parody, and then added the practice of blackface. The apparatus of colonial censorship in both the theatre and the press did not allow for outright celebrations of national content, but the Bufos Habaneros, like their many imitators, advertised themselves as a company devoted to 'championing' the 'tipos de este país'[29] (*types of this country*), and their popularity was palpable. The typically conservative *Diario de la Marina* waxed lyrical:

> Ya que según estamos mirando se ha despertado la manía de bufar, bufemos pues, y lancemos al aire nuestras bufonadas, puesto que ya se bufa en todas partes [...] el corcho sube por el consumo que

---

[27] James K. Kennard, 'Who Are Our National Poets?', in T. Allston Brown and Charles Day (eds), 'Black Musicians and Early Ethiopian Minstrelsy', *The Black Perspective in Music*, 3.1 (Spring 1975), pp. 83–85.
[28] William T. Lhamon, *Jim Crow, American: Selected Songs and Plays* (Cambridge, MA: Belknap Press of Harvard University Press, 2009).
[29] *Gaceta de la Habana* (31 May 1868).

de él hacen los tiznados bufadores, y los vinateros se quejan con el alza de alcornoque.[30]

Since, as we can see, the mania for bufo-*ing has awoken, let's all* bufo *then, and throw in the air our* bufo-*nades, now that there is* bufo-*ing everywhere [...] [the price of] cork is rising from the tinted* bufadors' *consumption and the vintners are complaining about the increase in oak cork.*

Another wary commentator was quick to relegate the *bufos'* impact to the local realm: 'tiene su mérito relativo, local, de circunstancias, y como tal lo aceptamos, sin reconocerle derecho a los honores del examen crítico. Hace reír y basta'[31] (*it has its merit—relative, local, of circumstance, and as such we can accept it, without granting it the honour of critical examination. It causes laughter, no more*). Such dismissals, like Kennard's irony, conceal a comparable class distaste for the vernacular with which both forms were initially received by the mainstream press.

An evening at the Chatham Theater in New York in the early 1840s or at the Teatro Villanueva in Havana in 1868 shared a basic structure, in which racial impersonation entailed the elaboration of ostensibly black speech, sound and movement as well as the use of burnt cork. Both alternated short, comic theatrical pieces with original song and dance and, in the fullness of national time, these would come to be understood as foundational to the development of national humour as well as the popular vernacular music and dance of both countries. In Cuba's first *bufo* performances, one-act plays alternated with *guarachas*, songs that had developed from rural music traditions and were usually sung by two voices, often as a duet, with the accompaniment of a guitar and, by 1868, also the *güiro*,[32] an inclusion that belied a trend toward 'nationalizing'—that is, Cubanizing—Spanish-based musics through the integration of Africa-derived instruments or rhythmic structure, becoming one early iteration of what we now recognize as Afro-Hispanic sound. *Guarachas* were known, and admired, for their often salacious or satirical lyrics and their *sandunguerísima* (most enchanting) rhythms (as the contemporary phrase went)—an alluring style associated over

---

[30] *Diario de la Marina* (4 October 1868); quoted in Leal, *La selva oscura* 2, 27.
[31] *Diario de la Marina* (6 June 1868); quoted in Leal, *La selva oscura* 2, 29.
[32] The *güiro* is a serrated, gourd-shaped percussion instrument, held in the hand and played by scraping a stick along one side.

time with black or African sound and movement. The *teatro bufo* would later incorporate other Cuban music and social dance, particularly the controversial and heavily eroticized *danzón*. In 1868, the most popular character of the *bufo* plays was the so-called *negro catedrático* (black professor), who debuted as the protagonist of the one-act play *Los negros catedráticos* (The Black Professors) written by Bufos Habaneros' company member, Francisco Fernández Vilaros;[33] a pompous social climber, the *catedrático* is ostensibly a satire of an urban, free, black man with apparently doomed pretensions to erudition. The contrast between the comedic theatre and the music established a tension between the economy of blackface (with both visual and oral dimensions, as we shall see) and the aural economy of an emergent Afro-Cuban music.

A night with Christy's Minstrels in New York in 1843 was structured as a concert with 20 different numbers. In one playbill examined by William J. Mahar, the evening is divided into two parts, the first purporting to represent 'the Free Blacks of the North' and the second 'Portraying the Peculiarities of the Southern Plantation Negroes'. Most were musical and/or dance numbers, for example the song 'Virginia Juba, Banjo Melody with Solo', the popular 'Jim Crack Corn', or a song called 'Down in Carolina' that purported to introduce a plantation 'cornshucking' dance—precisely the kind of repertoire that over time would shape American folk music and social dance. These were presented along with parodic lectures and comic dialogues, including one 'Fine Old Colored Gentleman Parody'.[34] Mahar's meticulous archival work teaches us that what we call the 'minstrel show' varied substantially in both form and content in the antebellum period, but all provided some combination of musical numbers and theatrical bits, if not full skits, plays or operas. That is to say that, as in the Cuban case, blackface performance happened on several simultaneous registers—speech, rhythm, gesture—which complicated each other in performance. We do well to remember that the power of T.D. Rice's signature 'Jump Jim Crow' did not lie primarily in the punch of the song's often politically pointed lyrics; it was foremost a *dance*, and as such engaged a range of real and imagined ideas about black rhythm, movement and style. Lhamon reminds us that 'clapping and slapping, double-timing and

---

[33] Francisco Fernández Vilaros, *Los negros catedráticos*, in Rine Leal (ed.), *Teatro bufo siglo XIX*, Vol. 1 (Havana: Editorial Arte y Literatura, 1975), pp. 131–62.

[34] William J. Mahar, *Behind the Burnt Cork Mask: Early Blackface Minstrelsy and Antebellum American Popular Culture* (Urbana, IL: University of Illinois Press, 1999), p. 45.

patting Juba, kicking and high-stepping, the staging and the lyrics were all part of dancing "Jim Crow"'.[35] Dale Cockrell shares an 1837 account of Rice as virtuosic dancer:

> he varies his jumpings to an infinite extent, starting with different steps, and terminating with different positions in each verse. Then there are eight verses to the song, and it is encored six times, which draws deeply upon Mr Crow's ingenuity to vary the pantomime.[36]

Rice's inimitable style notwithstanding, part of what made these forms so popular was that they were imitable—purportedly everyone (even the Queen of England)[37] wanted to Jump Jim Crow, just as later Cuban publics sang their favourite *guarachas* and danced the sensual *danzón*.

Both minstrelsy and the *teatro bufo* imagined themselves in contraposition to the imported opera (and in the Cuban case also the Spanish zarzuela)[38] that otherwise dominated the 'legitimate' stage in both countries, at times presenting comic parodies of the very operas on offer at competing theatres. Parodying this fare was itself a jab at the higher-class publics that patronized it, whether the elite and middle classes in New York or Philadelphia, or the ruling colonial class in Cuba. Over time, however, the commercial zeal of both the *bufos* and the minstrels led many to seek out these same 'respectable' audiences and, when possible, fill their playhouses. The *teatro bufo* usually replaced operatic scores with popular music, featuring *guarachas*, *danzones* or other 'Cuban' genres. One early press reviewer commended the *bufos'* repertoire of *guarachas*, noting that it would 'contentar mucho al público que le favorece, mejor que con los cantos italianos, que sólo suenan bien con su letra propia, y en boca de quienes los entienden'[39] (*greatly please their public, far more than with Italian songs, which only sound right in their own language, in the mouths of those who understand*

---

[35] William T. Lhamon, *Raising Cain: Blackface Performance from Jim Crow to Hip Hop* (Cambridge, MA: Harvard University Press, 2000), p. 181.
[36] Dale Cockrell, *Demons of Disorder: Early Blackface Minstrels and Their World* (Cambridge: Cambridge University Press, 1997), pp. 75–76.
[37] See Stephen Johnson, 'Death and the Minstrel Race, Madness, and Art in the Last (W)Rites of Three Early Blackface Performers', in Johnson (ed.), *Burnt Cork*, 85.
[38] On the zarzuela in Cuba, including its representation of race, see Susan Thomas, *Cuban Zarzuela: Performing Race and Gender on Havana's Lyric Stage* (Chicago, IL: University of Illinois Press, 2009).
[39] *Diario de la marina* (9 June 1868); also quoted in Leal, *La selva oscura* 2, 19.

them.) In *Traviata o La dama de las clavelinas* (Traviata or the lady of the carnations), written by José Tamayo and performed in Santiago de Cuba in 1879, Verdi's suffering protagonist becomes a charming black sex worker who, rather than meeting a tragic operatic end, is miraculously saved by performing a Cuban *danzón*.[40] Ignacio Saragacha's late play *Mefistofeles* (1896) parodies Gounod's operatic retelling of Goethe's *Faust*, and casts Faust as a *brujo* (a black witch doctor), whose world is filled with allusions to black Cuba, including the African-inflected dances of *la conga* and *el yambú*. When Irina Bajini claims of this play that 'la música parece imponerse con el objetivo de romper con la tradición europea' (*the music seems to impose itself with the aim of breaking with the European tradition*), it is true of the *bufo* repertoire as a whole.[41]

Among stage characters, the blackface star in Cuba in 1868 was the *negrito* who appeared in various iterations, including both the pompous *catedrático* and his counterpart the *bozal*, an unacculturated African, often but not always figured as an enslaved plantation worker. Both the *catedrático* and the *bozal* are defined at the intersection of race and language: both terms serve as nouns and adjectives, referring both to a black persona and a particular way of speaking—or poorly speaking—Spanish. *Los negros catedráticos* and its two popular sequels exploited the humour of both, pitting the pretentious *catedrático* patriarch Ancieto against his would-be son-in-law the *bozal* José, a hardworking dock worker. Ancieto roundly opposes José's bid to marry his daughter because, he says, 'ninguno de mi prosapia formará alianza ofensiva ni defensiva con ningún negro heterogéneo sino con los de su claise y condición' (*no one of my lineage will form any alliance, defensive or offensive, with any heterogeneous black man, but only with those of their class and condition*). José proudly counters that he meets all the requirements of a good husband: '[y]o so congo, trabajaore la muella [...] yo no toma guariente [...] yo so libre [...] yo gana do peso toitico lu día' (*I am a congo, a dock worker, I don't drink liquor, I am free, I earn two pesos every day*). On learning that José has saved his two daily pesos and is now wealthy, Ancieto approves the 'offensive' alliance promptly. His daughter Dorotea quips in verse '¡Todo cambia el dinero!/Si ayer pobre, era un borrico,/hoy, que sabemos que es rico,/es el congo un caballero'[42] (*Money changes everything!/If yesterday he was poor, and a drunk/today*

---

[40] See Irina Bajini, *Antología de teatro bufo Cubano* (Bogotá, Colombia: Ediciones Uniandes, 2018), pp. 54–55.
[41] Bajini, *Antología*, 42.
[42] Fernández Vilaros, *Los negros catedráticos*, 145, 144 and 149.

that we know he's rich/the congo *is a gentleman*). The *catedrático* and the *bozal* set the poles for a spectrum of representing the *negrito*. As the end of slavery approached, the *teatro bufo* added a number of colloquial black male figures, including *negros curros, negros cheches, brujos* and *negros de manglar*, each of which were associated with varying degrees of vagrancy or criminality.

As in the Cuban case, minstrelsy produced a number of iconic black male figures that lay at the intersection of racialized language and gesture, including Jim Crow, Zip Coon and Old Dan Tucker, all elaborated through the songs that were their primary vehicles. To these we can add the range of malaprop-spouting figures—parodies of doctors, politicians and preachers—that were the protagonists of countless stump speeches. For Lott, masculinity was at the heart of the complex cultural 'love and theft' of such blackface:

> to put on the cultural forms of 'blackness' was to engage in a complex affair of manly mimicry [...] To wear or even enjoy blackface was literally, for a time, to become black, to inherit the cool, virility, humility, abandon, or *gaité de coeur* that were the prime components of white ideologies of black manhood.[43]

Important to both the *teatro bufo* and minstrelsy was the representation of women of colour. In minstrelsy we find comic 'Mammies' and fancy 'yellar' girls, played by white men in racial drag, engaging a homosocial play of homosexual/homophobic desire and misogyny in the sexual banter between male actors.[44] The *teatro bufo*, in turn, witnessed the meteoric popularity of the *mulata*, particularly from the early 1880s, played by women usually in brownface. Often the object in a love triangle between two men, usually a *negrito* and a Spanish immigrant counterpart (over time, a heavily accented *gallego* or Galician immigrant), the *mulata* was (as I argue at length elsewhere)[45] a highly eroticized figure that became the literal and figurative embodiment of Cuban racial mixing or *mestizaje*, replete with the complex anticolonial investment, racist panic and nationalist desire that this implied. The competition between two men—one black, one white; one African, one Spanish—for the sexual

---

[43] Lott, *Love and Theft*, 54.
[44] On the minstrel 'wench', see Christian DuComb, *Haunted City: Three Centuries of Racial Impersonation in Philadelphia* (Ann Arbor, MI: University of Michigan Press, 2017), pp. 117–42.
[45] See my chapter 'Racial Ethnography and Literate Sex, 1888' in *Blackface Cuba*, 180–223.

favours of a biracial, island-born woman encapsulated the discourse of colonial contest and what Doris Sommer has called the 'national romance' foundational to nineteenth-century Latin American aesthetics.[46]

Notably, the *teatro bufo* and minstrelsy both incorporated a range of immigrant types in addition to black characters. In Cuba these included Catalans, Canarios (*isleños* or 'islanders' from the Canaries), *Chinos* (Chinese) and later the bumbling but imposing North American *Gringos*, among others, not played in blackface. In the USA, in later decades, the blackface mask became a technique for representing a wide range of local and immigrant groups, including 'Dutchmen' (Germans), Irishmen, 'Chinamen' and 'Indians'; these too were defined at the intersection of ostensibly characteristic gestural mannerisms and speech. As Kristina Wirtz writes of Cuba in the nineteenth century, 'language ideologies and [...] notions about how different social groups spoke Spanish were certainly intertwined with racial and national imaginaries, creating mutually reinforcing notions about accents and social identifications'.[47] Inés María Martiatu similarly argues that the *teatro bufo* uses language as an 'elemento de exclusión' (*element of exclusion*) that inherently 'subalterniza al negro' (*subalternizes the black*).[48] In both cases, as past scholarship suggests, the stage functioned as a vernacular engine for 'forging' national culture, in both senses of the verb 'to forge': to make and to fake. Lott writes 'blackface was at one and the same time a displaced mapping of ethnic Otherness and an early agent of acculturation'.[49] Both forms engaged a range of racial and ethnic elements that were imagined as particularly and peculiarly US American or Cuban and, over time, these theatrical genres helped delineate the criteria by which certain racial types would be integrated into a national imaginary and on what terms.

Theorizing blackface

This brief comparison needs qualification as it can produce a kind mirage: the unit of comparison, the nation, suggests more stability and uniformity than is warranted in fact. During the periods in question, the

---

[46] Doris Sommer, *Foundational Fictions: The National Romances of Latin America* (Berkeley, CA: University of California Press, 1993).
[47] Kristina Wirtz, *Performing Afro-Cuba: Image, Voice, Spectacle in the Making of Race and History* (Chicago, IL: University of Chicago Press, 2014), p. 275.
[48] Inés María Martiatu Terry, 'El negrito y la mulata en el vórtice de la nacionalidad', in Martiatu Terry (ed.), *Bufo y nación*, 77.
[49] Lott, *Love and Theft*, 100.

USA and Cuba were on opposite sides of the colonial divide. The status of 'the' nation was differently precarious in both locales, a fact partly obscured by the operation of comparison. More importantly, a methodological tautology can hide in our nationally bounded scholarship: the nation is both the object of study and the frame of analysis, potentially leading to an overdetermination of national meaning ascribed to these forms. I aim instead to gain some critical purchase on the ways that theatre may have helped to constitute what we understand as national in the first place—in the still young republic of the United States and especially in colonial Cuba.

We can rethink the nation as frame by instead engaging the underlying economy of slavery that links both the USA and Cuba, especially in this era of 'second slavery'. Blackface performance follows along the extensive transatlantic routes of chattel slavery, participating in what Alexander Weheliye has called 'racializing assemblages', which construe 'race not as a biological or cultural classification but as a set of sociopolitical processes that discipline humanity into full humans, not-quite-humans, and nonhumans'.[50] Michael Omi and Howard Winant earlier named this a 'racial formation', constituted by both the macro and micro sociohistorical processes 'by which racial categories are created, inhabited, transformed, and destroyed'.[51] Performance is one modality through which such racial meanings are produced. For Joseph Roach, performance is a privileged modality because, he argues at length, the situation of American conquest, colonization and slavery produced historically unprecedented social circumstances that required the complex cultural processes of public memory, surrogation and self-invention that performance makes possible.[52] For Roach, surrogation names a basic operation of all cultural (re)production—'the doomed search for originals by continuously auditioning stand-ins'[53]—and blackface is one of its most complex exemplars, through which circum-Atlantic societies invented themselves by, in part, 'performing who and what they were not'.[54]

---

[50] Alexander Weheliye, *Habeas Viscus: Racializing Assemblages, Biopolitics, and Black Feminist Theories of the Human* (Durham, NC and London: Duke University Press, 2014), p. 4.
[51] Michael Omi and Howard Winant, *Racial Formation in the United States: From the 1960s to the 1990s* (New York: Routledge, 1994), p. 55.
[52] Joseph Roach, *Cities of the Dead: Circum-Atlantic Performance* (New York: Columbia University Press, 1996), pp. 2–4.
[53] Roach, *Cities of the Dead*, 3.
[54] Roach, *Cities of the Dead*, 5.

Saidiya Hartman centres the extractive rather than referential logic of 'putting on' blackness (whether through visual marker, voice, sound or gesture), which from the outset assumes the 'fungibility' of blackness. The black body, blackness itself, is imagined as an 'empty' and available vehicle for white occupation, in every colonial sense of the word. Hartman writes:

> The fungibility of the commodity makes the captive body an abstract and empty vessel vulnerable to the projection of others' feelings, ideas, desires and values; and, as property, the dispossessed body of the enslaved is the surrogate for the master's body since it guarantees his disembodied universality and acts as the sign of his power and dominion.[55]

Thus, she continues, the desire to put on, occupy or somehow possess blackness 'as a sentimental resource or the *locus* of excess enjoyment is both founded upon and enabled by the material relations of chattel slavery'.[56] So long as slavery (and what Hartman calls 'the afterlife of slavery') is the socioeconomic frame through which race is lived and practised, there can be no innocent or non-racial uses of the performance of blackness.[57]

Building on the work of Roach and Hartman, Tavia Nyong'o develops the generative concept of the 'circum-Atlantic fold', which allows us to meaningfully frame a relational, rather than strictly comparative, approach to blackface. Inspired by both Foucault and Eve Sedgewick's use of 'the fold', Nyong'o employs it to conjure the 'nonteleological and complexly affective relationship to an imminent future that the present is already caught up in'. For Nyong'o, 'the fold' marks the time and space between 'the potential for Black freedom' and its actual enactment in which 'many of our conceptualizations of race, inheritance, and hybridity

---

[55] Saidiya Hartman, *Scenes of Subjection: Terror, Slavery, and Self-Making in Nineteenth Century America* (Oxford: Oxford University Press, 1997), p. 21. See the related discussion in Lane, 'ImpersoNación', 187–88.

[56] Hartman, *Scenes of Subjection*, 21.

[57] This does not preclude counterhegemonic uses of blackface. Witness Nicholas Jones' study of the *habla de negros* (black speech) in early modern Spanish theatre which aims to 'shed light on the recurring—not exceptional—instantiations where *habla de negros* texts showcase their black characters acting and speaking with agency and destabilizing the category of Whiteness': Nicholas R. Jones, *Staging Habla De Negros: Radical Performances of the African Diaspora in Early Modern Spain* (University Park, PA: Pennsylvania State University Press, 2019), p. 6.

were formulated'.[58] His study refers to the British Atlantic, but a broader geographic fold could be usefully redeployed to encompass colonial and postcolonial blackface practice in the Caribbean and the circum-Atlantic, marking the spatial and temporal zones in which blackness was rendered commodifiable, in Hartman's rich sense. We can imagine such a fold to begin with the first evidence of such (ab)uses of blackness and to extend to the aftermaths that we continue to live today. We can thereby find structural synergies between, say, New York or Philadelphia in the 1840s, and Havana in 1868, both moments of intense condensation of the expropriation of blackness, seeing them as part of a shared and recursive formation. Roach might map these theatre cultures as related 'vortices of behavior', whose function is to 'canalize specified needs, desires, and habits in order to reproduce them'. Such vortices are anchored by 'condensational events', which 'gain a powerful enough hold on collective memory that they will survive the transformation or the relocation of the spaces in which they first flourished'.[59]

A fundamental characteristic of blackface commodification across this fold is that, embodied by white actors, it almost invariably produces a counterfeit racial currency—a blackness in quotation. The concept of the 'counterfeit' is occasion for perennial debate in the field, raising vexing questions of originals and forgeries, authenticity and ownership. Lhamon, for one, does not posit a relation of commodity or counterfeit at the heart of blackface. He insists that when T.D. Rice copied the virtuosic gestures produced by black dancers at bustling labour sites like New York's Catherine Market, those gestures were already 'currency *for exchange*'; such blackface imitation was, he argues, the early churning of a dynamic economy of cultural transmission that he calls 'the Atlantic blackface lore cycle'.[60] Via the poet and theorist Fred Moten, we could insist that, to the contrary, those dancers were likely already moving in an economy in which they themselves had been commodified, an economy that failed to imagine meaning for those dances outside such exchange value. In his brilliant meditations on 'the resistance of the object', Moten teaches us to think about black expression in such scenes of subjection (glossing Hartman), underscoring 'the historical reality of commodities who spoke—of laborers who were commodities before, as it were, the abstraction of labor power from their bodies'.[61] The

---

[58] Nyong'o, *Amalgamation Waltz*, 18.
[59] Roach, *Cities of the Dead*, 28.
[60] Lhamon, *Raising Cain*, 1 and 3, my emphasis.
[61] Fred Moten, *In the Break: The Aesthetics of the Black Radical Tradition* (Minneapolis, MN: University of Minnesota Press, 2003), p. 6.

bodily expression that emanates from those human 'objects'—whether song, dance or, as he has it, screams—is the 'impossible speech' of the commodity, acts through which the 'object' produces itself as subject under and against the very logic of the commodity. 'This is the story of how apparent nonvalue functions as a creator of value; it is also the story of how value animates what appears as nonvalue', a material animation he finds at the ontological heart of the black radical tradition.[62] We can imagine the performances of those dancers at Catherine Market as part of that tradition, acts of improvisatory blackness that mark 'simultaneously both the performance of the object and the performance of humanity'.[63] Whatever else we may say about T.D. Rice's use of those dance moves, in the first instance he reanimates them within the normative and violent economy that commodified those black dancers to begin with. Lott calls this a 'raw' commodification, trafficking in 'the cultural commodities of human commodities'.[64]

The racial counterfeit emerges in this recursive and relentless process of commodification. This is to say more than that the commodified representation of black people on the minstrel and *bufo* stage was distorted or inauthentic, although that is true. It is to say also that blackness itself came to be partly defined through this dense operation of (re)commodification: such commodification is part of what is imagined to be (or seem) 'black' in the first place. That is, part of what felt 'authentic' to enthralled audiences is precisely the fungibility that is, through the very act of expropriation, ascribed to blackness. This is, of course, an extremely complex affair that cannot be reduced to that formula alone, but the underlying structure remains: the gesture of expropriation has a performative racializing force.

This complexity of the racial counterfeit is evident in the figure of the racial malaprop, which populated the minstrel stage through stump speeches and the *teatro bufo* through the figure of the *negro catedrático*. In the USA we find blackface burlesque lectures on the new sciences of magnetism, psychology or phrenology, as well as mock political oratory and the many burlesque lectures on women's rights delivered by cross-dressed blackface comedians.[65] In Cuba we find the figure of the black *catedrático*, usually male but at times female, who recurs as a character in a number of plays, and whose appeal lies in the contrast between his usually modest social standing and his

---

[62] Moten, *In the Break*, 18.
[63] Moten, *In the Break*, 2.
[64] Lott, *Love and Theft*, 40.
[65] See Mahar's chapter on such oratory in *Behind the Burnt Cork Mask*, 59–100.

aspirational, grandiloquent speech. That contrast characterizes both forms: what is funny in the first order is a black person undertaking such learned rhetoric. The humour of both forms further relies on the deep distortion of English or Spanish, abounding in mispronunciations (substituting the wrong vowels, adding consonants), catachresis and malapropism, often structured around comic alliterative puns. In the written texts of these speeches and plays, the speech is written out phonetically, as is the case for most other forms of black speech. Here orality is mobilized as the primary mode of racialization over the visual, a practice with a long tradition in the Iberian world dating to the so-called *habla de negros* (black speech) in the *siglo de oro* (Golden Age) drama or the related Neapolitan *moresche*, as argued by Noémie Ndiaye.[66]

Mahar is comfortable saying that these malaprop speeches were performed 'in dialect', as though there were in fact a dialect from which this distorted stage language borrowed or to which it referred, and he is careful in his consideration of its relation to Black Vernacular English. Some scholars of the *teatro bufo* are also comfortable in the assumption that the *catedrático* refers to an actual demographic, and have turned to the *teatro bufo* for evidence of authentic black speech.[67] Ángel Cristóbal García, for one, claims that *catedrático* speech could be found among 'negros libres urbanos que pretenden vivir "a la blanca" y que asumen de esta forma una actitud social inconsecuente con su realidad económica, racial y lingüística'[68] (*urban free blacks who aim to live 'as whites' and who thus assume a social attitude inconsistent with their economic, racial and linguistic reality*). Even as we can acknowledge the use and abuse of Black Vernacular English or *habla de negros*, I am inclined to believe that part of the (pernicious) work of these counterfeits is to produce the illusion of a coherent original, an illusion that may unwittingly extend into our scholarship. I would venture that in García's quick formulation that free blacks were living 'a la blanca' we hear a late echo of what I have called *catedrácismo*, a racial discourse elaborated in this theatre in which black people who behave outside the normative expectations of a racist society are structurally defined as pretenders (acting in whiteface,

---

[66] Noémie Ndiaye, 'Off the Record: Contrapuntal Theatre History', in Tracy Davis and Peter Marx (eds), *The Routledge Companion to Theatre and Performance Historiography* (New York: Routledge, 2021), pp. 229–48 (233). On the *habla de negros* see Jones, *Staging Habla De Negros*.

[67] On vernacular speech in the *teatro bufo*, see Sergio Valdés Bernal, *El teatro cubano colonial y la caracterización lingüístico-cultural de sus personajes* (Madrid: Iberoamericana, 2018).

[68] Ángel Cristóbal García, *Habla cubana en el Teatro Bufo del Siglo XIX* (Miami, FL: Letras Latinas Publishers, 2017), np.

as it were), interlopers in a white world. As pretenders, their speech and actions are overdetermined as showy, ostentatious; they are imagined to be inherently theatrical, ultimately producing the racial paradox Michael Eric Dyson describes in *Entertaining Race*: 'Black folk are forced to entertain race' and to make race entertaining. He writes '[i]t is the white world's demand to bow to racial hierarchy that grinds every Black limb, every Black thought, every Black word to performance inside the white world'.[69] It is not enough to say that these forms misrepresent or satirize free, educated, black people; the counterfeit operation at work in both introduces a false rate of exchange, one that defines a priori any desire for black people to be 'free' and 'educated' as a failed mimetic desire to be white.

We arrive, then, at a different question about nation, race and blackface performance: why and how did this counterfeit feel not only racial but national for so many audiences? This question admits entry into wider discussion of how national projects in the slaveholding Caribbean were racialized from the outset, and whether they were especially so during the colonial nineteenth century, when widespread projects of nationhood (like that of the USA) coexisted and competed with enduring colonial orders (like that of Spanish Cuba). We could usefully study the similar and different place of race in national imaginaries and in their correlative political and legal systems across this 'fold'. Our concern is with the work of the theatre in those processes, allowing us to ask how vernacular culture both captured and taught ways of feeling national through blackface across these different contexts.[70] We can sharpen the question as well: was the cultural commodification of blackness always implicated, already, in the production of national affect? To the extent

---

[69] Michael E. Dyson, *Entertaining Race: Performing Blackness in America* (New York: St Martin's Press, 2021), pp. 4 and 5.

[70] Consider the research on racial impersonation in 1780s Saint-Domingue by Julia Prest. She finds that the several references to locally produced blackface performance all involve use of the Creole language, as opposed to the normative colonial French. She considers it likely that a Creole blackface theatre tradition might have further expanded 'had public theatre in the colony not been overtaken by the momentous events of 1791 and beyond': Julia Prest, 'The Familiar Other: Blackface Performance in Creole Works from 1780s Saint-Domingue', in Jeffrey M. Leichman and Karine Bénac-Giroux (eds), *Colonialism and Slavery in Performance: Theatre and the Eighteenth-Century French Caribbean*, Oxford University Studies in the Enlightenment (Liverpool: Liverpool University Press, 2021), pp. 41–63 (59). See also Sarah J. Adams's analysis of the black-masked Harlequin figure as he appeared onstage in Suriname in Chapter Four of this volume.

that this is so, what is the specific work of the counterfeit in giving shape to national structures of feeling?

I return to Villoch and his political love story with the colonial *teatro bufo*, where the theatre presents a virtual Cuba 'on loan' from an unrealized future, the same theatre that Rine Leal casts as the unwitting understudy for a national theatre otherwise repressed by Spanish colonial rule. For both men, the theatre specifically conjured a national structure of feeling before the social and political conditions for such nationhood had emerged. In *Blackface Cuba* I argue that it was, paradoxically, through blackface performance that an emergent Cuba elaborated a national myth of *mestizaje*, in which the nation is the transcendent outcome of a colonial encounter between Spanish and African cultures. That myth, still prevalent today, would have us believe that performance—in particular, what we now call Afro-Cuban dance and music—'naturally' emerged as Cuba's national genres through the inevitable encounter of African and Spanish cultures. That story—part of the same political love story—forgets, as does Villoch, that a prime technology for such mixing in the colonial period was not racial integration but instead racial impersonation. And it turns out not to be a paradox at all, but rather the point. The technologies of blackface, of 'putting on' blackness, offered a precise mechanism for colonial white *criollos* to assert difference from colonial Spain via recourse to 'African' sound, gestures, dance and speech, while at the same time disciplining and constraining the participation of real, enslaved and free, black subjects in that very imaginary. Blackface emerges as a means of translation between the colonial order, structured around slavery and its aftermaths, and the imagined national future that believes itself to have transcended that past; it becomes the language of nation but in its very ontology carries forward its colonial racial logic. The 'condensational' practice of blackface served as the means to produce a racialized national affect that is, at the same time, a nationalized racial affect. The *negrito*, the blackface counterfeit, serves as both uncomfortable remainder and alibi for the otherwise unmarked whiteness that organizes national imagining in the colony. Our challenge as scholars is to resist the usual love stories, decolonizing our narration such that the stories we tell about these performance forms do not perpetuate the racialized national narrative those forms embodied.

Bibliography

Anderson, Benedict. *Imagined Communities: Reflections on the Origin and Spread of Nationalism* (London: Verso, 1991).

Bajini, Irina. *Antología de teatro bufo Cubano* (Bogotá, Colombia: Ediciones Uniandes, 2018).

Boudet, Rosa Ileana. *La chimenea encantada: Francisco Covarrubias* (Santa Monica, CA: Ediciones la Flecha, 2017).

Chude-Sokei, Louis. *The Last 'Darky': Bert Williams, Black-on-Black Minstrelsy and the African Diaspora* (Durham, NC: Duke University Press, 2006).

Cockrell, Dale. *Demons of Disorder: Early Blackface Minstrels and Their World* (Cambridge: Cambridge University Press, 1997).

Cole, Catherine. 'American Ghetto Parties and Ghanaian Concert Parties: A Transnational Perspective on Blackface', in Stephen Johnson (ed.), *Burnt Cork: Traditions and Legacies of Blackface Minstrelsy* (Amherst, MA: University of Massachusetts Press, 2012), pp. 223–57.

Cruz, Mary. *Creto Gangá* (Havana: Contemporaneo, 1974).

del Monte, Laureano. *Con don, sin don, ayer y hoy, caricatura trágico-bufa, lírico bailable en un acto y 5 cuadros, y en prosa* (Havana: Imprenta El Aerolito, 1894).

DuComb, Christian. *Haunted City: Three Centuries of Racial Impersonation in Philadelphia* (Ann Arbor, MI: University of Michigan Press, 2017).

Dyson, Michael E. *Entertaining Race: Performing Blackness in America* (New York: St Martin's Press, 2021).

Fernández de la Reguera Tayà, Tànit. *Cuba y Cataluña en la segunda mitad del siglo XIX: Teatro popular e identidades (proto)nacionales* (Madrid: Editorial Pliegos, 2020).

Fernández Vilaros, Francisco. *Los negros catedráticos*, in Rine Leal (ed.), *Teatro bufo siglo XIX*, Vol. 1 (Havana: Editorial Arte y Literatura, 1975), pp. 131–62.

Ferrer, Ada. *Cuba: An American History* (New York: Scribner, 2021).

Ferrer, Ada. *Freedom's Mirror: Cuba and Haiti in the Age of Revolution* (Cambridge: Cambridge University Press, 2016).

García, Ángel Cristóbal. *Habla cubana en el Teatro Bufo del Siglo XIX* (Miami, FL: Letras Latinas Publishers, 2017).

Gibbs, Jenna M. *Performing the Temple of Liberty: Slavery, Theater, and Popular Culture in London and Philadelphia, 1760–1850* (Baltimore, MD: Johns Hopkins University Press, 2014).

Hartman, Saidiya. *Scenes of Subjection: Terror, Slavery, and Self-Making in Nineteenth Century America* (Oxford: Oxford University Press, 1997).

Johnson, Stephen. 'Death and the Minstrel Race, Madness, and Art in the Last (W)Rites of Three Early Blackface Performers', in Stephen Johnson (ed.), *Burnt Cork: Traditions and Legacies of Blackface Minstrelsy* (Amherst, MA: University of Massachusetts Press, 2012), pp. 73–103.

Jones, Nicholas R. *Staging Habla De Negros: Radical Performances of the African Diaspora in Early Modern Spain* (University Park, PA: Pennsylvania State University Press, 2019).

Kennard, James K. 'Who Are Our National Poets?', in T. Allston Brown and Charles Day (eds), 'Black Musicians and Early Ethiopian Minstrelsy', *The Black Perspective in Music*, 3.1 (Spring 1975), pp. 83–85.

Lane, Jill. *Blackface Cuba (1840–1895)* (Philadelphia, PA: University of Pennsylvania Press, 2005).

Lane, Jill. 'ImpersoNación', in Inés María Martiatu Terry (ed.), *Bufo y nación: interpelaciones desde el presente* (Havana: Letras Cubanas, 2009), pp. 172–206.

Leal, Rine. *Breve historia del teatro Cubano* (Havana: Editorial Letras Cubanas, 1980).

Leal, Rine. *La selva oscura*, Vol. 1 (Havana: Arte y Literatura, 1975).

Leal, Rine. *La selva oscura*, Vol. 2: *De los bufos a la neocolonia, Historia del teatro cubano de 1868 a 1902* (Havana: Arte y Literatura, 1982).

Lhamon, William T. *Jim Crow, American: Selected Songs and Plays* (Cambridge, MA: Belknap Press of Harvard University Press, 2009).

Lhamon, William T. *Raising Cain: Blackface Performance from Jim Crow to Hip Hop* (Cambridge, MA: Harvard University Press, 2000).

Lott, Eric J. *Love and Theft: Blackface Minstrelsy and the American Working Class* (New York: Oxford University Press, 1993; 2013).

Mahar, William J. *Behind the Burnt Cork Mask: Early Blackface Minstrelsy and Antebellum American Popular Culture* (Urbana, IL: University of Illinois Press, 1999).

Marquese, Rafael, Tâmis Parron and Márcia R. Berbel. *Slavery and Politics: Brazil and Cuba, 1790–1850*, trans. Leonardo Marques (Albuquerque, NM: University of New Mexico Press, 2016).

Martiatu Terry, Inés María. 'El negrito y la mulata en el vórtice de la nacionalidad', in Inés María Martiatu Terry (ed.), *Bufo y nación: interpelaciones desde el presente* (Havana: Letras Cubanas, 2009), pp. 68–104.

Moten, Fred. *In the Break: The Aesthetics of the Black Radical Tradition* (Minneapolis, MN: University of Minnesota Press, 2003).

Ndiaye, Noémie. 'Off the Record: Contrapuntal Theatre History', in Tracy Davis and Peter Marx (eds), *The Routledge Companion to Theatre and Performance Historiography* (New York: Routledge, 2021), 229–48.

Nowatzki, Robert. *Representing African Americans in Transatlantic Abolitionism and Blackface Minstrelsy* (Baton Rouge, LA: Louisiana State University Press, 2010).

Nyong'o, Tavia. *The Amalgamation Waltz: Race, Performance and the Ruses of Memory* (Minneapolis, MN: University of Minnesota Press, 2009).

Omi, Michael and Howard Winant. *Racial Formation in the United States: From the 1960s to the 1990s* (New York: Routledge, 1994).

Perez, Louis. *Cuba Between Reform and Revolution*, Third edition (New York and Oxford: Oxford University Press, 2006).

Prest, Julia. 'The Familiar Other: Blackface Performance in Creole Works from 1780s Saint-Domingue', in Jeffrey M. Leichman and Karine Bénac-Giroux (eds), *Colonialism and Slavery in Performance: Theatre and the Eighteenth-Century French Caribbean*, Oxford University Studies in the Enlightenment (Liverpool: Liverpool University Press, 2021), pp. 41–63.

Roach, Joseph. *Cities of the Dead: Circum-Atlantic Performance* (New York: Columbia University Press, 1996).

Sommer, Doris. *Foundational Fictions: The National Romances of Latin America* (Berkeley, CA: University of California Press, 1993).

Soria, Mar. 'Colonial Imaginings on the Stage: Blackface, Gender, and the Economics of Empire in Spanish and Catalan Popular Theater', in N. Michelle Murray and Akiko Tsuchiya (eds), *Unsettling Colonialism: Gender and Race in the Nineteenth-Century Global Hispanic World* (Albany, NY: State University of New York Press, 2019), pp. 135–69.

Thomas, Susan. *Cuban Zarzuela: Performing Race and Gender on Havana's Lyric Stage* (Chicago, IL: University of Illinois Press, 2009).

Tomich, Dale. *Through the Prism of Slavery: Labor, Capital, and World Economy* (Lanham, MD: Rowman and Littlefield, 2004).

Valdés Bernal, Sergio. *El teatro cubano colonial y la caracterización lingüístico-cultural de sus personajes* (Madrid: Iberoamericana, 2018).

Villoch, Federico. 'Los Bufos de Salas', *Carteles*, 27.1 (29 September 1946), pp. 22–23.

Weheliye, Alexander. *Habeas Viscus: Racializing Assemblages, Biopolitics, and Black Feminist Theories of the Human* (Durham, NC and London: Duke University Press, 2014).

Wirtz, Kristina. *Performing Afro-Cuba: Image, Voice, Spectacle in the Making of Race and History* (Chicago, IL: University of Chicago Press, 2014).

Six

Contextualizing Late Eighteenth-Century Jamaican Oratorio: Obstacles and Opportunities

Wayne Weaver

When Maria Nugent, wife of the British governor of Jamaica George Nugent, wrote in her diary in 1802 about attending a militia mustering ceremony in Spanish Town, she recalled that 'it was ridiculous to hear the negroes, who were spectators, laugh at the Jew company when it fired, which it did very badly—"Now Massa Jew! Dat right! Dat well, Massa Jew!" &c.'[1] Around a year later, in February 1803, she noted that at the local theatre she had been part of an audience comprising 'all colours and descriptions; blacks, browns, Jews and whites'.[2] Nugent's persistent observation of the behaviours and complexions of the people around her during her residence in Jamaica raises important questions about constructions of white identity, nationhood and the racialization of human difference. But Nugent was a foreign visitor with no intention of remaining in Jamaica beyond her husband's posting. She had arrived with her own metropolitan perspectives which did not necessarily correspond with those of her Jamaican contemporaries. Few sources survive to inform on these Creole perspectives. In this chapter I explore how musico-theatrical sources might be deployed to contextualize—and thereby elucidate—local dynamics (and vice versa).[3]

---

[1] Maria Nugent, *Lady Nugent's Journal: Jamaica One Hundred Years Ago*, ed. Frank Cundall, Cambridge Library Collection, Slavery and Abolition (Cambridge: Cambridge University Press, 2012), p. 76.

[2] Nugent, *Lady Nugent's Journal*, 193. For a compelling contextualization and discussion of this moment, see Errol Hill, *The Jamaican Stage, 1655–1900: Profile of a Colonial Theatre* (Amherst, MA: University of Massachusetts Press, 1992), p. 189; see also Elizabeth Maddock Dillon, *New World Drama: The Performative Commons in the Atlantic World, 1649–1849* (Durham, NC: Duke University Press, 2014), p. 178.

[3] Various publications come close to studying these themes through the literary analysis of texts from eighteenth-century Jamaica. One example is Vincent Carretta (ed.), *Unchained Voices: An Anthology of Black Authors*

In adopting a contextualizing approach, I am mindful of Tracy Davis's caution that 'one scholar's criterion for *Gestalt* may be another's idea of irrelevance'.[4] However, in the little-known case of eighteenth-century Jamaican oratorio, context nonetheless offers meaningful opportunities for researchers.

In light of the substantial efforts that have been made to provide insights into life within, notably, the chattel slavery regime in Jamaica, it is striking that the music and theatre of the time, and the ways in which eighteenth-century Jamaicans engaged with these art forms, remain virtually unknown.[5] Little information about local perspectives has appeared in the few books that cover Jamaican theatre and art music in the late eighteenth and early nineteenth centuries.[6] Both Errol Hill's *Jamaican Stage, 1655–1900* and Ivy Baxter's *Arts of an Island [...] 1494–1962* rely on the expansive chronology provided in Richardson Wright's *Revels in Jamaica 1682–1838*.[7] In this chapter, I explore obstacles to and opportunities for interrogating constructions of nationhood and whiteness through the examination of oratorios—which I argue were understood as theatrical (as well as religious) works—composed by a Jamaican Creole, Samuel Felsted (1743–1802).

Samuel Felsted and the oratorio genre

Felsted, who is not mentioned in the books listed above, was a white Jamaican born to Anglo-American migrants. He is well summarized by the expression 'Renaissance man' on account of his wide-ranging talents

---

  in the English-Speaking World of the Eighteenth Century (Lexington, KY: University Press of Kentucky, 1996).
[4] Tracy C. Davis, 'The Context Problem', *Theatre Survey*, 45.2 (2004), pp. 203–09 (204).
[5] As Elizabeth Maddock Dillon has noted, 'eighteenth-century Jamaica seldom appears in accounts of the history of Anglophone theatre, culture, or aesthetics: Jamaica did not become wholly independent from Great Britain until 1962 and, as a result, has been written out of nationally oriented accounts of British and American literature and culture, despite the fact that Jamaica stood at the center of the Anglophone Atlantic colonial system': Dillon, *New World Drama*, 182–83.
[6] Hill's brief commentary on Jamaica's locally produced theatre is an exception to this statement: Hill, *The Jamaican Stage*, 159–62.
[7] Hill, *The Jamaican Stage*; Ivy Baxter, *The Arts of an Island: The Development of the Culture and of the Folk and Creative Arts in Jamaica, 1494–1962 (Independence)* (Metuchen, NJ: Scarecrow Press, 1970); Richardson Wright, *Revels in Jamaica, 1682–1838* (Kingston, Jamaica: Bolivar Press, 1986).

in art, music, poetry, botany and invention.[8] Although he appears never to have left Jamaica, it is clear from the fact that his music was published in England that Felsted enjoyed connections with musical professionals there. *Jonah,* the first of his oratorios, was published in London in 1775 by a subscription of more than 200 individuals. Later, around 1783 (when Felsted left his first post at Half-Way Tree to become the organist at Kingston Parish Church), he published a set of six voluntaries for the organ or harpsichord. I discuss Felsted's *Jonah* in this chapter alongside his second, and lesser-known, oratorio *The Dedication*.[9]

Samuel Felsted stands out as the first Anglophone composer of oratorios of the early modern Americas. Although he was unparalleled in his area and time, the genre was already popular in England. Oratorios are large-scale musical works for voices and orchestral accompaniment. Like opera, oratorio is structured as a series of aria, recitative, chorus and instrumental movements. However, unlike opera, oratorio is typically based on biblical texts, with most being derived from the Old Testament. In order to emphasize their spiritual qualities, oratorios are customarily performed without staging in ecclesiastical settings, but their biblical subject matter makes them inherently dramatic.

The first oratorios of George Frideric Handel (1685–1759) had received highly acclaimed performances in early 1730s and 1740s England.[10] Their success helped make Handel the chief exponent of the genre in his day and the main name associated with it for several generations. Surviving

---

[8] My use of the term 'Renaissance man' to describe Samuel Felsted is borrowed from Pamela O'Gorman, '*Jonah*: An Eighteenth-Century Jamaican Oratorio', *Jamaica Journal*, Institute of Jamaica, Kingston, 22.4 (1990), pp. 41–45 (43). Further information about Felsted's life and music can be found in my forthcoming doctoral thesis and in the following articles: Thurston Dox, 'Samuel Felsted of Jamaica', *The American Music Research Center Journal*, 1 (1991), pp. 37–46; Thurston Dox, 'Samuel Felsted's *Jonah*: The Earliest American Oratorio', *Choral Journal*, 32.7 (1992), pp. 27–32; Pamela O'Gorman, 'An Eighteenth-Century Jamaican Oratorio Part Two, The Music of Samuel Felsted's *Jonah*', *Jamaica Journal*, Institute of Jamaica, Kingston, 23.1 (1990), pp. 14–19.

[9] A copy of the published edition of *Jonah* is held by the British Library and an original edition of Felsted's organ voluntaries is held by the Bristol Central Library. *The Dedication* only survives as a manuscript held at the British Library (reference R.M.21.f.2).

[10] Although performed initially as a staged work for a private audience, Handel's *Esther* (1718) received its first public—unstaged—performance in 1732. Two further oratorios by Handel (*Deborah* and *Athalia*) were performed in 1733: Howard E. Smither, 'Oratorio', *Grove Music Online*. 2001, https://doi.org/10.1093/gmo/9781561592630.article.20397.

commentaries show that Handel's music was also well known in late eighteenth-century Jamaica.[11] Indeed, Felsted owned copies of some of Handel's works and was clearly influenced by his musical style.[12] After Handel's death, some of his works were turned into *pasticcio* oratorios and new oratorios were performed to varying acclaim. These include *The Song of Deborah and Barak* (1732) by Maurice Greene, *David's Lamentation over Saul and Jonathan* (1736) by William Boyce, *Jephtha* (1757) by John Stanley and *Judith* (1761) by Thomas Arne. Felsted's direct contemporary, Samuel Arnold (1740–1802), also wrote oratorios. *The Prodigal Son* was performed in 1773 and *Omnipotence* (a Handel *pasticcio*) was performed in 1774.[13] Each of these organist-composers held eminent musical appointments in churches, in theatres or as musicians appointed to the royal family. By composing and having his own music published, Felsted was engaging in practices common among established municipal musicians in Britain.

Felsted clearly conceived of his oratorios in theatrical terms. *The Dedication* (the longer of the two surviving oratorios that he composed) is split into two parts comprising three scenes. Each scene opens with a brief paragraph of staging information. Despite only being 'intended as an assistance to the imagination', Felsted's staging details add an extra dramatic element to the score.[14] The scene descriptors demonstrate that he was well aware of his music's dramatic qualities, and also indicate how he took inspiration from Handel's oratorios, several of which include similar details. Felsted's scene descriptions also resemble the kinds of sets that were designed for similar dramatic performances in Kingston and in Spanish Town around the time that he served as the organist of Kingston Parish Church (1783–90).[15]

[11] Excerpts from oratorios by Handel were performed at the funeral of the Countess of Effingham (wife of the serving governor at the time) at St Catherine's Church in Spanish Town: *Daily Advertiser* (Kingston), 4 November 1791, p. 3. See also note 48 below.

[12] For more information about Felsted's Handel manuscripts, see David Hunter, 'Music and the Use of the Profits of the Anglo-American Slave Economy (c. 1610–c. 1810)', in Anna Morcom and Timothy D. Taylor (eds), *The Oxford Handbook of Economic Ethnomusicology* (Oxford: Oxford Academic, 2020) https://doi.org/10.1093/oxfordhb/9780190859633.013.5.

[13] For more detailed information about eighteenth-century oratorio, see Howard E. Smither, *A History of the Oratorio*, Vols 2 and 3: *The Oratorio in the Baroque Era: Protestant Germany and England* and *The Oratorio in the Classical Era* (Chapel Hill, NC: University of North Carolina Press, 1977).

[14] Felsted, *The Dedication*, np.

[15] See, for example, Smither, *A History of the Oratorio* 2, 287–89; Wright, *Revels in Jamaica*, 287. Further details about Felsted's employment at Kingston

The paucity of information surrounding Samuel Felsted is the most obvious reason why he has escaped the attention of earlier researchers. Yet his oratorios constitute the majority of a tiny corpus of sheet music surviving from late eighteenth-century Jamaica. As well as Creole perspectives on issues like those identified above, Felsted's oratorios offer hitherto unexplored opportunities for the interrogation of 'non-white' aspects of Jamaican experience. This chapter considers what it might mean to step up to Olivia Bloechl's challenge to revisit existing scholarship in order to develop it in ways that permit an interrogation of how it formed part of a process in which racialized versions of whiteness and blackness were constructed.[16] I will reflect here on the opportunities and challenges that arise when we attempt to garner deeper understandings of the implicit meanings of Felsted's oratorios, advocating a more comprehensive understanding of their social and political microclimate, but also a better understanding of how British ideas played an integral role in shaping Jamaican society. First, I will provide background information including details about the structure of the Jamaican society of Felsted's day, his musical network and his sources of inspiration. I will then turn to an extract from *The Dedication* as a case study on the ways in which Felsted's libretti can been seen to contribute to—and reflect—eighteenth-century constructions of concepts like whiteness, nation, enslavement and a racialized understanding of human difference. Thinking about the links between Felsted's libretti and the construction of racial difference is a way to bring his music—which is devoid of the kinds of sonic elements that might make it locatable outside Britain—into a dialogue with its complex colonial context.

The Jamaican society of Felsted's day

Jamaica, during the era of chattel slavery, has been described in confusing and contradictory ways. For some, it was 'the brightest jewel in the British diadem' on account of its strategic location, size (in comparison with the other West Indian colonies) and the huge

---

Parish Church (and his dismissal in 1790), are forthcoming in my doctoral thesis.

[16] Olivia Bloechl, 'Race, Empire, and Early Music', in Olivia Bloechl, Melanie Lowe and Jeffrey Kallberg (eds), *Rethinking Difference in Music Scholarship* (Cambridge: Cambridge University Press, 2015), p. 79.

wealth it generated.[17] Jamaica was seen as a kind of 'prodigious mine', quite literally to the detriment of its raw materials and the lives of its inhabitants, most of whom were of African origin.[18] But the island's reliance on imports of enslaved Africans to bolster its stagnant demographics and its 'transitory and impermanent characteristics' as the result of having few long-term white settlers means that it has been described by scholars of the period as a 'failed settler society'.[19] Life in colonial-era Jamaica was overshadowed by (at least) three things. Firstly, displacement—because the majority of the population were trafficked Africans or European migrants. Secondly, absence—owing to the absence of 'life-yielding' social institutions like marriage and the family unit, and also the absenteeism of many estate owners who preferred to live in Britain and delegate the management of their affairs to Jamaican overseers and attorneys. And thirdly, by the extremely elevated rates of mortality.[20] Only the colony's rising class of 'people of colour', typically the racially mixed offspring of white men and enslaved black women, increased naturally.[21] Jamaica was also home

---

[17] Christer Petley, *White Fury: A Jamaican Slaveholder and the Age of Revolution* (Oxford: Oxford University Press, 2018), p. 143. For details about Jamaica's historic wealth, see Trevor G. Burnard, '"Prodigious Riches": The Wealth of Jamaica before the American Revolution', *The Economic History Review*, 54.3 (2001), pp. 506–24.

[18] The terms 'prodigious' and 'mine' have been applied to Jamaica by several writers. See, for instance, Trevor G. Burnard, *Planters, Merchants, and Slaves: Plantation Societies in British America, 1650–1820* (Chicago and London: University of Chicago Press, 2015), p. 165. For further details about the use of Jamaica's wealth for musical purposes, see David Hunter, 'The Beckfords in England and Italy: A Case Study in the Musical Uses of the Profits of Slavery', *Early Music*, 46.2 (2018), pp. 285–98 and Hunter, 'Music and the Use of the Profits of the Anglo-American Slave Economy'. Details about the use of Jamaican woods in musical instrument construction may be found in Michael G. Zadro, 'Woods Used for Woodwind Instruments since the Sixteenth Century—1', *Early Music*, 3.2 (1975), pp. 134–36.

[19] Burnard, *Planters, Merchants, and Slaves*, 157; Trevor G. Burnard, 'A Failed Settler Society: Marriage and Demographic Failure in Early Jamaica', *Journal of Social History*, 28.1 (1994), pp. 63–82.

[20] For detailed research about perspectives of life and death in Jamaica in the eighteenth century, see Vincent Brown, *The Reaper's Garden: Death and Power in the World of Atlantic Slavery* (Cambridge, MA and London: Harvard University Press, 2008).

[21] For more detail about the rise of people of colour in Jamaica in the late eighteenth century, see Daniel Livesay, *Children of Uncertain Fortune: Mixed-Race Jamaicans in Britain and the Atlantic Family, 1733–1833* (Williamsburg, VA and Chapel Hill, NC: University of North Carolina Press,

to a significant and conspicuous population of Jewish people of Iberian descent, many descended from Portuguese *conversos* (converts) who had been left behind when the Spanish occupation of Jamaica came to an end around 1670 (the year when Spain formally recognized Jamaica as an English colony).[22] This all made Jamaica into something of a social crucible, with an established and wealthy white elite administration operating at its uppermost level, a category of 'poor whites' (which included the Jewish community) in the middle and, at the lowest level, a huge underclass of African-descended people (enslaved and free, black and mixed).[23]

The Jamaican Assembly of 1797 adopted a different method of distinguishing between the colony's social groups. Their system, which also differs from Maria Nugent's categorization of 'blacks, browns, Jews and whites' (quoted above), portrayed the colony in four tiers according to their social privileges: 'whites, free people of color having special privileges granted by private acts, free people of color not possessing such privileges, and slaves'.[24] But this view failed to acknowledge the fact that certain groups of white people were denied some of the 'special privileges' supposed to have been automatically allocated. Whites who were not members of the island's established (Anglican) church, such as people who were Jewish, Catholic or members of Dissenter churches, were not granted the same privileges. This means that they were conceived of as a kind of 'white other'.[25] At the turn of the nineteenth century, people who were white others, along with the African-descended people living in Jamaica, were still being subjected

---

2018). See also Edward Brathwaite, *The Development of Creole Society in Jamaica, 1770–1820* (Kingston, Jamaica and Miami, FL: Ian Randle, 2005).

[22] Further details about the Jewish people of eighteenth-century Jamaica are to be found in Stanley Mirvis, *The Jews of Eighteenth-Century Jamaica: A Testamentary History of a Diaspora in Transition* (New Haven, CT: Yale University Press, 2020).

[23] Trevor Burnard has pointed out that Kingston contained more enslaved people and free people of colour combined than all of the urban centres in British North America: Trevor G. Burnard, 'Slaves and Slavery in Kingston, 1770–1815', *International Review of Social History*, 65.S28 (2020), pp. 39–65. He has noted that Jamaican settlers were unable to establish a 'consensus about what Jamaican identity should be' and that the tone of the society was set by people who did not see it as their home: Burnard, 'A Failed Settler Society', 63–64.

[24] Brathwaite, *The Development of Creole Society*, 105.

[25] This is in spite of the passing of the Plantation Act in 1740, which was supposed to encourage people like Dissenters to settle in Jamaica: Mirvis, *The Jews of Eighteenth-Century Jamaica*, 69.

to forms of discrimination that were legally enforced.[26] They vied for 'special privileges' but also for status and recognition from the white elite authorities; the Jews and free people of colour would receive their respective emancipations just a few years apart in the 1830s. As an Anabaptist, and thus a Dissenter, Felsted was part of this questionable subgroup within the white population.[27] With this in mind, we now turn to his influences and his musical network. Here I will note, where applicable, the involvement of people who would not necessarily have been considered as white.

Felsted's musical network, influences and the question of *whiteness*

The existence of Felsted's music is due, in part, to the lively cultural environment created by an assortment of talented civilian and military performers who relocated to Jamaica between 1770 and the mid-1790s. Their activities saw Jamaica's most populous towns—especially Kingston—transform the island into a key location in a complex theatrical network spanning the Anglophone Atlantic region. In order to understand the themes arising in the libretti of Felsted's musical scores, we need to first delve a little further into his locale. Who were the white and non-white people that made up Felsted's musical and theatrical network and what sorts of performances might have been sources of inspiration for our composer?

The exact nature of Felsted's involvement with the theatre is not known, but the American Company was arguably the most important group to arrive in Jamaica during his maturity, and other performers travelled to the island after the American War of Independence (1775–83). Some of them only stayed for a short time, but others (who are mentioned below) remained on the island for life. The American Company offered full theatrical seasons and concert performances in the periods between. The seasons involved three or four performances per week, with a weekly or fortnightly change of bill. They performed a variety of material, but typically opted for works that

---

[26] Such people were forbidden (among other aspects of civic life) from bearing arms, standing for public office or serving on juries: Mirvis, *The Jews of Eighteenth-Century Jamaica*, 29–30. As separate Jewish and black militia regiments were established towards the end of the eighteenth century, Jamaican lawmakers remained suspicious and constantly vigilant of residents whose behaviour did not conform to their established norms.

[27] Dox, 'Samuel Felsted of Jamaica', 41.

had met with acclaim on London's stages and that contained themes of local interest.

Many of these stage works reflected the desire of local people to see visual representations of themselves and the other people living around them in Jamaican society performed on stage. An example of this is Richard Cumberland's *The West Indian* (1771), which was performed in Kingston in 1777 and again in 1784. This work was probably the source of inspiration for *A West-India Lady's arrival in London* (1781), a comedy written by the actor-singer Margaret Cheer.[28] Reflecting the increasing Jewish patronage of the Kingston theatre, Cumberland's *Jew Outwitted* was performed in 1783. This followed a locally published and probably adapted edition of Richard Brinsley Sheridan's comic opera *The Duenna* in 1779.[29] Meanwhile, other works that were performed contained themes surrounding enslavement like Dibdin's *The Padlock* (1768), which was staged in Kingston in 1777 and several times in the 1780s, and George Colman the younger's *Inkle and Yarico*, which was staged in 1788.[30]

Some of the most visible people who were part of the Kingston theatre scene were not typically 'white'.[31] Mr Morales, who might have been descended from a local Ibero-Jewish family, was an original member of the American Company. When the troupe departed, he and another actor-singer (Mr Roberts) remained behind and worked as part of a troupe led by the Irish actor-singer James Mahon. Mahon was active in

---

[28] Wright, *Revels in Jamaica*, 154–55. Miss Cheer was an actress in the American Company led by Lewis Hallam the younger (1740–1808). Like all of the original Jamaican plays from this period, the text has not survived, but previous researchers have suggested that it was probably based on Cumberland's *The West Indian*, the opening scene of which features the arrival of Belcour (a wealthy, West Indian estate owner), at a busy London dockyard. The advertisement for the performance includes '4 blacks etc.' in the cast listing. These people might well have been of African heritage and, if they were, this advertisement would constitute the earliest recorded instance of black actors performing in a Jamaican theatre. It is also possible that these actors could have been people of European heritage performing in blackface. This issue is examined in more detail in my doctoral thesis. For the full newspaper advertisement see *Royal Gazette* (Kingston), 6 October 1781.

[29] Hill, *The Jamaican Stage*, 80.

[30] Hill, *The Jamaican Stage*, 79. Wright, *Revels in Jamaica*, 202; 264–65.

[31] As well as the fact that the actors working on Jamaican stages played to audiences that were mixed, Jamaican theatres relied on the labour of servants and enslaved people. Jamaica's theatrical scene was thus composed of people from a variety of European and African backgrounds.

Kingston in the late 1780s and early 1790s.[32] As well as Morales, another Jewish musician living in Kingston around this time was Myer Lyon (*d.* 1796). Lyon, who was also known by his stage name Michael Leoni, had a background in operatic and oratorio performance in London. He left for Jamaica (probably to escape his creditors) in 1789.[33] Around the same time, French and Italian performers were arriving in Jamaica, fleeing revolutionary Saint-Domingue. These people (who are likely to have been Catholics) included the 'Italian Music Master' Monsieur Bifari, Monsieur Yanda a 'professor of Music', and a Mademoiselle Dubourg.[34] The final name I wish to mention here is Felix Byrne, another musician of Catholic faith. Byrne returned to Jamaica in the 1790s after a period in London under the tutelage of Samuel Arnold.[35] Among various pursuits, he sold and maintained musical instruments, owned a long room that was used as a performance venue and, in 1804, founded the Jamaican equivalent of London's Vauxhall Pleasure Gardens at Harmony Hall.[36] So what can we do with these names and theatre pieces? What do they actually tell us?

Felsted was surrounded by people whose whiteness (like his own) was problematic because of their choice of religion. Being white did not necessarily entitle a person to 'white', or rather, elite status. The

---

[32] Wright, *Revels in Jamaica*, 261–62. Back in England, Mahon had been a 'favourite and frequent bass singer at Bath and the Salisbury Festivals' and an occasional singer at the Vauxhall Pleasure Gardens, in addition to his regular work at the Covent Garden theatre. He had also taken part in the Handel Memorial Concerts of 1786: Philip H. Highfill, *A Biographical Dictionary of Actors, Actresses, Musicians, Dancers, Managers and Other Stage Personnel in London, 1660–1800* (Carbondale, IL: Southern Illinois University Press, 1973), p. 55.

[33] As Stanley Mirvis has noted, Leoni could have chosen Jamaica above other locations in order 'to take part in the island's blossoming theatre culture': Mirvis, *The Jews of Eighteenth-Century Jamaica*, 106. Lyon served as the 'Principal Reader' and almost certainly as a *hazan* (cantor) in the synagogue in Kingston, where where he was later buried. Although his life in Jamaica is shrouded in mystery, like that of many migrants residing there in the late eighteenth century, it seems likely that he would have found opportunities to take part in the local musical and theatrical scene. What is more, the fact that Leoni's burial inscription records him as 'one of the first singers of the age' suggests that his talents were known in Kingston. For further details about Leoni, see Uri Erman, 'The Operatic Voice of Leoni the Jew: Between the Synagogue and the Theater in Late Georgian Britain', *Journal of British Studies*, 56.2 (2017), pp. 295–321.

[34] Wright, *Revels in Jamaica*, 297–98.

[35] Wright, *Revels in Jamaica*, 285.

[36] Wright, *Revels in Jamaica*, 311.

theatrical performances these people helped to create for the mixed Jamaican audiences raise issues about how white identity was delineated. Felsted's own libretti are, therefore, likely to have been inspired by a variety of people and literary works connected to the Kingston theatre, as well as by his lived experiences. The variety found in the backgrounds of the people connected to musico-theatrical performance in Jamaica, like the variety found in the pieces performed on stage, encourages us to consider how Felsted's understandings of what it meant to be white (or not) are portrayed in his self-authored libretti. I now turn to these libretti for evidence of how they portray ideas about nation and difference.

Felsted's portrayals of nation and difference

Opportunities to interrogate nationhood and ideas about human sameness and difference surface at several moments in Felsted's libretti and are most apparent in terms like 'nation', 'race', 'empire', 'heathen' (and thereby implicitly its antonym 'gentile'). The libretti also mention different national groups such as 'Ninevites', 'Chaldeans',[37] 'Israelites' and 'Babylonians', as well as more localized groups within Old Testament society, for example 'nobles', 'servants' and 'slaves'. I want to focus here on the concept of the nation, but before examining Felsted's treatment of the word, it is helpful to understand what it might have meant to others at the time.

Each of the terms mentioned above is linked to the concept of 'identity', which Samuel Johnson's dictionary of 1755 defines as 'sameness; not diversity'.[38] Johnson defined a 'nation' as 'a people distinguished from another people; generally by their language, original, or government'.[39] The imprecision of the use of 'original' here suggests that the word nation could, in fact, encompass a wide variety of distinctions between different groups of people. Some of these might be physically visible and others less concrete, like a group's religious convictions or political persuasion. My point here is that the definition of 'nation' could encompass meanings that relate to things that are intangible but also physical, and that might therefore be racialized. This makes it possible

---

[37] The Chaldeans were indigenous to the geographical area over which the Babylonians ruled, and gradually became fully assimilated into the Babylonian population.
[38] 'Johnson's Dictionary Online', https://johnsonsdictionaryonline.com.
[39] 'Johnson's Dictionary Online', https://johnsonsdictionaryonline.com.

to observe how eighteenth-century perceptions of 'race' and 'nation' could become conflated. In Felsted's day, few Jamaicans would have been able to imagine 'the British Nation' in the way that today it comprises people of different national and racial backgrounds.

As well as understanding the eighteenth-century meanings of terms such as those mentioned above, we also need to find ways to try to understand what Felsted's agendas or motivations might have been. His portrayal in the libretti of the interactions between different social groups, for example, could have served as metaphors for the interactions between the Jewish people, enslaved and free people of African origin and the white peoples in Felsted's locality. His libretti need to be considered from the perspective of how they either directly quoted or in various ways manipulated their biblical source material. They also need to be studied in ways that call into question historic analyses of the same biblical texts by Felsted's contemporaries. The fact that the composer was an Anabaptist and a church musician who wrote oratorios based on Old Testament narratives means that he might have had religious and moral concerns with his chosen texts. It is to be expected that a person like Felsted would have been well versed in contemporary interpretations of the Bible, but also older ones that were still prevalent in his lifetime. Such ideas were circulating in the Caribbean via books, pamphlets and periodicals, many of which were being imported and sold locally. Some were republished in local newspapers.

Felsted's *Jonah* is an adaptation of the biblical text in which God sends the prophet Jonah to preach to the people of Nineveh and warn them to mend their wicked ways or face destruction.[40] His references to the Ninevite community as a cohesive group of wrong-doers might have led Felsted's audience to draw correlations between the Ninevites and themselves. The Ninevites needed a God-ordained intervention (Jonah's message) in order to turn from their wrongfulness and thus avoid disaster, and Jamaica needed a similarly God-inspired intervention in order to turn from its wrongfulness (in the form of the anti-royalist sentiment that was rife in Jamaica on the eve of the American war) in order to avoid disaster by pledging its allegiance to King George III.[41]

---

[40] Jonah 1–3.

[41] This point draws on an idea posited by Arthur Marks. Marks mentions that 'by the time that *Jonah* was published, the tensions and turmoil between the principals were already well established, even if the actual conflict had not yet erupted [...] Felsted, as a Jamaican [...] may have been [...] concerned about the fate of the island colony. Certainly, many settlers in the West Indies shared the increasing political resentment of mainland

The Dedication, like *Jonah*, is based on an Old Testament narrative. In this case, Felsted chose the third chapter in the book of the prophet Daniel. Daniel, who incidentally, was a royal captive, does not appear in this narrative.[42] Rather, *The Dedication* is Felsted's retelling of the story of how Daniel's friends (also captives) were sentenced to die in King Nebuchadnezzar's fiery furnace for refusing to worship an idol. God delivered the men from the furnace because they were good people and because they remained true to their faith, even at their time of greatest peril. Essentially enslaved and forcibly removed to Babylon, Daniel and his friends were renamed Belteshazzar (Daniel), Hananiah (Shadrach), Mishael (Meshach) and Azariah (Abednego). Felsted's choice to base his oratorio narrative on the plight of a group of enslaved Israelites seems like a clear indication of how he was influenced by the Jewish and African people surrounding him in late eighteenth-century Kingston. It may also hint at his own feelings of displacement within the Jamaican society—despite being a person of Anglo-American descent, because of his religion Felsted did not fit all of the contemporary expectations of what a 'white person' was.

The densest collection of identity-related rhetoric in Felsted's oratorios occurs in Part I, scene 2 of the *Dedication*. He set this scene in '[a] wild, romantic view of rocks and spreading foliage [with] A cascade [...] river [...] Ferns and aquatic plants on the margin'.[43] The text, which I quote below, is presented over two movements. The first, a solo aria, is performed by Mishael, and the other, an aria and duet (for the final stanza), is performed by Mishael and Azariah, first separately then together.

Air
Mishael   O God, will Thou for ever veil Thy Face.
Wilt Thou no more regard Thy chosen Race?

Anglo-Americans regarding the distant Crown's excessive and merciless authority over their affairs.' Arthur S. Marks, 'Benjamin West's "Jonah": A Previously Overlooked Illustration for the First Oratorio Composed in the New World', *The American Art Journal*, 28.1 (1997), pp. 122–37 (131).

[42] Felsted's decision to turn to the book of Daniel might be related to the literature of his day. The figure of the royal captive (or slave) may have first appeared as a trope in Anglophone literature in Aphra Behn's tragic novella *Oroonoko*, written in 1688 and set in colonial Suriname. The work was rewritten as a dramatic production by Thomas Southerne and staged in 1695 at the Theatre Royal with music written by Henry Purcell (1659–95)—a composer from whom Handel took inspiration.

[43] Felsted, *The Dedication* I, 2.

>   Must Israel's captive Sons for ever mourn
>   Their nativeland, oh never to return?
>   Shall Heathens in derision to Thy Name
>   Our adoration for their Idol claim?

Air
Azariah   The glitt'ring ray,
             Which pours the Day,
             O'er Salem's Splendid tow'rs;
             To Hill and Stream
             Extends its beam
             And cheers the drooping flow'rs.

Mishael   The mighty force
             Which points the course
             Of Empire and of Fate;
             To humbler scenes,
             Protection deigns,
             And guards our captive state.

Duet [*Mishael and Azariah*]
             Then strike the string
             To Judah's King,
             His Works with joy record:
             Whose tender Care
             Alike we Share
             With Asia's haughty lord.[44]

What can be inferred here about Felsted's notions of race and nationhood—and, indeed, exile? And how might his text have resonated with his audience of people who, as I have pointed out, were marked by displacement, absence and death? The text above represents Felsted's imagined version of a conversation between two of the Israelite slaves. Mishael laments their state of captivity, while Azariah offers words of comfort which, by the end of the aria, seem to have met with success. Felsted's interest here seems to be in portraying the Jews as displaced and unhappy, but also as a special group. As 'God's chosen race', the Jews are cared for and watched over by God who protects them in moments of trial and danger. How does this appearance of the word 'race' here resonate with the types of difference that existed in his world? Two

---

[44] Felsted, *The Dedication* I, 2.

things become apparent here: firstly, that the word 'race' does indeed appear to be interchangeable with the word 'nation'; and secondly, that this extract can be interpreted in various ways that draw parallels between national and social groups like Europeans, Britons, Africans, 'free' or 'indentured people' and 'slaves'. Kingston audiences living long before the concept of Babylon was attached to Jamaica by the Rastafari community in the twentieth century would have found resonances in Felsted's text because of its potential application to their own liminal and transitory 'Babylonian' experiences.

What is also apparent is the way in which Felsted's presentation of a text that seems to be venerating Jewishness is in tension with the fact that the Jewish people were a marginalized group within Jamaican society. However, without primary sources like contemporary letters and diaries, or commentaries detailing experiences and perceptions of his oratorios, it is difficult to tell how Felsted and his audiences linked the Jewish people in his libretti with those living in Jamaica, or why exactly the composer might have been interested in portraying them in the manner cited above. Perhaps Felsted sought to flatter Jewish people known to him personally. He could have been relying on Jewish patronage from a wealthy merchant like Emmanuel Baruh Lousada,[45] or from the prominent Jewish residents who had previously supported the subscription scheme that had paid for his first oratorio *Jonah* to be published.[46]

Alternatively, the extract might point to Felsted's use of a contemporary writing convention in British literature. The 'British-Israel paradigm' is a way of thinking about Britain and Britons through the image of Israel that is presented in the Bible. As Deborah Rooke has explained, the paradigm assumes that 'Britain was the Israel of its

---

[45] Felsted's 1778 painting of Lousada's lavish manor, which stood between central Kingston and Half-Way Tree, suggests that he was well connected with the local Jewish population. See also Mirvis, *The Jews of Eighteenth-Century Jamaica*, 193–94.

[46] The majority of the subscribers to *Jonah* (who are listed in the opening pages of the published edition) were Jamaican residents. It is not known whether any of the subscribers were people of African heritage, but the presence of names like de Cordova, Feurtado [*sic*], Dias Fernandes and Mendes Pereira makes it clear that several prominent Ibero-Jewish family members took part. Neither the details of the first performance of *Jonah* nor the costs for publishing the score are known, but between them the subscribers contributed to the costs for around 300 copies to be produced and shipped to Jamaica. Pamela O'Gorman's article contains an image of the subscription list taken from the opening pages of the *Jonah* score: O'Gorman, '*Jonah*: An Eighteenth-Century Jamaican Oratorio', 44.

day' and that, like the Israelites in the Bible, Britons 'had been chosen by God to preserve the true faith against the surrounding idolatrous nations'.[47] The British-Israel paradigm is evident in the Israelite oratorios of Handel, which are likely to have been sources of inspiration for Felsted. As well as Jamaican organists, various members of the Jamaican elite were well acquainted with Handel's music.[48]

The British-Israel paradigm is helpful in as much as it offers insights into metropolitan constructs of British identity of the kind that might have been familiar to Maria Nugent. But how did this change for the British subjects living abroad in what were called 'torrid' environments?[49] The idea that the Caribbean climate had a lasting and physically degenerative effect on (white) people's characteristics was still common in Felsted's world.[50] Jamaicans, like Britons, shared the similarity of

---

[47] Deborah W. Rooke, *Handel's Israelite Oratorio Libretti: Sacred Drama and Biblical Exegesis* (Oxford: Oxford Univeristy Press, 2012), p. xxii. For more information about how the British-Israel paradigm is evident in Handel's music see Ruth Smith, *Handel's Oratorios and Eighteenth-Century Thought* (Cambridge: Cambridge University Press, 1995).

[48] See notes 11 and 32 above. Handel's four coronation anthems were performed in Jamaica as part of a ceremony marking the coronation of George III in 1761: Barry W. Higman, *Proslavery Priest: The Atlantic World of John Lindsay, 1729–1788* (Kingston, Jamaica: University of West Indies Press, 2011), pp. 119–20. Further details about the performance of Handel's music in late eighteenth-century Jamaica are forthcoming in my doctoral thesis.

[49] The idea that foreign travel created difference is very evident in theatre works performed in Jamaica in Felsted's lifetime. Richard Sheridan's comedy *A School for Scandal* (1777), which was performed on multiple occasions in Jamaica in 1781 and 1784, offers one of many examples in the form of the character Sir Oliver Surface. Having travelled to India as a merchant, Surface is referred to as a Nabob on his return to England. Similarly, as Linda Colley has pointed out, people who travelled to the Caribbean returned as changed 'planters' or 'West Indians': Linda Colley, *Britons: Forging the Nation, 1707–1837* (London: Pimlico, 2003), p. 16. For further details about the 'torrid zone', see Louis H. Roper, *The Torrid Zone* (Columbia, SC: University of South Carolina Press, 2018). For further discussions on the topic of West Indian identity in Britain, see Andrew Jackson O'Shaughnessy, *An Empire Divided: The American Revolution and the British Caribbean*, Early American Studies (Philadelphia, PA: University of Pennsylvania Press, 2000).

[50] At this point in history, it was believed in Europe that it would take around ten generations for people of European ancestry to 'turn into Negroes' or vice versa. The effects were believed to be partially compounded or remedied if an individual adopted the manners and foods of the other. Roxann Wheeler, *The Complexion of Race: Categories of Difference*

being relatively vulnerable people living in Protestant lands that were surrounded by potentially dangerous Catholic territories (like France and Spain or, in the case of Jamaica, Saint-Domingue and Cuba). Their geographical separation in physical space was something that was said to be God-ordained, and this served to add greater legitimacy to their autonomous religious alterity.

Protestantism was a unifying aspect of identity in mainland Britain so, by extension, it became an aspect of what it was to be part of the white ruling class in Jamaica. However, because the ideals of different Protestant denominations resonated to varying degrees with the ideals of Jamaican society, the only version of Protestantism that was fully accepted was the Anglicanism of the established church. Other Protestants like Quakers (who had long condemned the premise of slavery in the Americas), and even those who encouraged the baptism of enslaved people but did little to disturb the colonial order, like the Moravians, were subjected to derision, suspicion and marginalization.

Felsted's music, with its grandeur and inherent emphasis on metropolitan musical customs, its conspicuous Handelian traits, and hundreds of affluent and educated subscribers (in the case of *Jonah*), was clearly intended to cater to a certain impression of elite metropolitan whiteness. Yet the inclusion of people who were not Anglican, nor even Protestant, in the *Jonah* subscription list, the involvement of Catholic and possibly Jewish performers as mentioned above, and the fact that the supposedly elite forms of Jamaican music were being performed and consumed in environments that were heavily populated with large numbers of people of African heritage or people that were conspicuously 'white others', means that the comparison between Felsted's music and that of his metropolitan contemporaries can only go so far.[51] How might the excerpts quoted above have resonated with the lives of black, mixed and 'white other' Kingstonians? Did they draw parallels between the plight of the Israelite slaves and the ways that in their own society they were stigmatized and systematically denied social equality? In the final section of my analysis, I turn to the premise

in *Eighteenth-Century British Culture* (Philadelphia, PA: University of Pennsylvania Press, 2000), pp. 4–5.

[51] It is not currently known whether any of the subscribers to Felsted's *Jonah* were black, but given the fact that 'free blacks' and 'people of colour' were typically baptized and, as contemporary eyewitness accounts suggest, were regular attendees at church, it is plausible that they formed part of Felsted's (real or imagined) oratorio audiences: Nicholas M. Beasley, *Christian Ritual and the Creation of British Slave Societies, 1650–1780* (Athens, GA and London: University of Georgia Press, 2010), p. 33.

of slavery and the question of what it might have meant to Felsted's Jamaican contemporaries. Thinking about historic Jamaican responses to slavery is a way in which we can begin to consider what the libretto of Felsted's *Dedication* might have meant to its non-white—and especially its African-descended—audience.

Felsted's *Dedication* and slavery

In Felsted's *Dedication*, Azariah, Mishael and Hananiah are referred to alternately as slaves and servants. They are called slaves when they are commanded by King Nebuchadnezzar in exclamations like '[n]o more, audacious Slaves, my strength deride' and '[s]peak Slaves, and ease my tortur'd heart'.[52] But the men are referred to quite differently in the context of their prayer and religious devotion. In the movement that opens Part II, scene 3, which is imagined as being set in '[a]n extensive plain' and sung by a chorus of kneeling Chaldeans,[53] the Israelites are defined in terms that emphasize their obedience and the dutiful morality of their character. The chorus sings, for instance: 'Obedient to the pleasing sound,/Lo! We close thy shrine around,/Off'ring up the servant prayer,/Anxious to obtain thy care./Bless thy servants' daily toil,/Yield us floods of wine and oil'.[54] Similarly, in the 'Elegy' movement the Israelites pray for God to 'save [...] thy servants from the flame and vindicate Thy Holy Name'.[55] Finally, at the moment King Nebuchadnezzar realizes that the Israelites' trust in God is justified (in Part II, scene 2), he calls for them to '[c]ome hither Servants of the LORD'.

These moments in Felsted's libretto show how the Israelites are called to serve God but must also serve their mortal king. They are an oppressed group who pray for God's blessing in order to help them manage the trials that confront them. When the Israelites' behaviour diverges from Babylonian expectations, they are ruthlessly exposed (by the Chaldeans), and described as 'audacious' and 'caitiffs',[56] yet their actions are suggestive of a people who are humble yet steadfast in their

---

[52] Felsted, *The Dedication* II, 1 and 2.
[53] Felsted's scene description here is particularly evocative: 'An extensive plain. A golden statue and Pedestal. A Band of Musicians, with ancient Instruments, arranged in a semicircle behind the Pedestal. Toward the close of the Symphony, the Chaldeans enter from different places, kneel around and sing the Chorus.' Felsted, *The Dedication* II, 3.
[54] Felsted, *The Dedication* I, 3.
[55] Felsted, *The Dedication* II, 2.
[56] Felsted, *The Dedication* II, 3.

beliefs—beliefs directly linked with their community's autonomous identity.

Perhaps Felsted saw in this passage from the book of Daniel an opportunity to remind the communities of enslaved, abused and disenfranchised people living around him in Kingston to put their trust in God (as the Jewish people had done) and to look towards the reward of a happier afterlife in heaven in return for their good moral behaviour in their earthly lives. Such tenets were dominant in the preaching of the various missionaries who visited Jamaica in the eighteenth century, including those of the Moravian church. The Moravians were treated similarly to the Quakers and Baptists (and Anabaptists) in Jamaican society in as much as they were also viewed as Dissenters. The Moravians, however, never became well-established in Jamaican's urban environments.[57] Whether or not Felsted was connected to the Dissenting missionaries who were active in Jamaica or their philosophies is as yet uncertain, but it is certainly possible.

In this chapter, I have reflected on how Felsted's oratorios might be meaningfully contextualized with reference to the ethnic variety of the Kingston population and the complex nature of Jamaican identity at the time. Jamaica, as I have pointed out, was regarded in a liminal and transitory way by many of the people who lived there, especially those who influenced its government and culture. These people were part of a white elite minority in Jamaican society. I have also provided a literary analysis of certain passages from Felsted's self-authored libretti, focussing in particular on extracts from his second oratorio, *The Dedication*. Felsted's libretti offer opportunities for speculation about the meanings, for eighteenth-century Jamaican residents, of concepts like nation and white identity and also about slavery and servanthood around the time they were written.

My examination of Felsted's oratorio libretti has brought to the surface some of the tensions of the society in which they were written. These tensions revolved around the constructions of white identity. 'White' is a racialized term and, like all of the terms that I have discussed in this chapter, it is perhaps best understood in opposition to something else. Something, or rather a type of identity, that is *other* than white. This is more complicated than the distinction that might be drawn between 'white' and 'black'; it is not a question of 'race' in the modern sense. Felsted's libretti, rather, demonstrate the fluidity of

---

[57] Richard S. Dunn, *A Tale of Two Plantations* (Cambridge, MA and London: Harvard University Press, 2014), p. 225.

whiteness and that a number of attributes that might not be thought of as 'white' could contribute to the term's meaning. The ambiguity of the meaning of 'white' in Felsted's world, I would argue, is intrinsically linked to the ambiguity of the term 'nation' in Felsted's libretti. For instance, the 'daily toil' of the enslaved Israelites (who, nevertheless, were part of God's 'chosen race'), was something that might have been viewed as dutifulness, and a respect for sovereign authority. The way in which Jewish people appear in Felsted's libretti relates to the British-Israel paradigm, in which certain positive attributes of Jewishness (like the dutifulness shown by the Israelites in ancient Persia) were seen as British ideals. Meanwhile, in Jamaican society, the same trope created a dissonance in the face of the way in which enslaved people, Jewish people or those with any religious background that was not Anglican were treated by Jamaican lawmakers. The concurrent use of the terms 'slaves' and 'servants' in Felsted's libretto for *The Dedication* can be viewed as one of several examples of this tension.

This chapter has demonstrated how the contextual investigation of Jamaican oratorio offers unique opportunities for scholars to garner deeper understandings of the relationships between religious music, theatre and the complex social environment that existed in colonial towns like Kingston. Felsted's libretti are, inevitably, a product of the society in which they were written. In order to begin to understand what purposes they served in their original space, it is necessary to draw on a wide range of sources—sources that reveal the common or prevalent philosophies alongside which the libretti existed. The fact that much of the surviving material that can be used to contextualize eighteenth-century Jamaican sources originates in Britain is a challenge. But I believe that this is a limitation that can be mitigated by the kinds of questions that are posed about the source material, and the ways in which circumstantial evidence can be brought into play as the basis for historically informed speculation about it.

One of the clearest things about *The Dedication* is that Felsted's decision to compose a work based on the experiences of a group of Israelite captives (or slaves) offers a rare but telling indicator of how his local circumstances directly influenced his music's themes. The themes that are relevant to Felsted's oratorios, including enslavement, work differently from other examples of the genre that existed in different contexts and environments. Above all, in order to meaningfully contextualize works like the oratorios of Samuel Felsted, we need to understand what effect their place of origin and, more importantly, the place where they were performed had on their construction and interpretation. The true value and relevance of the compositions of Felsted and other colonials of the early Americas may only be known today by revisiting and recontextualizing them in ways that consider their broader social frameworks and philosophies.

Bibliography

Baxter, Ivy. *The Arts of an Island: The Development of the Culture and of the Folk and Creative Arts in Jamaica, 1494–1962 (Independence)* (Metuchen, NJ: Scarecrow Press, 1970).

Beasley, Nicholas M. *Christian Ritual and the Creation of British Slave Societies, 1650–1780* (Athens, GA and London: University of Georgia Press, 2010).

Bloechl, Olivia. 'Race, Empire, and Early Music', in Olivia Bloechl, Melanie Lowe and Jeffrey Kallberg (eds), *Rethinking Difference in Music Scholarship* (Cambridge: Cambridge University Press, 2015).

Brathwaite, Edward. *The Development of Creole Society in Jamaica, 1770–1820* (Kingston, Jamaica and Miami, FL: Ian Randle, 2005).

Brown, Vincent. *The Reaper's Garden: Death and Power in the World of Atlantic Slavery* (Cambridge, MA; London: Harvard University Press, 2008).

Burnard, Trevor G. 'A Failed Settler Society: Marriage and Demographic Failure in Early Jamaica', *Journal of Social History*, 28.1 (1994), pp. 63–82.

Burnard, Trevor G. *Planters, Merchants, and Slaves: Plantation Societies in British America, 1650–1820* (Chicago and London: University of Chicago Press, 2015).

Burnard, Trevor G. '"Prodigious Riches": The Wealth of Jamaica before the American Revolution', *The Economic History Review*, 54.3 (2001), pp. 506–24.

Burnard, Trevor G. 'Slaves and Slavery in Kingston, 1770–1815', *International Review of Social History*, 65.S28 (2020), pp. 39–65.

Carretta, Vincent (ed.). *Unchained Voices: An Anthology of Black Authors in the English-Speaking World of the Eighteenth Century* (Lexington, KY: University Press of Kentucky, 1996).

Colley, Linda. *Britons: Forging the Nation, 1707–1837* (London: Pimlico, 2003).

Davis, Tracy C. 'The Context Problem', *Theatre Survey*, 45.2 (2004), pp. 203–09.

Dillon, Elizabeth Maddock. *New World Drama: The Performative Commons in the Atlantic World, 1649–1849* (Durham, NC: Duke University Press, 2014).

Dox, Thurston. 'Samuel Felsted of Jamaica', *The American Music Research Center Journal*, 1 (1991), pp. 37–46.

Dox, Thurston. 'Samuel Felsted's *Jonah*: The Earliest American Oratorio', *Choral Journal*, 32.7 (1992), pp. 27–32.

Dunn, Richard S. *A Tale of Two Plantations* (Cambridge, MA and London: Harvard University Press, 2014).

Erman, Uri. 'The Operatic Voice of Leoni the Jew: Between the Synagogue and the Theater in Late Georgian Britain', *Journal of British Studies*, 56.2 (2017), pp. 295–321.

Felsted, Samuel. *The Dedication* R.M.21.f.2, British Library.

Felsted, Samuel. *Jonah* (London: Longman, Lukey and Broderip, 1775).

Felsted, Samuel. *Six Voluntarys for the Organ or Harpsichord* (London: Thompson, nd).

Highfill, Philip H. *A Biographical Dictionary of Actors, Actresses, Musicians, Dancers, Managers and Other Stage Personnel in London, 1660–1800* (Carbondale, IL: Southern Illinois University Press, 1973).

Higman, Barry W. *Proslavery Priest: The Atlantic World of John Lindsay, 1729–1788* (Kingston, Jamaica: University of West Indies Press, 2011).

Hill, Errol. *The Jamaican Stage, 1655–1900: Profile of a Colonial Theatre* (Amherst, MA: University of Massachusetts Press, 1992).

Hunter, David. 'The Beckfords in England and Italy: A Case Study in the Musical Uses of the Profits of Slavery', *Early Music*, 46.2 (2018), pp. 285–98.

Hunter, David. 'Music and the Use of the Profits of the Anglo-American Slave Economy (c. 1610–c. 1810)', in Anna Morcom and Timothy D. Taylor (eds), *The Oxford Handbook of Economic Ethnomusicology* (Oxford: Oxford Academic, 2020) https://doi.org/10.1093/oxfordhb/9780190859633.013.5.

Johnson, Samuel. 'Johnson's Dictionary Online', https://johnsonsdictionaryonline.com.

Livesay, Daniel. *Children of Uncertain Fortune: Mixed-Race Jamaicans in Britain and the Atlantic Family, 1733–1833* (Williamsburg, VA and Chapel Hill, NC: University of North Carolina Press, 2018).

Marks, Arthur S. 'Benjamin West's "Jonah": A Previously Overlooked Illustration for the First Oratorio Composed in the New World', *The American Art Journal*, 28.1 (1997), pp. 122–37.

Mirvis, Stanley. *The Jews of Eighteenth-Century Jamaica: A Testamentary History of a Diaspora in Transition* (New Haven, CT: Yale University Press, 2020).

Nugent, Maria. *Lady Nugent's Journal: Jamaica One Hundred Years Ago*, ed. Frank Cundall, Cambridge Library Collection, Slavery and Abolition (Cambridge: Cambridge University Press, 2012).

O'Gorman, Pamela. 'An Eighteenth-Century Jamaican Oratorio Part Two, The Music of Samuel Felsted's *Jonah*', *Jamaica Journal*, Institute of Jamaica, Kingston, 23.1 (1990), pp. 14–19.

O'Gorman, Pamela. '*Jonah*: An Eighteenth-Century Jamaican Oratorio', *Jamaica Journal*, Institute of Jamaica, Kingston, 22.4 (1990), pp. 41–45.

O'Shaughnessy, Andrew Jackson. *An Empire Divided: The American Revolution and the British Caribbean*, Early American Studies (Philadelphia, PA: University of Pennsylvania Press, 2000).

Petley, Christer. *White Fury: A Jamaican Slaveholder and the Age of Revolution* (Oxford: Oxford University Press, 2018).

Rooke, Deborah W. *Handel's Israelite Oratorio Libretti: Sacred Drama and Biblical Exegesis* (Oxford: Oxford University Press, 2012).

Roper, Louis H. *The Torrid Zone* (Columbia, SC: University of South Carolina Press, 2018).

Smith, Ruth. *Handel's Oratorios and Eighteenth-Century Thought* (Cambridge: Cambridge University Press, 1995).

Smither, Howard E. *A History of the Oratorio*, Vol. 2: *The Oratorio in the Baroque Era: Protestant Germany and England* (Chapel Hill, NC: University of North Carolina Press, 1977).

Smither, Howard E. *A History of the Oratorio*, Vol. 3: *The Oratorio in the Classical Era* (Chapel Hill, NC: University of North Carolina Press, 1977).

Smither, Howard E. 'Oratorio.' Grove Music Online. 2001, https://doi.org/10.1093/gmo/9781561592630.article.20397.

Wheeler, Roxann. *The Complexion of Race: Categories of Difference in Eighteenth-Century British Culture* (Philadelphia, PA: University of Pennsylvania Press, 2000).

Wright, Richardson. *Revels in Jamaica, 1682–1838* (Kingston, Jamaica: Bolivar Press, 1986).

Zadro, Michael G. 'Woods Used for Woodwind Instruments since the Sixteenth Century—1', *Early Music*, 3.2 (1975), pp. 134–36.

Part III

Sources and Gaps

Seven

Silences in the Archive: The Mysterious One-Night Stand of John Fawcett's *Obi; or, Three-Finger'd Jack* in Kingston, Jamaica (1862)

Jenna M. Gibbs

In September 1862, John Fawcett's pantomime *Obi; or Three Finger'd Jack* was produced by J. Thompson for a single performance at the Theatre Royal in Kingston, Jamaica. Popular on stages throughout the British Atlantic, including the British Caribbean, since its London debut in 1800 and throughout the early to mid-nineteenth century, Fawcett's pantomime loosely dramatized a real-life 1780–81 Jamaican slave revolt instigated and led by a maroon, Jack Mansong. Jack led a prolonged revolt and evaded capture by hiding in the mountains from 1779–81. He earned the moniker 'three finger'd Jack' after losing two fingers in a fight. In 1781, he was apprehended and killed by two maroons in the employ of the British, in exchange for a £100 bounty. But before then, Jack had led a series of raids on plantations and incited unrest among enslaved people. White slaveholders' perception of Jack as a fearsome rebel was enhanced by his reputation of having supernatural powers through the African-derived practice of *obeah* (*obi*), which Fawcett emphasized in his pantomime.[1] The piece also featured a slave plantation rendition of Jonkanoo, a vernacular performative tradition

---

[1] There are no extant script or stage directions for the 1862 production. I am basing my comments about the plotline and content on what is known of its performance elsewhere in the British Atlantic from its 1800 debut through the early-to-mid-nineteenth century, grounded in theatrical reviews of the 1800 debut in London and on the extant manuscript, John Fawcett, *Obi; or, Three Finger'd Jack* (1825 text) reproduced in Peter J. Kitson and Debbie Lee (eds), *Slavery, Abolition and Emancipation: Writings in the British Romantic Period*, 8 vols (London: Pickering and Chatto, 1999), Vol. 5: *Drama*, ed. Jeffrey N. Cox, pp. 203–19.

of dance, music, costuming and parade with West African roots.[2] Thus, in addition to dramatizing a 'true' story of Jamaican history, Fawcett's pantomime also featured some aspects of Afro-Caribbean culture, which—as this chapter will seek to demonstrate—is relevant to the archival silence on its 1862 revival.

As Errol Hill has noted, this 1862 performance eludes historical documentation.[3] No reviews of this pantomime's performance in any of the local newspapers survive. No information is available about the audience composition. In the late eighteenth century, theatre audiences were primarily 'the planters, well-to-do merchants, military and naval officers, government officials and civic leaders'.[4] But little is known about audience composition when *Obi* took the Kingston stage almost 30 years after emancipation—other than records noting that the audiences could be rambunctious and that in the late nineteenth century there were calls for more policemen to address disorder and lawlessness inside and outside the theatre.[5] Were there black audience members? We do not know. If black audience members were present, how did they respond? We do not know. How did white audience members respond? We do not know that either. Moreover, no commentary exists—or none that any scholar of Caribbean theatre has been able to find—as to why this piece, perennially popular throughout the British Atlantic, garnered only a single production on this occasion. This one-night stand is especially puzzling given that both amateur and professional productions of other plays that were either set in or relevant to the British Caribbean became production staples.[6] The mysterious one-night stand of *Obi; or, Three Finger'd Jack* in Kingston in 1862 is shrouded in silence and erasure.

For scholars of the Caribbean, these silences and erasures are a significant part of practising history. This reality pertains when reading against the grain of governmental sources to illuminate the lives

---

[2] Jenna M. Gibbs, 'Jonkanoo Performances of Resistance, Freedom and Memory', in Evelyn O'Callaghan and Tim Watson (eds), *Caribbean Literature in Transition, 1800–1920* (Cambridge and New York: Cambridge University Press, 2020), pp. 52–66 (52–53).

[3] Errol Hill, *The Jamaican Stage 1655–1900: Profile of A Colonial Theatre* (Amherst, MA: University of Massachusetts Press, 1992), p. 101.

[4] 'Introduction to Caribbean Theatre', in Martin Banham, Errol Hill and George Woodyard (eds), *The Cambridge Guide to African and Caribbean Theatre* (Cambridge and New York: Cambridge University Press, 1994), pp. 141–52 (146).

[5] Hill, *The Jamaican Stage*, 95.

[6] Banham, Hill and Woodyard, *African and Caribbean Theatre*, 146.

of enslaved and formerly enslaved people. Combatting the silence includes exploring formerly enslaved people's possible participation in theatre and related performances, probing audience reactions to a play through trace evidence written by local authorities and explaining the otherwise inexplicable using contextual evidence. There is now a plethora of older and newer works that articulate these and other methodological approaches to tackling archival gaps and silences. Some of the referenced theoretical perspectives are iconic methodological works that are not specific to the Caribbean but that can nonetheless be broadly applied. Others are more recent works that specifically address Caribbean historical and literary research. This chapter will discuss a few works that highlight three key issues of archival silence, and then apply that discussion to the one-night stand of *Obi; or Three Finger'd Jack* in Kingston, 1862. Firstly, it will explore the difficulties—but also the benefits—of using works from governmental or other 'top-down' sources to try to illuminate behaviours 'from below'. Secondly, and interrelatedly, the chapter explores using contextual evidence to read into an otherwise unknowable moment or event. Thirdly, it concludes by examining the way our retrospective view of history shapes what we deem worthy of excavating.

Let us start with the challenge of using works from 'top-down' sources to interrogate behaviours and lives 'from below' (a question that is also addressed briefly in the context of military documents in Chapter Eight of this volume). A beginning point to any discussion of this methodological conundrum must surely be Carlo Ginzburg's classic *The Cheese and the Worms*, no matter what one's field or period of scholarship. The book is a vibrant recovery of the life, worldview and agency of a sixteenth-century miller, Menocchio. Ginzburg recounts the story solely through the records of Menocchio's trial by the Inquisition, in which we never hear the voice of the miller himself, only those of his interrogators. As Ginzburg notes, 'the scarcity of evidence about the behaviour and attitudes of the subordinate classes of the past is certainly the major, though not the only, obstacle facing research of this type'.[7] He then discusses how we, as historians, can understand culture in our investigations of non-written or elusive pasts: 'the existence of different cultural levels with in so-called civilized societies is the premise of the discipline that has come to be defined cautiously as folklore, social anthropology, history of popular traditions, and

---

[7] Carlo Ginzburg, *The Cheese and the Worms: The Cosmos of a Sixteenth-Century Miller*, trans. John and Anne C. Tedeschi (Baltimore, MD: Johns Hopkins University Press, 1980), p. 3.

European ethnology', but demands of us, the researchers, that we carefully investigate 'the reciprocal movement between [...] two levels of culture', that is top-down *vis-à-vis* popular folkloric culture.[8] While more recent work has questioned the bifurcation between 'two levels' of culture—that is, high and low—Ginzburg's observation is nonetheless highly pertinent to the case study of the one-night stand of *Obi* with its animation of Jonkanoo. At the time of that 1862 production, the vernacular performances of Jonkanoo (which dated from colonial-era slavery and continued after emancipation) had been clamped down on by the local white legislature for the performances' allegedly rebellious potential. Not only is Ginzburg's use of the 'top-down' archive alongside an understanding of the relationship of authority to the preservation of folkloric cultural performances relevant here, but so too is his and Anna Davin's incisive article on the 'historian as detective', and how to use almost ephemeral 'trace evidence' to build a case; that is, using 'clues', the historical ear and psychological intuition as the guiding axes of a 'scientific' methodology.[9]

The challenges of recovering the disenfranchised through the records of the powerful, and the use of evidentiary traces, have been powerfully addressed by more recent works that are specific to the Caribbean. Some of this scholarship relates directly to the recovery of the lives of black women and men. In Saidiya Hartman's 2007 book, *Lose Your Mother*, for example, she asserts that 'to read the archive is to enter a mortuary; it permits one final viewing and allows for a last glimpse of persons about to disappear into the slave hold'.[10] These last glimpses, she makes clear, are from the records left by slave ship owners, slave owners and overseers—evidentiary traces of silenced lives and the violence inflicted upon them, recorded by those in power. In a subsequent article, 'Venus in Two Acts', she examines how what we know of the Black Venus figure is a product of the power relations in the archival contexts in which she appears: 'the hollow of the slave ship, the pest-house, the brothel, the cage, the surgeon's laboratory, the prison, the case-field, the kitchen, the master's bedroom'.[11] Hartman quotes Foucault to conclude that what we know of Venus is 'little more than a register of her encounter with

---

[8] Ginzburg, *Cheese and the Worms*, xxii.
[9] Anna Davin and Carlo Ginzburg, 'Morelli, Freud and Sherlock Holmes: Clues and Scientific Method', *History Workshop*, 9 (Spring 1980), pp. 5–36.
[10] Saidiya Hartman, *Lose Your Mother: A Journey Along the Atlantic Slave Route* (New York: Farrar, Straus and Giroux, 2007), p. 17.
[11] Saidiya Hartman, 'Venus in Two Acts', *Small Axe*, 12.2 (June 2008), pp. 1–14 (1).

power' that provides 'a meager sketch of her existence'.[12] Hartman then embarks on trying to read against the grain to recover the Black Venus as a figure that is more than 'traces in the archive'.[13]

Similarly, Marisa Fuentes' recent book, *Dispossessed Lives: Enslaved Women, Violence and the Archives*, is a tour de force in recovering the lives of black women by 'employing a methodology that purposely subverts the overdetermining power of colonial discourses'.[14] As she notes, we do not have a paucity of sources about the Caribbean. Rather, the problem is that 'most are the words and perspectives of white authorities and slave owners'.[15] She lays out a methodology for using archival fragments to read '*along the bias grain* to eke out extinguished and invisible but no less historically important lives'.[16] While Fuentes is specifically concerned with recovering the lives of black women and the violence they experienced, her larger observations about how these experiences did/did not make their way into the colonial archive hold true for any attempt to write colonial and postcolonial Caribbean history. Her advice to read 'along the bias grain' is particularly pertinent to challenging the 'overdetermining power' of colonial archive-keeping, including that of the white-dominated, mid-nineteenth-century Kingston theatre. Ginzburg, Hartman and Fuentes thus all use 'traces in the archive' to read against the grain of sources born of oppressive power relations—recovering Menocchio from the records of the Spanish Inquisition that condemned him to be burned at the stake, animating Venus from the records of the slave holders and slave owners and their violence, and recovering the lives of black women and their agency.

The second critical approach to the problem of gaps in the archive explored here is the importance of using *context* to read through silences (an approach also adopted in Chapter Six of this volume). Not at all a new suggestion, of course: Natalie Zemon Davis, in her 1990 book *Fiction in the Archives*—and in several consequential later articles—posited the methodological approach of applying our historical and literary analysis to grasping the context and using that knowledge of context to read back into, interrogate and explain otherwise unknowable people and events.[17]

---

[12] Michel Foucault, 'Lives of Infamous Men', in Paul Rabinow and Nicolas Rose (eds), *The Essential Foucault* (New York: New Press, 2003), p. 284. Quoted in Hartman, 'Venus in Two Acts', 2.
[13] Hartman, 'Venus in Two Acts', 2.
[14] Marisa J. Fuentes, *Dispossessed Lives: Enslaved Women, Violence, and the Archive* (Philadelphia, PA: University of Pennsylvania Press, 2016), p. 4.
[15] Fuentes, *Dispossessed Lives*, 4.
[16] Fuentes, *Dispossessed Lives*, 7.
[17] Natalie Zemon Davis, *Fiction in the Archives: Pardon Tales and Their Tellers*

This approach has more recently been embraced and expanded upon by scholars working in colonial contexts. Ann Laura Stoler's *Along the Archival Grain* pursues how colonial lives are recorded in government and how colonial administrations recorded 'traces' in constructed categories because, in her words, 'colonial administrations were prolific producers of social categories'.[18] These constructed categories make it necessary to read closely the context in which they were created. As well as building on Zemon Davis, she draws on Claude Lévi-Strauss's vision of anthropology to argue for reading below the surface for 'the pliable coordinates of what constitutes colonial common sense in a changing imperial order'.[19] But it is equally important to account for what Antoinette Burton defines as trace evidence that is *separate* from what is found in official imperial sources. As she puts it: 'archives—that is, traces of the past collected either intentionally or haphazardly as "evidence"—are by no means limited to official spaces or state repositories [...] scholars have been "reading' historical evidence off of any number of different archival incarnations for centuries'. She goes on to cite oral history, body tattoos and tapestries as examples of 'unofficial' repositories.[20] Her observations are applicable to an investigation of the elusive performance of *Obi; or Three Finger'd Jack*, because we can, for example, use the unofficial evidence of vernacular Jonkanoo performances to supplement the official imperial—and silent—records of the pantomime's performance, including its rendition of a Jonkanoo scene. In sum, context and 'unofficial' evidence matter: whether it's the pliable coordinates of colonial understandings or using larger cultural-political contexts. Context is itself a contested category because, as Tracy Davis puts it, 'though it is provided for the sake of "completeness", one scholar's criterion for *Gestalt* may be another's idea of irrelevance'.[21] Put differently, performances and audience reception of them are ephemeral, so using context to read into what the performance might have meant does not establish conclusive interpretations upon which all can agree. Context is, nonetheless, what guides historical analysis and helps us combat gaps and silences in the archives, as Davis also makes clear: '"[c]ontext" is instrumental in helping to convey the immediacy of performances in

---

   in Sixteenth-Century France (Stanford, CA: Stanford University Press, 1990).
[18] Ann Laura Stoler, *Along the Archival Grain: Epistemic Anxieties and Colonial Common Sense* (Princeton, NJ and Oxford: Princeton University Press, 2009), p. 1.
[19] Stoler, *Along the Archival Grain*, 3.
[20] Antoinette Burton (ed.), *Archive Stories: Facts, Fictions and The Writing of History* (Durham, NC and London: Duke University Press, 2005), pp. 2–3.
[21] Tracy C. Davis, 'The Context Problem', *Theatre Survey*, 45.2, pp. 203–09 (204).

the past, compensates for their perishability, and conveys their relevance to the past and present'.[22]

A third important issue is what Michel-Rolph Trouillot, in his now classic *Silencing the Past*, identified as one of the key archival creations of silence: the moment of retrospective significance, that is, how history is archived or 'made' in the final instance.[23] Since Trouillot's pioneering work, scholars' perspective on and making *of* the archive has changed: erased peoples and silenced events have been very creatively resurrected. Scholars of Caribbean literature, theatre and history, for example, have embarked on a remaking of the archive that pushes back on the eighteenth- and nineteenth-century dismissal of the significance of scholarly concerns with race, slavery and—in the instance of the 1862 production of *Obi; or Three Finger'd Jack* in Kingston, Jamaica—the performance and reception of race and slavery. Yet, as Trouillot himself is quoted as stating in Hazel Corby's foreword to the twentieth anniversary edition of his book, 'history is the fruit of power, but power itself is never so transparent that its analysis becomes superfluous. The ultimate mark of power may be its invisibility; the ultimate challenge, the exposition of its roots.'[24] In other words, it is incumbent on scholars of the Caribbean to consider how the imperial and state power structures have constructed the archives, and this still holds true despite the creative reconstruction of hitherto silenced events.

Indeed, there is now a plethora of work, inspired by Fanon, Foucault, Trouillot and others, that explicitly engages with the relationship between colonial/imperial authoritarian state power and archival silences about cultural and performative memory. This scholarship includes studies of Algerian anticolonial history and art, the Brazilian Amazon and the 'sounds' of indigenous *encantados* (enchantments, or delights), and the decorative and sartorial history of Dutch Suriname.[25] An exciting 2021 volume edited by Michael Moss and David Thomas,

---

[22] Davis, 'The Context Problem', 204.
[23] Michel-Rolph Trouillot, *Silencing the Past: Power and the Production of History* (Boston, MA: Beacon Press, 2015).
[24] Trouillot, *Silencing the Past*, 1.
[25] See Érika Nimis, 'Small Archives and the Silences of Algerian History', *African Arts*, 48.2 ('African Art and the Archive') (Summer 2015), pp. 26–39; Maria Fantinato Géo de Siqueira, '"We are Losing Our *Encantados* because We Can't Hear Them Anymore": Silence, Extractivism, and Politics of Listening in/to the Brazilian Amazon', *The World of Music*, 10.2 ('Audibilities of Colonialism and Extractivism') (2021), pp. 21–50; Paul Bilj, 'Re-Dressing Silence: Surinamese Dutch Clothing and the Memory of Slavery in the

Archival Silences: Missing, Lost and, [sic] Uncreated Archives, takes as its axiomatic organizing theme 'how authoritarian regimes, not surprisingly, tend to result in archival silences', and its contributors explore a variety of colonial/imperial examples.[26] In Chapter Four, for example, Stanley H. Griffin examines the creation of the Jamaican state archives that began with the establishment of the Island Secretary's Office (ISO) in 1659 as the 'record-keeping arm of the colonial government', continued with the dismantling of the colonial-era ISO in 1879 and formal transference of records to the Island Records Office (IRO) in 1897, and the consolidation of official government archives and their oversight between the mid-1950s and early 1980s. Griffin examines how 'the prejudices and injustices documented within the holdings mirrored [those] of the white ruling minority of colonisers and planter classes' and shows how these biases shape the difficulties we encounter in tracing the history and culture of people of African and Indian descent, including the documentation of Rastafari—his specific area of concern.[27] Similarly, in Chapter Two, Michael Piggott discusses the imperial Australian archival construction in relation to indigenous peoples, yet he draws a larger contextual point that is pertinent here when he states:

> As a silencing force, colonization has few equals. In the Caribbean for example, the consequences of Spanish, French, British and Dutch expansions there in the seventeenth and eighteenth centuries included enslavement and indentureship for some and decimation of the indigenous populations. In eighteenth and nineteenth century Australia [...] there was a similar impact on communities within which oral traditions, cultural practices and languages had flourished for millennia.[28]

This somewhat lengthy digression into colonial/imperial contexts unrelated to the 1862 Kingston stage on which *Obi* briefly appeared before vanishing is, in fact, not the detour it might appear to be.

Netherlands', *The Journal of Decorative and Propaganda Arts*, 27 ('Souvenirs and Objects of Remembrance') (2015), pp. 214–31.

[26] Michael Moss and David Thomas (eds), *Archival Silences: Missing, Lost and, Uncreated Archives* (London and New York: Routledge, 2021), p. 3.

[27] Stanley H. Griffin, 'Noises in the Archives: Acknowledging the Present Yet Silenced Presence in Caribbean Archival Memory', in Moss and Thomas (eds), *Archival Silences*, pp. 81–99 (81 and 86).

[28] Michael Piggott, 'What are Silences: The Australian Example', in Moss and Thomas (eds), *Archival Silences*, 26–53 (28).

Rather, the lack of records reflects the white-constructed archives of state imperial authority, and particularly the suppression of African or indigenous-derived folkloric vernacular traditions, a point that is further discussed below.

This chapter will now turn to a discussion of the lone performance of *Obi; or Three Finger'd Jack* in Kingston in 1862, with the three methodological approaches outlined above employed to counteract the archival gaps and silences: the 'trace evidence' or 'clues' from those in power that help us 'read against the grain'; the use of context and unofficial evidence to assist our understanding; and the retrospective significance of how and why the archives were created, bearing in mind the significance of state and imperial power structures in that process. The use of trace evidence to counter the erasure of people, the challenges of using colonial records written by the powerful and the retrospective silences that have shaped the archives all shed light on the performance of the pantomime and its obscurity in the archive, despite its larger Atlantic popularity.

Reading against the grain

The elision of knowledge about the only performance of this Jamaican story on the Kingston stage has its roots in the original narratives of Jack's resistance, his use of *obeah* and the linkage to vernacular, African-derived performances. As outlined in the introduction to this chapter, the pantomime was based on an armed challenge to slavery that took place in Jamaica in 1780 and 1781. *Obi* debuted in London in 1800 and in Philadelphia in 1801, against the backdrop of the ongoing Haitian Revolution. The piece, explicitly advertised as a 'trans-atlantic pantomime', was wildly popular on both sides of the Atlantic and migrated throughout the Atlantic and Pacific worlds well into the nineteenth century.[29] While Fawcett's pantomime is romanticized—he invents, for example, a romantic subplot between the British Captain Orford (charged with supervising the hunt for Jack) and the plantation owner's daughter, Rosa—he nonetheless draws closely upon the contemporary documentation of the real-life Jack, his rebellion and his capture by British-employed bounty-hunting maroons.

The story was well known throughout the Anglophone world not only because of the popularity of the pantomime but also because, as

---

[29] Anon., 'Theatrical Intelligence', *Thespian Mirror: A Periodical Comprising a Collection of Dramatic Biography* (15 March 1806), p. 98.

several scholars have explained, three key sources Fawcett used for his pantomime were each known to varying degrees.[30] Perhaps the most influential of these was Benjamin Moseley's 1799 *A Treatise on Sugar*. Moseley, a physician who practised in Jamaica from 1768–84, strongly links *obeah* with slave resistance, 'setting the stage', as Frances R. Botkin points out, 'for subsequent accounts'.[31] Moseley, while acknowledging Jack as 'having ascended from Spartacus', emphasized his use of *obeah* and depicted him as a criminal who 'had a mortal hatred to white men'.[32] William Earle Jr's more sympathetic account highlights the democratic rights of man in rebelling against slavery; he also referenced the classical Spartacus and asserted that Jack was 'as bright a luminary as ever graced the Roman annals'.[33] In contrast to Moseley, however, Earle concluded that Jack's cause was 'great and noble […] for he stood alone[,] a bold and daring defender of the Rights of Man'.[34] Although published in the United States in 1804, Earle's tract was not available in the early nineteenth-century Caribbean,[35] and thus was less likely to have been widely read in mid-century Jamaica at the time of *Obi*'s appearance on the Kingston stage. The third account Fawcett may have drawn on was William Burdett's *Life and Exploits of Mansong, Commonly Called Three-Finger'd Jack* (1800), which portrayed Jack's exploits as an adventure story and went into ten editions as well as generating numerous anonymous adaptations up to 1870.[36]

So why, given the notoriety of the story and the trans-national popularity of the pantomime did it garner only one paltry performance in Kingston? One explanation for this (and for the archival silence about it) pertains to the amateur nature of that performance. Produced at

---

[30] William Earle Jr, *Obi; or The History of Three-Fingered Jack*, ed. Srinivas Aravamudan (London: Broadview, 2015), Introduction, 10–17; Frances R. Botkin, *Thieving Three-Fingered Jack: Transatlantic Tales of a Jamaican Outlaw, 1780–2015* (New Brunswick, Camden and Newark, NJ, and London: Rutgers University Press, 2017), pp. 2–4; Fawcett, *Obi; or, Three-Finger'd Jack*, in *Slavery, Abolition, and Emancipation*, 5: 201–02; Jenna Gibbs, 'Toussaint, Gabriel, and Three Finger'd Jack: "Courageous Chiefs" and the "Sacred Standard of Liberty" on the Atlantic Stage', *Early American Studies*, 13.3 (Summer 2015), pp. 626–60 (634).

[31] Botkin, *Thieving Three-Fingered Jack*, 37.

[32] Benjamin Moseley, *A Treatise on Sugar* (London: G.G. and J. Robson, 1799), pp. 198–99.

[33] William Earle Jr., *Obi; or, The History of Three Fingered Jack* (London: 1800, repr. Worcester, MA: Isiah Thomas, 1804), p. 4.

[34] Earle Jr., *Obi* (1804), 4.

[35] Gibbs, 'Toussaint, Gabriel and Three-Finger'd Jack', 653.

[36] Botkin, *Thieving Three-Fingered Jack*, 47.

the Theatre Royal, Kingston, on 16 September, the piece was a benefit performance for J. Thompson, who, as Hill notes, was 'a member of the traveling Lanergan troupe who had elected to remain in Jamaica after the company moved on'.[37] *Obi* was performed by amateurs, in part because in the early 1860s the American Civil War had hampered the usual flow of touring professionals hailing from the United States.[38] Yet these production details do not explain its absence from the Kingston stage *prior* to 1862.

To explain the phantom performance of *Obi; or Three Finger'd Jack* we must take Saidiya Hartman's advice to read against the grain and also play detective to search for, as Carlo Ginsburg puts it, 'trace evidence'. One way of pursuing these research objectives is to recognize, as outlined above, that the pantomime and its eponymous rebel hero had widespread resonance in the Anglophone African diaspora as performances of resistance. For example, famed black Shakespearian actor Ira Aldridge regularly performed the *Obi* pantomime as Jack, and he bookended these performances (on stages in London and Europe in the 1820s, 1830s and 1840s) with antislavery oratory.[39] Similarly, the all-African American theatre company, the African Grove, performed *Obi* in an 1822 season that also included a play written by the founder and leader of the company, William Brown, about slave revolt in Saint-Domingue, *King Shotaway*.[40] And the African Grove also performed a fiery antislavery, antiracist ballad that advocated armed resistance to slavery and oppression, 'Soliloquy of a Maroon chief in Jamaica'.[41] 'Soliloquy' was published in a New York periodical, *St Tammany's Magazine*, in 1821.[42] Although the author is

---

[37] Hill, *The Jamaican Stage*, 101.
[38] Hill, *The Jamaican Stage*, 101.
[39] Gibbs, *Performing the Temple of Liberty*, 223–24.
[40] Shane White, *Stories of Freedom in Black New York* (Cambridge, MA and London: Harvard University Press, 2002), p. 68. See also Jenna M. Gibbs, 'Protesting Slavery, Asserting Freedom, and Defying Racism: The African Grove Theatre in New York, 1821–1824', in Sarah J. Adams, Jenna M. Gibbs and Wendy Sutherland (eds), *Staging Slavery: Performances of Colonial Slavery and Race in International Perspective (1770–1850)* (London and New York: Routledge, 2023), pp. 250–72.
[41] Michael Warner, Natasha Hurley, Luis Iglesias, Sonia Di Loreto, Jeffrey Scraba and Sandra Young collectively wrote an article on which I have drawn: 'A Soliloquy "Lately Spoken at the African Theatre": Race and the Public Sphere in New York City, 1821', *American Literature*, 73.1 (2001), pp. 1–46.
[42] Anon., 'Negro Melodies—No. III. "Soliloquy of a Maroon Chief in Jamaica" (lately spoken at the African Theatre)', *St Tammany's Magazine*, 4 (4 December 1821), p. 52, in George Thompson, *A Documentary History of*

unknown, the verses were a radical statement of violent resistance to both slavery and white racism. The soliloquy explicitly attacked 'scientific' racist theories pitting biologically superior 'whiteness', at the head of racial taxonomy, against biologically inferior 'blackness' at the bottom—the latter depicted as a link between human and ape. The maroon chief—presumably Jack Mansong—decries how whites 'exult in [their own] liberty yet ask for no change for others'.[43] The chief also threatens to avenge the 'mealy infamy' and 'disgrace' of racism and the denial of liberty.[44] He offers to first disgrace racist infamy by reason: he claims he will prove African-descended peoples' equality and liberty 'by his word'. But the chief then unequivocally threatens that if his attempts at proving liberty and equality by reason fail, he will 'avouch it by my sword'![45] *Obi; or Three Finger'd Jack* thus had long-standing connotations of black rebellion and antiracist protest, a fearsome prospect for white Jamaicans, even in 1862.

Moreover, the piece was indelibly associated with the spectre of the Haitian Revolution which, for some white Jamaicans, was still a lived and terrifying memory. At the time of the Revolution, the full-scale uprising of enslaved people had threatened to spread through the Greater Caribbean and numerous plots—and alleged plots—to spread the revolution were uncovered and punished by white authorities.[46] Reading against the grain, we can surmise that even in 1862 the resonance between *Obi* and the Haitian Revolution would likely have been twofold: the timing of its most notable productions, and its prominent staging of Jack's adherence to *obeah* practices. The pantomime's original debut in London in 1800 took place as Toussaint L'Ouverture was leading the alliance of enslaved rebels and free people of colour in a full-scale revolt against French colonial

---

the *African Theatre* (Evanston, IL: Northwestern University Press, 1998), pp. 218–19.

[43] 'Soliloquy', in Thompson, *A Documentary History*, 219.
[44] 'Soliloquy', in Thompson, *A Documentary History*, 219.
[45] 'Soliloquy', in Thompson, *A Documentary History*, 219.
[46] David Barry Gaspar and David Patrick Geggus (eds), *A Turbulent Time: The French Revolution and the Greater Caribbean* (Bloomington, IN: Indiana University Press, 1997); Laurent Dubois, *A Colony of Citizens: Revolution and Slave Emancipation in the French Caribbean, 1787–1804* (Chapel Hill, NC: University of North Carolina Press, 2004); Alfred N. Hunt, *Haiti's Influence on Antebellum American: Slumbering Volcano in the Caribbean* (Baton Rouge, LA: Louisiana State University Press, 1988); Eugene Genovese, *From Rebellion to Revolution: Afro-American Slave Revolts in the Making of the Modern World* (Baton Rouge, LA: Louisiana State University Press, 1979).

rule. The pantomime was one of several topical pieces through which playwrights, despite being prohibited by censorship laws from directly staging contemporary political events, capitalized on the revolution to protest against the injustice of slavery while also dramatizing the horrors of slave revolt. One example is John Cartwright Cross's *King Caesar; or the Negro Slaves*, produced at the Royal Circus in London in 1801 and featuring the 1750s Saint-Domingue revolt led by François Mackendal.[47] In North America, the pantomime's debut in Philadelphia in 1800 coincided with the discovery of a slave revolt conspiracy in Southampton, Virginia, led by Gabriel, a slave of plantation owner Thomas Henry Prosser. Their attempted revolt was aided by two Frenchmen in Philadelphia, and betrayed by two enslaved men, leading to the trial and execution of Gabriel and 23 other rebels.[48] The sensationalist press coverage made clear the grave threat slave revolt posed to American stability and repeatedly linked Gabriel with Toussaint—just as Jack was taking the stage in *Obi*.[49] And later productions were staged to highlight slave insurrection, such as the African Grove's production in 1821, which took the boards just as Denmark Vesey's South Carolina slave revolt conspiracy was exposed.[50]

Secondly, the pantomime also invoked the strong linkage of *obeah/ vodou* with rebellion by enslaved and oppressed black people. Not only in Jack Mansong's real-life Jamaican revolt but also in the Haitian Revolution, *vodou* had played a distinct role in leadership, and—as numerous scholars have shown—for white Anglo-Americans there was an indelible link in literary and performative sources between slave revolt and African-derived religious practices.[51] Fawcett, meanwhile,

[47] George Taylor, *The French Revolution and the London Stage, 1789–1805* (New York: Cambridge University Press, 2000), p. 215; L.W. Connolly, *The Censorship of English Drama, 1737–1824* (San Marino, CA: Huntington Library, 1976), p. 95.
[48] Douglas Egerton, *Death or Liberty: African Americans and Revolutionary America* (New York: Oxford University Press, 2009), p. 279.
[49] Gibbs, 'Toussaint, Gabriel and Three Finger'd Jack', 647–48.
[50] Even as late as 1849, Gabriel and his fellow conspirators were extolled in song and verse, in such examples as 'Uncle Gabriel, the Negro General', 'de Chief of de Insurgents/Way down in Southampton' and 'Uncle Gabriel. The Negro General'. In Lawrence Gellert, *Mainstream*, 16.2 (February 1963), p. 19; *Ethiopian Glee Book*, Christy Minstrels, 1849, p. 120; printed in full in Mat Callahan, *Songs of Slavery and Emancipation* (Jackson, MI: University Press of Mississippi, 2022), pp. 86–87.
[51] Alan Richardson, 'Romantic Voodoo: *Obeah* and British Culture, 1797–1807', in Margarite Fernández Olmos and Lizabeth Paravisini-Gebert (eds), *Sacred Possessions: Vodou, Santeria, Obeah, and the Caribbean* (New Brunswick, NJ:

amplified contrast by making Jack and his fellow rebels practise *obeah* and their captors explicitly Christian. Reputed to have supernatural powers through this practice, Jack, as we have seen, was apprehended by maroon bounty hunters in real life, but in the pantomime Fawcett instead identified them as Christian slaves loyal to their good 'massa', who freed them after they captured Jack.

While we do not know black or white Jamaicans' reactions to the 1862 production of *Obi; or Three Finger'd Jack*, we can surmise that a pantomime that associated antiracist armed resistance with *obeah*—which was, in turn, associated with the Haitian Revolution—may not have been popular with the white theatrical and state authorities in mid-nineteenth-century Jamaica (although it may have been popular with black audience members, if any were present).

Interpolating the context

In addition to Fawcett's pitting of *obeah* against Christianity, he also staged the African-derived tradition of Jonkanoo. Following the British Emancipation Bill in 1833, and the end of the subsequent 'apprenticeship' system that kept enslaved people tied to the land and in continued service to their former owners, white Kingston officials enacted a massive crackdown on black protests, including attempting to suppress annual Jonkanoo parades. In 1840, Hector Mitchell, the mayor of Kingston, and the Kingston Common Council banned the 'debauchery and demoralization' of Jonkanoo's 'disgusting orgies of African barbarism'.[52] When the Jonkanoo revellers defiantly paraded anyway, the police were called in, killing several women and injuring others. Despite this brutality, an outraged crowd member of African descent told officials that they had a right to the parade because 'they were freed and would not be made slaves of'.[53] Church and civic authorities' attempts to suppress Jonkanoo continued, but free black Jamaicans boldly continued to celebrate their African-derived masking, dancing and drumming in the Christmas season and on the annual 1 August Freedom Day commemorations of emancipation.

Rutgers University Press, 1997), pp. 171–95 (171–72). See also Gibbs, 'Toussaint, Gabriel, and Three Finger'd Jack', 637–39.

[52] Colonial Office Papers, CO 137/256, Metcalfe to Stanley, 29 October 1841. Quoted in Swithin Wilmot, 'The Politics of Protest in Free Jamaica: The Kingston John Canoe Christmas Riots, 1840 and 1841', *Caribbean Quarterly*, 36 (1990), pp. 65–75 (65).

[53] Quoted in Wilmot, 'The Politics of Protest', 65.

During the mid-nineteenth-century, violent suppressions of Jonkanoo by white authorities give us contextual insight into the pantomime's near-absence from the Jamaican stage. The pantomime features an elaborate scene of the Jonkanoo festival performed at Christmas and Boxing Day on Jamaican—and Bahamian and Bermudian—plantations. This striking dance scene was led by 'Jonkanoo', a 'master of ceremonies' decked out in 'motley coloured dress ornamented with feathers and beads' and a 'cap with small bells and feathers', according to the stage directions in the extant 1825 manuscript.[54] Similarly, the annual Jonkanoo parade featured in the pantomime was firmly an emblem of Afro-Caribbean resistance, both during slavery and after emancipation. In colonial Jamaica, Jonkanoo had been a ritualized masquerade of dance, song and parade performed by enslaved Africans, a brief 'world turned upside down', as Mikhail Bahktin articulated.[55] The Jonkanoo character, sometimes also known as John Konny or Kooner John, was derived from a tribal chief from Axim (present-day Ghana) who, adorned in a horned headdress, led an armed rebellion against Dutch merchant-settlers in 1702. He had eventually been captured and sent as a slave to Jamaica, where he became a folk hero featured in enslaved peoples' Jonkanoo parades. These performances, described repeatedly by white observers like absentee plantation owner William Beckford, resident plantation owner Edward Long and novelist, playwright and absentee plantation owner Matthew 'Monk' Lewis, entailed elaborate headdresses, drumming, banjos, marches and dancing.[56] Long, for example, described the 'masqueraders as dressed up in grotesque habits, and a pair of oxhorns on their head' who performed a parade to fife and drums.[57] This description was echoed by the theatre critic Timothy Dutton who, when reviewing the 1800 London debut, described Jonkanoo's leader as 'a grotesque character, equipped with a ludicrous and enormously

---

[54] Fawcett, *Obi*, in *Slavery, Abolition and Emancipation* 5, 203.

[55] Mikhail Bahktin, *Rabelais and His World*, trans. Hélène Iswolsky (Bloomington, IN: Indiana University Press, 1984), p. 15.

[56] William Beckford, *A Descriptive Account of the Island of Jamaica*, 2 vols (1790) (London: Forgotten Books, 2017), Vol. 1, pp. 390–92; Edward Long, *The History of Jamaica, or, General Survey of the Antient and Modern State of That Island, with Reflections on its Situation, Settlements, Inhabitants, Climate, Products, Commerce, Laws, and Government*, 3 vols (1774) (Cambridge: Cambridge University Press, 2010), Vol. 2, pp. 423–25; Matthew Lewis, *Journal of a West India Proprietor Kept during a Residence in the Island of Jamaica*, ed. Judith Terry (1816) (Oxford: Oxford University Press, 1999), p. 36.

[57] Long, *History of Jamaica* 1, 439.

large false head' who 'presides [...] in the capacity as master of the ceremonies'.[58]

While these sources do not tell us how *Obi* was performed in Kingston in 1862, what we *can* learn from reading the governmental records—in combination with interrogating the 1860s context—is that the white governmental powers considered Jonkanoo to be very threatening. We know from the top-down records that black Jamaicans performed Jonkanoo defiantly, even when under actual gunfire. These African diasporic commemorations of slavery, resistance and freedom persisted in the street as well as on the stage, especially in Jamaica and the Bahamas—and, most notably, among the Jamaican maroon communities, as Kathleen Wilson has cogently shown.[59]

We turn to one last contextual source of trace evidence 'clues': the American Civil War. In Warwick Crescent, Jamaica, there stands a monument—known variously as the 'Soldiers Monument' or 'Soldiers and Sailors Monument' that commemorates the residents of Jamaica who served in the Union and gave their lives in the American Civil War.[60] As it seems unlikely that white Jamaicans would have rallied to the Union cause, we must assume that these soldiers and sailors were black Jamaicans. Meanwhile, what we know about *white* Jamaican traders' and legislators' responses to the American Civil War is that they were mightily displeased with its disruptive effect on their trade. As one Jamaican writer to *The New York Times* put it in 1861:

> This colony is fully realizing the evil which I predicted in one of my previous letters to arise from the civil war in America. Jamaica is almost entirely dependent upon the United States for the breadstuffs and provisions which she consumes, and it is quite evident that anything which leads to a stoppage of supplies must occasion us very great suffering. What, with the known activity of the Southern privateers and the sparsity of arrivals, the people of this colony have very great cause for anxiety, and with them the continuance of the civil war must be a matter deeply to be deplored. Our trade has been crippled, that leads

---

[58] Timothy Dutton, *Dramatic Censor; or, Monthly Epitome of Taste, Fashion, and Manners* (London: J. Roach and C. Chapple, 1801), Vol. 3, p. 20.
[59] Gibbs, 'Jonkanoo Performances', 61–62; Kathleen Wilson, 'The Performances of Freedom: Maroons and the Colonial Order in Eighteenth-Century Jamaica and the Atlantic Sound', *William and Mary Quarterly*, 66 (2009), pp. 45–86.
[60] 'American Civil War Memorial Jamaica', https://www.tracesofwar.com.

to a falling off of revenue, and that in its turn must lead to an increase of taxation.[61]

There is no documentation that directly links white Jamaicans' unease with the American Civil War to the evident unsuitability of *Obi* on the Kingston stage in 1862. Yet it is hard for the historian to imagine that white Jamaicans would have been pleased to see a play about black revolt in Jamaica take the stage amidst this civil war trauma, and with the reality of black Jamaicans joining and dying for the Union cause.

We can read this context of the suppression of Jonkanoo and black resistance and anxieties over the American Civil War into the absences of theatrical or governmental records of *Obi; or Three Finger'd Jack*. This one-night stand, however, remains mysterious given that both amateur and professional productions of other plays that were either set in or relevant to the British Caribbean became production staples. Examples include Richard Cumberland's *The West Indian* (1771), Isaac Bickerstaffe's comic operetta *The Padlock* (1768) and George Colman Jr's *Inkle and Yarico* (1787), set in Barbados.[62] Based on context and reading between the lines of government records, we can conclude that the subject matter of Jack's resistance was too risky, even after emancipation—fears that echoed in the post-emancipation crackdown on Jonkanoo celebrations and unease over the American Civil War.

(Re)constructing the archive

In conclusion, we come back to Trouillot's point about 'silences' being, in part, to do with our retrospective archival creation: that is, what we—in the here and now—deem important has a strong bearing on how we record and organize archives. In the years since Trouillot wrote his *magnum opus*, however, much has changed, as evidenced by the exciting fresh perspectives on the Caribbean archives cited at the beginning of this chapter. Numerous historians, myself included, have combatted the colonial/imperial construction of archival records and silences by shifting the emphasis of what we consider important in the historical record, and by reading against the grain. As Fuentes concludes, 'it is the historian's job to substantiate all the pieces with more archival evidence, context, and historiography and put them together into a coherent

---

[61] Correspondence of *The New York Times*, Kingston, Jamaica, Monday 5 August 1861.
[62] Banham, Hill and Woodyard, *African and Caribbean Theatre*, 146.

narrative form'.[63] Meanwhile, one indication of this shift in emphasis is that *Obi; or Three Finger'd Jack* is still resonant and, indeed, has been renewed as a memory of resistance: Botkin has written eloquently about Ted Dwyer's 1980 production *Mansong*, a rewrite of *Obi; or, Three Finger'd Jack* that was staged at the War Theatre in Kingston and featured a Jonkanoo band. Let us conclude, then, by flipping on its head Trouillot's notion that our retrospective construction of the archive is one of the silences: because now, our retrospective understanding of the importance of Jonkanoo and *Obi; or, Three Finger'd Jack* as cultural markers of memory and resistance are a counter to the archival silences and the way we can read through top-down sources.

Mysteries nonetheless remain. I would, for example, love to know why J. Thompson chose *Obi; or Three Finger'd Jack* to serve as his charity benefit. Given the context of coercive oppression of black vernacular expression; given the absence and evident undesirability of the staging of revolt; what was his motivation? How did he react to its performance? Who made up the audience, and what was their response to a play about a Jamaican slave revolt, with strong resonances of the Haitian Revolution, performed as the American Civil War was under way? We may never know the answers to these kinds of questions. But reading against the grain, teasing out trace evidence and using our best gauge of historical contextual understanding allows us nonetheless to disrupt the archival silence.

Bibliography

'American Civil War Memorial Jamaica', https://www.tracesofwar.com.

Anon. 'Negro Melodies—No. III. "Soliloquy of a Maroon Chief in Jamaica" (lately spoken at the African Theatre)', *St Tammany's Magazine*, 4 (4 December 1821), p. 52, in George Thompson, *A Documentary History of the African Theatre* (Evanston, IL: Northwestern University Press, 1998), pp. 218–19.

Anon. 'Theatrical Intelligence', *Thespian Mirror: A Periodical Comprising a Collection of Dramatic Biography* (15 March 1806).

Banham, Martin, Errol Hill and George Woodyard (eds). *The Cambridge Guide to African and Caribbean Theatre* (Cambridge and New York: Cambridge University Press, 1994).

Beckford, William. *A Descriptive Account of the Island of Jamaica*, 2 vols (1790) (London: Forgotten Books, 2017), Vol. 1.

---

[63] Fuentes, *Dispossessed Lives*, 146.

Bilj, Paul. 'Re-Dressing Silence: Surinamese Dutch Clothing and the Memory of Slavery in the Netherlands', *The Journal of Decorative and Propaganda Arts*, 27 ('Souvenirs and Objects of Remembrance') (2015), pp. 214–31.

Botkin, Frances R. *Thieving Three-Fingered Jack: Transatlantic Tales of a Jamaican Outlaw, 1780–2015* (New Brunswick, Camden and Newark, NJ and London: Rutgers University Press, 2017).

Burton, Antoinette (ed.). *Archive Stories: Facts, Fictions, and the Writing of History* (Durham, NC and London: Duke University Press, 2005).

Callahan, Mat. *Songs of Slavery and Emancipation* (Jackson, MI: University Press of Mississippi, 2022).

Colonial Office Papers, CO 137/256, Metcalfe to Stanley, 29 October 1841.

Connolly, L.W. *The Censorship of English Drama, 1737–1824* (San Marino, CA: Huntington Library, 1976).

Davin, Anna and Carlo Ginzburg. 'Morelli, Freud and Sherlock Holmes: Clues and Scientific Method', *History Workshop*, 9 (Spring 1980), pp. 5–36.

Davis, Natalie Zemon. *Fiction in the Archives: Pardon Tales and Their Tellers in Sixteenth-Century France* (Stanford, CA: Stanford University Press, 1990).

Davis, Tracy C. 'The Context Problem', *Theatre Survey*, 45.2 (2004), pp. 203–09.

de Sigueira, Maria Fantinato Géo. '"We are Losing Our *Encantados* because We Can't Hear Them Anymore": Silence, Extractivism, and Politics of Listening in/to the Brazilian Amazon', *The World of Music*, 10.2 ('Audibilities of Colonialism and Extractivism') (2021), pp. 21–50.

Dubois, Laurent. *A Colony of Citizens: Revolution and Slave Emancipation in the French Caribbean, 1787–1804* (Chapel Hill, NC: University of North Carolina Press, 2004).

Dutton, Timothy. *Dramatic Censor; or, Monthly Epitome of Taste, Fashion, and Manners* (London: J. Roach and C. Chapple, 1801), Vol. 3.

Earle Jr, William. *Obi; or, The History of Three Fingered Jack* (London: 1800, repr., Worcester, MA: Isiah Thomas, 1804).

Earle Jr, William. *Obi; or The History of Three-Fingered Jack*, ed. Srinivas Aravamudan (London: Broadview, 2015).

Egerton, Douglas. *Death or Liberty: African Americans and Revolutionary America* (New York: Oxford University Press, 2009).

Fawcett, John. *Obi; or, Three Finger'd Jack* (1825 text) reproduced in Peter J. Kitson and Debbie Lee (eds), *Slavery, Abolition and Emancipation: Writings in the British Romantic Period*, 8 vols (London: Pickering and Chatto, 1999), Vol. 5: *Drama*, ed. Jeffrey N. Cox, pp. 203–19.

Fuentes, Marisa J. *Dispossessed Lives: Enslaved Women, Violence, and the Archive* (Philadelphia, PA: University of Pennsylvania Press, 2016).

Gaspar, David Barry and David Patrick Geggus (eds). *A Turbulent Time: The French Revolution and the Greater Caribbean* (Bloomington, IN: Indiana University Press, 1997).

Genovese, Eugene. *From Rebellion to Revolution: Afro-American Slave Revolts in the Making of the Modern World* (Baton Rouge, LA: Louisiana State University Press, 1979).

Gibbs, Jenna M. 'Jonkanoo Performances of Resistance, Freedom, and Memory', in Evelyn O'Callaghan and Tim Watson (eds), *Caribbean Literature in Transition, 1800–1920* (Cambridge and New York: Cambridge University Press, 2020), pp. 52–66.

Gibbs, Jenna M. *Performing the Temple of Liberty: Slavery, Theater and Popular Culture in London and Philadelphia, 1760–1850* (Baltimore, MD: Johns Hopkins University Press, 2014).

Gibbs, Jenna M. 'Protesting Slavery, Asserting Freedom, and Defying Racism: The African Grove Theatre in New York, 1821–1824', in Sarah J. Adams, Jenna M. Gibbs and Wendy Sutherland (eds), *Staging Slavery: Performances of Colonial Slavery and Race in International Perspective (1770–1850)* (London and New York: Routledge, 2023), pp. 250–72.

Gibbs, Jenna M. 'Toussaint, Gabriel and Three Finger'd Jack: "Courageous Chiefs" and the Sacred Standard of Liberty: On the Atlantic Stage', *Early American Studies*, 13.3 (Summer 2015), pp. 626–60.

Ginzburg, Carlo. *The Cheese and the Worms: The Cosmos of a Sixteenth-Century Miller* trans. John and Anne C. Tedeschi (Baltimore, MD: Johns Hopkins University Press, 1980).

Griffin, Stanley H. 'Noises in the Archives: Acknowledging the Present Yet Silenced Presence in Caribbean Archival Memory', in Michael and David Thomas (eds), *Archival Silences: Missing, Lost and, Uncreated Archives* (London and New York: Routledge, 2021), pp. 81–99.

Hartman, Saidiya. *Lose Your Mother: A Journey Along the Atlantic Slave Route* (New York: Farrar, Straus and Giroux, 2007).

Hartman, Saidiya. 'Venus in Two Acts', *Small Axe*, 12.2 (June 2008), pp. 1–14.

Hill, Errol. *The Jamaican Stage, 1655–1900: Profile of a Colonial Theatre* (Amherst, MA: The University of Massachusetts Press, 1992).

Hunt, Alfred N. *Haiti's Influence on Antebellum American: Slumbering Volcano in the Caribbean* (Baton Rouge, LA: Louisiana State University Press, 1988).

Lewis, Matthew. *Journal of a West India Proprietor Kept during a Residence in the Island of Jamaica* (1816), ed. Judith Terry (Oxford: Oxford University Press, 1999).

Long, Edward. *The History of Jamaica, or, General Survey of the Antient and Modern State of That Island, with Reflections on its Situation, Settlements, Inhabitants, Climate, Products, Commerce, Laws, and Government*, 3 vols (1774) (Cambridge: Cambridge University Press, 2010), Vol. 2.

Moseley, Benjamin. *A Treatise on Sugar* (London: G.G. and J. Robson, 1799).

Moss, Michael and David Thomas (eds). *Archival Silences: Missing, Lost and, Uncreated Archives* (London and New York: Routledge, 2021).

Nimis, Érika. 'Small Archives and the Silences of Algerian History', *African Arts*, 48.2 ('African Art and the Archive') (Summer 2015), pp. 26–39.

Piggott, Michael. 'What are Silences: The Australian Example', in Michael Moss and David Thomas (eds), *Archival Silences: Missing, Lost and, Uncreated Archives* (London and New York: Routledge, 2021), pp. 26–53.

Richardson, Alan. 'Romantic Voodoo: *Obeah* and British Culture, 1797–1807', in Margarite Fernández Olmos and Lizebeth Paravisini-Gebert (eds), *Sacred Possessions: Vodou, Santeria, Obeah, and the Caribbean* (New Brunswick, NJ: Rutgers University Press, 1997), pp. 171–95.

Stoler, Ann Laura. *Along the Archival Grain: Epistemic Anxieties and Colonial Common Sense* (Princeton, NJ and Oxford: Princeton University Press, 2009).

Taylor, George. *The French Revolution and the London Stage, 1789–1805* (New York: Cambridge University Press, 2000).

Thompson, Jr., George A. *A Documentary History of the African Theatre* (Evanston, IL: Northwestern University Press, 1998).

Trouillot, Michel-Rolph. *Silencing the Past: Power and the Production of History* (Boston, MA: Beacon Press, 2015).

Warner, Michael, Natasha Hurley, Luis Iglesias, Sonia Di Loreto, Jeffrey Scraba and Sandra Young. 'A Soliloquy "Lately Spoken at the African Theatre": Race and the Public Sphere in New York City, 1821', *American Literature*, 73.1 (2001), pp. 1–46.

White, Shane. *Stories of Freedom in Black New York* (Cambridge, MA and London: Harvard University Press, 2002).

Wilmot, Swithin. 'The Politics of Protest in Free Jamaica: The Kingston John Canoe Christmas Riots, 1840 and 1841', *Caribbean Quarterly*, 36 (1990), pp. 65–75.

Wilson, Kathleen. 'The Performances of Freedom: Maroons and the Colonial Order in Eighteenth-Century Jamaica and the Atlantic Sound', *William and Mary Quarterly*, 66 (2009), pp. 45–86.

Eight

Using Military Documents to Study Colonial-Era Theatre and Performance in Saint-Domingue

Logan J. Connors

Delafosse de Rouville was a young officer when he arrived in Port-au-Prince. In the 1780s, the city was an important hub of military and commercial activity in Saint-Domingue, France's 'pearl of the Antilles', a profitable and brutal slave colony whose residents would successfully revolt against the French to become the independent nation of Haiti in 1804. Years later, after the fall of Napoleon and riding the Bourbon restoration's wave of aristocratic energy, the anti-Republican de Rouville published his memoirs in the form of an *Éloge* to his former commander in Saint-Domingue, Colonel Mauduit-Duplessis, followed by an *Essai sur la situation de Saint-Domingue à cette époque*.[1] The *Éloge* centres on the death of Mauduit-Duplessis who, in 1791, was dragged through the streets of Port-au-Prince, mutilated and killed by French soldiers under his command because he had refused to recognize the new Republican government in Paris. De Rouville, who avoided death himself by means of deception and disguise, recounts Mauduit-Duplessis's murder as a procession of violence and brutality that ultimately turned theatrical when the members of the Artois division stripped the Colonel of his service medals and uniform, which were then 'portés en triomphe dans les bals et les comédies' (*worn triumphantly to dances and plays*) by his military assassins.[2]

De Rouville's *Éloge* and *Essai sur la situation de Saint-Domingue* are documents that focus on colonial military activity, but also reveal insights about the island's theatrical and performance cultures. This

---

[1] Delafosse de Rouville, *Éloge historique du Chevalier Mauduit-Duplessis, suivi d'un Essai sur La Situation de Saint-Domingue à cette époque* (Senlis: Tremblay, 1817).
[2] De Rouville, *Éloge historique*, 46. The account of Mauduit-Duplessis's death was truly theatricalized when it became the subject of a play by Marsollier de Vivetières: *La Mort du Colonel Mauduit ou Les Anarchistes au Port-au-Prince, fait historique en un acte et en prose* (Paris: Cailleau, 1800).

chapter describes and evaluates some of the ways in which scholars can utilize military documents, including institutional military archives, military memoirs and documents written by civilians about the military, to better understand theatre and other forms of performance in colonial Saint-Domingue. This goal appears straightforward, but the very existence of French-language theatre and of the complex political, social and military structures that supported the performing arts in a colonial space of mostly enslaved black labour warrant a critical approach. Military documentation, and particularly the institutional military archive—a 'technology' that 'bolstered the production' of a plantation society that exploited over half a million enslaved people—help illuminate how Saint-Domingue's white-centric theatre cultures existed and prospered.[3] Many of the documents in this chapter show 'extractive' value for scholars of theatre who (understandably) lack knowledge of French military institutions and processes. But the scholarly 'extraction' process should not mirror other extraction processes uncritically. Military documents, and especially the military's own archives, are situated within the goals of France at the time—a competitive and politically turbulent European empire that viewed theatre as a key means to please and 'occupy' the people (planters, bankers, soldiers, attorneys) who were largely responsible for installing and executing colonial extraction and exploitation. Another goal of this chapter is thus to describe some of the challenges and analytical drawbacks of using military documents as sources for the study of colonial theatre and performance.

In the eighteenth-century Caribbean French colonial territories were highly militarized spaces with particular geopolitical strategies and tensions. Colonies were administered by the military, mainly by the navy, starting in the late seventeenth century and with increasing vigour following France's embarrassing defeat in the Seven Years' War (1756–63).[4] Owing to the outsized presence of military personnel, institutions and cultures on French Caribbean islands, military documentation was diverse and pervasive. Naval governors and *intendants* created a considerable paper trail on everything from meteorology to demographics to the region's popular theatrical culture. Inspired by what were viewed

---

[3] Ann Laura Stoler, 'Colonial Archives and the Arts of Governance', *Archival Science*, 2 (2002), pp. 87–109 (98). Stoler is correct to urge scholars to look 'to colonial archives as both transparencies on which power relations were inscribed and intricate technologies of rule in themselves' (87).

[4] For more information, see Boris Lesueur, *Les Troupes coloniales d'Ancien Régime: Fidetilate per Mare et Terras* (Paris: SPM Kronos, 2014).

by European settlers and soldiers as 'exotic' locales, military officers wrote about their colonial experiences in times of both war and peace.

This chapter explores military relationships and tensions that informed and influenced theatre and public performances in the French Caribbean, and particularly in colonial Saint-Domingue. The first part will provide an overview of several types of military documents in institutional defence archives that reveal, or with further inquiry have the potential to reveal, the military's role in financing and participating in theatrical performances in Saint-Domingue's principal cities Cap-Français (now Cap-Haïtien) and Port-au-Prince. Many of these are, of course, examples of what Jenna Gibbs called (in Chapter 7 in this volume) the 'white-constructed archives of state imperial authority' and must be treated with due caution. Accordingly, in this part I also discuss a series of documents written by civilians, but which comment on the colonial 'military–theatrical complex'—a network of military–theatrical overlaps and interactions that emerged, at least as far as the French-speaking world is concerned, in the second half of the eighteenth century.[5]

In the second part of the chapter, I describe the dual role of military documents in the formation of a larger archive of French colonial theatre and performance practices. First, a military document can provide empirical evidence about public theatres in Saint-Domingue (which is important, given the relatively meagre archival sources about colonial French Caribbean theatre); and second, military documents can sometimes help explain some of the ephemeral, 'embodied practices [that] offer a way of knowing' about colonial Saint-Domingue and its social performances of military anxiety and power.[6] The traces of these performances in soldier memoirs and in other documents sometimes add human contours and experiences to the information in the institutional defence archive, thus complementing and confirming what the military says about itself. At other times, however, civilian texts intervene in contradiction to the archive's institutional framing and help fill gaps where the military archive is purposefully or inadvertently silent. All in all, when read either 'along' or 'against' the grain, military documents can help researchers better comprehend the performance environment

---

[5] This chapter will inform a larger project on the relationships between theatre and the French military from the Seven Years' War to the beginning of the Haitian Revolution, tentatively titled 'Military-Theatrical Experiences in the Age of the French Revolution'.

[6] Diana Taylor, *The Archive and the Repertoire: Performing Cultural Memory in the Americas* (Durham, NC and London: Duke University Press, 2003), p. 3.

in colonial Saint-Domingue; they can decentre eighteenth-century French studies from the Paris-based venues and metropolitan theatrical performances on which scholars have traditionally focussed, and detail several ways in which armed conflict and the colonial endeavour helped nurture dynamic (and in hindsight, highly problematic) artistic productions and experiences.[7]

Colonial theatre and the military archive

What constitutes a 'military document'? First, there are institutional military archives. Military archives, especially in relatively centralized governments like that of old-regime France, allow researchers, to borrow James Scott's phrasing, to 'see like a state'.[8] And seeing like a state can be an interesting exercise in the context of Saint-Domingue where the state was overrepresented in comparison with provincial France, particularly the military. From the late seventeenth century, administration in Saint-Domingue (and this is also the case for Martinique, Guadeloupe, French Guiana and other French Caribbean colonies) was the responsibility of the navy (Secrétariat d'État de la marine) and, when the navy was not in charge, such as during a few years in the 1760s and 1770s, of the army (Secrétariat d'État de la guerre) because the navy was put under control of the army in a panic-driven set of reforms after the Seven Years' War.[9]

The hyper-presence of state organs, policies, rules and administrators, as well as the military's integration into what were often civilian institutions in metropolitan France, provoked tension on the island. The military was tasked with enabling the colony's plantation complex to thrive by securing the seas against foreign attack, catching enslaved

---

[7] Stoler underscores the importance not only of reading 'against' the themes in colonial records but also of reading 'along' their grain in order to better understand the logic of colonial societies. About the archive, she writes 'we need to read for its regularities, for its logic of recall, for its densities and distributions, for its consistencies of misinformation, omission, and mistake—along the archival grain' ('Colonial archives', 100).

[8] James C. Scott, *Seeing Like a State: How Certain Schemes to Improve the Human Condition Have Failed* (New Haven, CT and London: Yale University Press, 1998).

[9] For a concise history of the development of the French armed forces in the Caribbean and on the shifting power structures at play during the old regime, see Boris Lesueur, 'Les troupes coloniaux aux Antilles sous l'Ancien Régime', *Histoire, Économie et Société*, 28.4 (2009), pp. 3–19.

people who had escaped, eliminating piracy and policing the streets in larger towns and cities. The navy failed to achieve many of these goals, especially in its altercations with larger and more efficient British forces, much to the dismay of both locals on the island and administrators in Versailles. Moreover, the military was often in conflict with the financial and cultural power centres of the island—the successful white planters and bourgeois financiers who, starting in the 1740s, were the impetus behind the development of public theatre in the colony.[10] Saint-Domingue's elite resented the crown and its reach because of the limited judicial powers invested in local officials on the island by Versailles. And, much to the dismay of French naval officers who were tasked with monitoring the island's ports, locals often rebelled against the *exclusif*, the crown's policy that banned or heavily regulated trade to places other than metropolitan France.[11]

The colonial 'state' was in many ways synonymous with 'the military', and there are military documents that deal with nearly every issue, institution or practice in the colony, from soil analysis to meteorology to medicine, or from marriage practices to slavery to theatre.[12] For example, many actors and theatre professionals travelled to Cap-Français (the island's main cultural hub) aboard naval vessels or boats that were subject to naval quartermaster logs because the navy was paying private shipowners to transport soldiers and military equipment. These documents reveal circulations, relationships and pathways that were shared between sailors and actors. Some of the logs are located at the Service Historique de la Défense in Vincennes, near Paris (where most of France's military archives are stored), but others are found in regional military archives in the western cities of Brest, Lorient and Rochefort. As the naval historian Boris Lesueur writes,

---

[10] For more information on the origins of public theatre in Saint-Domingue, see Jean Fouchard, *Le théâtre à Saint-Domingue* (Port-au-Prince: Imprimerie de l'État, 1955), pp. 4–10; see also David M. Powers, *From Plantation to Paradise? Cultural Politics and Musical Theatre in French Slave Colonies, 1764–1789* (East Lansing, MI: Michigan State, 2014), pp. 27–35.

[11] Paul Cheney provides a compelling account of conflict between planters and (mostly metropolitan) military officers through the story of Vice-Commander Ferron de la Ferronnays and his doomed marriage to a woman from the Creole elite. See Paul Cheney, *Cul de Sac: Patrimony, Capitalism, and Slavery in French Saint-Domingue* (Chicago and London: University of Chicago Press, 2017).

[12] See, for example, James E. McClellan, *Colonialism and Science: Saint Domingue and the Old Regime* (Chicago: University of Chicago Press, 1992; 2010).

naval documents are plentiful, but attempting to locate exhaustive documentation on any subject is notoriously difficult because the papers are always 'dispersés à travers différents dépôts d'archives et nécessitent un traitement complexe de compilation des données afin de parvenir à des conclusions significatives' (*dispersed across different archives and require a complex process of data collection in order to reach any significant conclusions*).[13]

Military archives reveal various requests to army and navy administrators in Versailles or to local military officials for what are essentially bailouts of theatrical venues. This occurred in cities and towns throughout France and its colonies where there were significant military bases or training facilities.[14] In Saint-Domingue, the principal theatres in Cap-Français and Port-au-Prince were owned by private stockholder companies—groups of local businessmen, plantation owners, officials and others who were tasked with raising money for the theatre and administering its budget.[15] However, as with many private arrangements related to the performing arts, past and present, the stockholder model proved to be insufficient to keep the Comédie (*theatre*) afloat. In a 1774 letter Dutrejet, Lavanis and Drieux, three stockholders at the theatre in Le Cap, asked Ferron de la Ferronnays, the Vice-Commander of its military force at the time, to contribute funds to the theatre, which had apparently overspent during its spring season.[16]

---

[13] Lesueur, *Les Troupes coloniales*, 28. All translations are mine, unless otherwise indicated.

[14] For example, in 1779 theatre directors in the eastern city of Metz conducted a study to see how many *livres* military battalions were paying for theatre subscriptions in garrison towns throughout northern and eastern France. Unhappy with what the local officers were paying, Metz's directors wrote to them, arguing that in Nancy and Valenciennes subscriptions were about 200 *livres* per battalion, and even as much as 300 in the military town of Douai—far more than the 80 *livres* that battalions were paying in Metz. See 'Correspondance from the Directeurs du spectacle to the Maréchal de Broglie', in Henri Tribout de Morembert, *Le théâtre à Metz*, Vol. 1 (Paris: Publications de la société d'histoire du théâtre, 1952), p. 87. Local leaders in Toulouse, Saumur, Arras and other provincial cities made similar requests for military officials to fund theatres better.

[15] For more information on the administration of private-stock theatre companies in the colonial Caribbean, see Lauren R. Clay, *Stagestruck: The Business of Theater in Eighteenth-Century France and Its Colonies* (Ithaca, NY and London: Cornell University Press, 2013), pp. 196–210.

[16] Daniel Dutrejet, Lavanis and Drieux, *Mémoire concernant le spectacle de la ville du Cap* (28 June 1774), Archives nationales (AN), Vol. 210, in Fouchard, *Le théâtre à Saint-Domingue*, 15–18.

It is possible, although difficult to confirm, that the theatre's request was at least partly responsible for a letter from Ferron de la Ferronnays to officials in Versailles, asking that they augment his commission and provide him with more discretionary use of the crown's funds in Saint-Domingue. As Paul Cheney writes, the truth is that the money was not for the theatre or for the Vice-Commander's troops, but for his new wife—a wealthy woman from a prominent Creole family, who was bleeding the French officer dry with her lovers, gambling and nights at the theatre in the small coastal town of Léogane.[17]

The theatrical money trail leads to two related documents: one is the annual pricing of subscriptions to the Comédie du Cap, the theatre in Port-au-Prince, and perhaps other venues—this was sent each year to the commanders in Cap-Français. These prospectuses show special pricing for military patrons, with increasing specificity as the 1780s progressed. For example, in 1776 the prospectus for the Comédie du Cap makes no explicit reference to special prices for military patrons.[18] But by 1784 the prospectus indicates that 'une portion des troisième loges sera occupée par [...] Sergens ou personnes de la Troupe qui ont leur entrée, ou qui paient en entrant, auxquels cette place seule sera alignée à l'instar des villes de garnison en France' (*a section of the third box shall be for Sergeants or other members of the military who have a subscription or who pay at the entrance, and to whom that location will be assigned following the norms of military towns in France*).[19] Saint-Domingue, it seems, followed a general trend of French military–theatrical cooperation in the second half of the eighteenth century. Military administrators from Cambrai to Cap-Français encouraged and compelled soldiers and sailors to attend what they hoped would be instructive and enjoyable nights at the theatre.

The military's reach into the leisure practices of its men was not appreciated by all. A linked series of documents are the numerous letters that Versailles received from officers complaining about the obligatory theatre subscriptions. With the promulgation of article 23 of title XX in the Ordonnance du roi pour régler le service dans les places et dans les quartiers du 1er mars 1768, officers were required to maintain subscriptions whenever they were garrisoned in a town with a public theatre. Many higher-ranking officers were even required to purchase subscriptions for their squadron or unit. Mandatory subscriptions

---

[17] Cheney, *Cul de Sac*, 130–40.
[18] *Prospectus pour l'Année 1776*, Archives nationales d'outre-mer (ANOM) COL F3 160 F10 F21, 4.
[19] *Prospectus pour l'Année 1784*, ANOM COL F3 160 F10 F21, 6.

exacerbated inequities and tensions among officers and undoubtedly influenced the behaviour of soldiers in colonial auditoriums by turning the theatrical experience into another military commitment, and not necessarily a break from the difficulties and doldrums of armed service to the crown.

Another type of archival document is the *règlement* detailing the structure and nature of military service in French Caribbean colonies. In the 1740s, for example, the armed forces set up new criteria for access to military academies and created a cadet school for the colonies in Rochefort (a port city in western France with its own naval archive). The school was reserved exclusively for the sons of noble colonists who were then supposed to go back to French Guiana, Martinique, Guadeloupe, Saint-Domingue and elsewhere across the Caribbean to lead squadrons and other units. These reforms have a heavy paper burden; one example is a Tableau des tous les officiers des troupes du Roy dans les Isles du Vent de l'Amérique,[20] a sweeping document that reveals the name and rank of each officer who was posted to the Windward Islands in the 1740s. Although the work falls beyond the purview of this chapter, it would be possible to cross-check the Tableau with the major players in Martinique's early theatre scene in order to find new overlaps and relationships between its military establishment and the colony's dramatic enterprise. Other documents in this vein of inquiry include a royal decree from 3 March 1781 that reorganized the militia system across French Caribbean colonies, and a decree from 28 March 1766 that established and delineated the *légion de Saint-Domingue*—the colony's new fighting force consisting of 54 companies across roughly a dozen locations (most of which had a public theatre or built one during the 1770s and 1780s).[21] These documents (and others) provide future avenues for researchers to connect, trace and map routes of military–theatrical interaction across the Atlantic and the Caribbean.

One treasure trove of military documents about theatre is not from the colonial Caribbean *per se*, but its resources could help explain key relationships, including theatrical networks, shared practices and common soldierly behaviours between France and its colonies. The Théâtre de la Marine in Brest (Brittany) was the only public performance venue ever financed by the French navy. The project started in the 1750s at the urging of some particularly theatrophilic commanders and *intendants* at the port city's naval training grounds and barracks. The most vocal advocate was Joseph Aymar, comte de Roquefeuil, a

---

[20] AN, D2A 18 (1741).
[21] Lesueur, *Les Troupes coloniales*, 42.

Commandant in Brest who wrote to the duc de Choiseul, France's Minister of the Navy in 1762, praising the effects of theatrical performance on his men. De Roquefeuil remarked that he was pleased by a 'petit spectacle qui est ici depuis deux ans' (*a modest theatre that has been here for two years*) because it 'semble y faire du bien; le spectacle détourne le goût du jeu, de la table, des querelles, ce qui n'a que trop régné ici' (*seems to help; the theatre turns attention away from gambling, from drinking, from the fights that have taken over for too long*), even adding that he thought it was prudent to expand the theatre's offerings by making it a permanent feature in the military town.[22]

The navy infused the project with a considerable amount of funding, justifying the expense not only as a means to keep officers and sailors away from 'vile occupations', such as frequenting the sex workers near the port, but also for forging beneficial relationships with Brest's bourgeois civilian population, which the navy relied upon for a host of duties and services, including armament and shipbuilding projects.[23] The navy financed and built the theatre in 1766, yet from a financial or a community-building perspective, its success was limited. Its paper trail, which is scattered across municipal archives and a regional outpost of the naval archives in Brest, a departmental archive in Quimper and the main Service Historique de la Défense in Vincennes, reveals a non-stop onslaught of requests for money, mandates to punish fighting in and outside the theatre, agreements to partition space in the auditorium among different companies and units to prevent discord and more. Documents about the Théâtre de la Marine portray a menacing performance environment where military presence often led to violence among sailors and complaints (and a refusal to purchase subscriptions) by the local civilian population. Of course, scholars should regard this type of medium with critical distance because the military, like any institution, never creates a flurry of documents when things are going well. Overreporting of bad behaviour is typical of this sort of documentation, as in the case of old-regime police reports—a methodological concern that, Lesueur, Ilya Berkovich, Jeffrey Ravel and other historians argue, leads to historiographical exaggeration.[24]

---

[22] Lettre de Roquefeuil à Choiseul du 8 décembre 1762. Services Historique de la Défense (SHD) 1 A 106, in Nolwenn Kerdraon-Duconte, 'Théâtre et pouvoir à Brest au XVIIIe siècle: Le costume et l'uniforme', *Annales de Bretagne et des Pays de l'Ouest*, 119.2 (2012), pp. 143–72 (148).

[23] Kerdraon-Duconte, 'Théâtre et pouvoir', 148.

[24] On the problem of overreporting in cases of desertion, see Lesueur, *Les Troupes coloniales*, 28; on the overreporting of bad behaviour among troops to justify tactical losses, see Ilya Berkovich, *Motivation in War:*

Of course, Brest's social, racial and economic features were starkly different from the situation in the colonial Caribbean. Any comparison between a western port in France and a colonial city where racial exclusion and violence undergirded nearly every aspect of society risks diluting or even normalizing the exceptional callousness of the colonial endeavour. However, the military–theatrical context in Brest will interest scholars of eighteenth-century Caribbean performance environments for at least two reasons: first, Brest is where many soldiers, sailors and officers were trained and stationed immediately before they arrived in the Caribbean colonies, and it stands to reason that soldiers and sailors did not shed every aspect of their identity when they sailed across the Atlantic Ocean. Indeed, it was in Brest where the men who massacred Mauduit-Duplessis trained and lived before they set sail for Saint-Domingue in 1791. Brest replaced Toulon as France's primary military port during the eighteenth century, mostly owing to an increase in naval incursions to the Atlantic and Caribbean before, during and immediately after the Seven Years' War (which added to the general increase in Caribbean activity resulting from the sugar boom and associated rise in the trade of enslaved peoples). Second, although the situation in Brest was not identical to that in Saint-Domingue, the flurry of paperwork surrounding the Théâtre de la Marine constitutes perhaps the most complete set of documents detailing the relationship between soldiers and eighteenth-century public theatre in the French-speaking world—and as such can be used to probe the Caribbean context as well. There are requests from soldiers to take the programming rights away from stage directors and give them directly to the military; documents from religious orders complaining about the new naval theatre; and of course, numerous requests for money.[25] These documents can help us better understand the culture of theatregoing in Le Cap where, as in Brest, Metz, Valenciennes and other *villes de garnison*, nights at the theatre were heavily populated and policed by members of the armed forces.

The Experience of Common Soldiers in Old-Regime Europe (Cambridge: Cambridge University Press, 2017), pp. 3–7; on the limits of police reports, see Jeffrey S. Ravel, *The Contested Parterre: Public Theatre and French Political Culture, 1680–1791* (Ithaca, NY and London: Cornell University Press, 1999), pp. 1–12.

[25] See Auguste-Aimé Kernéis, 'Contribution à l'Histoire de la ville et du port de Brest', *Société académique de Brest*, 36 (1912), pp. 97–285 (110); Bruno Baron, 'Élites, pouvoirs et vie municipale à Brest, 1750–1820' (PhD thesis, Université de Bretagne occidentale, 2012), p. 10; and Kerdraon-Duconte, 'Théâtre et pouvoir', 147–50.

There are limitations and drawbacks to comparing colonial theatres to French provincial venues such as the Naval Theatre in Brest. Colonial theatres were frequented by more civilian patrons (and many more patrons overall) than in Brest; as mentioned earlier, race was a pervasive exclusionary principle in colonial spaces but virtually absent in discussions of theatre in the French provinces;[26] and colonial playhouses, particularly the theatre in Le Cap, were far more complex in theatrical genre and aesthetically dynamic than in a military outpost such as Brest. However, as several scholars have demonstrated in their studies of eighteenth-century French theatre or military cultures, there exist several cultural, programmatic and managerial overlaps (as well as illustrative differences) between (mostly Atlantic) French port cities and the crown's Caribbean colonies.[27] These connections to the metropole in no way prevent scholarship on other links, such as those from the French Caribbean to other European powers (Spain, England, the Netherlands, etc.) or to the new United States of America. Moreover, the Brest link can complement other potential connections to France or even island-to-island overlaps, such as those between Saint-Domingue and Jamaica or Cuba—bonds that are arduous to reveal owing to the complexity of working across multiple archival traditions and languages—but bonds that would nevertheless centre eighteenth-century colonial studies in the Caribbean rather than in traditional metropolitan frames.

Military archives can reveal, connect, add and elaborate, but they can also conceal, camouflage and falsify. Archives are heterogeneous in their media: there are many different types of documents. The motivations behind military documentation, the reasons why documents exist, however, are relatively stable. Institutional archives

---

[26] 'Race' as such did not feature in discussions about theatre, but the massive capital earned from the colonial plantation complex and the slave trade contributed considerably to urban embellishment projects (including theatre building) in Nantes, Bordeaux, La Rochelle and other French cities, particularly on the Atlantic coast.

[27] See Clay's *Stagestruck* for a comparative discussion of theatre finances. For more information on the differences in religious concerts between Saint-Domingue and metropolitan France, see Andrei Pesic, 'The Flighty *Coquette* Sings on Easter Sunday: Music and Religion in Saint-Domingue, 1765–1789', French Historical Studies, 42.4 (2019), pp. 563–93; for several discussions on military cultures shared between provincial France and colonial spaces, see Christy Pichichero, *The Military Enlightenment: War and Culture in the French Empire from Louis XIV to Napoleon* (Ithaca, NY and London: Cornell University Press, 2017).

are produced by the administration to detail and describe military entities (enlistment roles, officer transfers, equipment inventories, building plans, etc.). There are documents to compel military personnel into acting or ceasing to act (rules, orders, sanctions, etc.) and there are complaints by officers addressed to their local commanders or from local commanders to Versailles. The objections, however, are usually narrow in scope, hesitant to address structural or pervasive issues and understandably optimistic about the military endeavour. The officer in question is part of the command structure and sensitive to the normative discourses and hierarchical nature of military life. Officer complainants are watchful of their tone and concerned about the reception of their requests because they are asking for something from a military superior. As Boris Lesueur reminds us, military documentation often produces a 'vision faussée' (*falsified vision*) of any issue pertaining to a soldier's life because of esprit de corps, political manoeuvring and fear of reprisals.[28] Scholars of military cultures should therefore embrace other types of writing as well in order to gain a more holistic picture of a soldier's experience.

Civilian commentaries and soldier memoirs

To better understand the goals, limits and scope of military–theatrical interactions in French colonies, it is essential to look to documents outside the institutional military archive. Civilian commentators and the personal writings of soldiers supplement the military archive, which understandably limits, curates and presents the military within a certain frame. The examples are again numerous, so the last part of this chapter is limited to two types of military media, each of which comment very differently on military influences and performances in colonial Saint-Domingue.

The first example comes from a series of *Réflexions, Descriptions* and other quasi-historical, quasi-anthropological accounts of life on the island. The most famous were penned by the Martinican lawyer and long-term resident of Saint-Domingue, Médéric Louis Élie Moreau de Saint-Méry, including his *Description topographique, physique, civile, politique et historique de la partie française de l'isle Saint-Domingue* and his *Loix et constitutions des colonies françoises de l'Amérique sous le Vent*.[29] Other long-form accounts of life on the island that comment on

---

[28] Lesueur, *Les Troupes coloniales*, 28.
[29] Médéric Louis Élie Moreau de Saint-Méry, *Description topographique*,

the military include Michel-René Hilliard d'Auberteuil's *Considérations sur l'état présent de la colonie française de Saint-Domingue* and Justin Girod de Chantrans's *Voyage d'un Suisse dans différentes colonies d'Amérique*, to name two.[30]

The advantage of these texts is that they are not penned by soldiers, but they are often about soldiers and can thus add to or contradict what the military writes about itself. In addition, they are most often written by or for 'outsiders', so the emphasis is on description and discovery. One particularly revealing example is Moreau de Saint-Méry's account of the performance space at the Comédie du Cap. The military is everywhere: in the seating arrangements, in the artwork on the ceiling and in plain view of virtually any spectator in the auditorium:

> Les deux premières loges du premier rang vers le théâtre, n'en forment qu'une de chaque côté; celle de la droite est pour le gouverneur-général, ceux qu'il y invite, ou les officiers de la garnison; celle de la gauche appartient à l'intendant, et les officiers d'administration s'y placent [...] Des 10 loges qui sont le plus au fond du troisième rang, sept reçoivent les mulâtresses et trois les négresses. Il y a le long du parterre trois loges grillées de chaque côté. En arrière de l'orchestre, on a pris sur le parterre de quoi former un banc de toute la largeur; c'est là que se met l'état-major de la place et des corps militaires. Le spectacle peut contenir 1,500 personnes. La salle qui était peinte en mosaïque jaune de Naples sur un fond bleu de roi, a été mis en 1784 en blanc cendré avec des panaux et des filets bleus, et l'on a ôté de deux en deux loges les piliers de bois et de forme carrée qui gênaient la vue [...] Les deux loges des Administrateurs ont sur le devant un tapis peint avec des attributs militaires ou de marine.[31]

---

physique, civile, politique et historique de la partie française de l'isle Saint-Domingue, 2 vols (Philadelphia, PA: Moreau de Saint-Méry, 1797); and *Loix et constitutions des colonies françoises de l'Amérique sous le Vent suivies d'un tableau raisonné des différentes parties de l'administration*, 6 vols (Paris: Moreau de Saint-Méry, 1784–90).

[30] Michel-René Hilliard d'Auberteuil, *Considérations sur l'état présent de la colonie française de Saint-Domingue. Ouvrage politique et législatif; Présenté au Ministre de la Marine*, 2 vols (Paris: Grangé, 1776–77); Justin Girod-Chantrans, *Voyage d'un Suisse dans différentes colonies d'Amérique pendant la dernière guerre, avec une table d'observations météorologiques faites à Saint-Domingue* (Neuchâtel: Société Typographique, 1785).

[31] Moreau de Saint-Méry, *Description topographique* 1, 361–62.

> *The first two boxes at the front of the theatre each have one only one entrance; the right one is for the Governor-General, his guests, or the officers from the barracks; the left one is for the* intendant, *and the administrative officers [also] sit there [...] Of the ten boxes at the back of the third row, seven are for mixed-race women* (mulâtresses) *and three are for black women* (négresses). *At the back of the pit there are three boxes behind grilles on each side. Behind the orchestra, space has been made in the pit to create a large row; placed there are the military leaders and the soldiers. The theatre can hold 1,500 people. The auditorium, which was painted in a Neapolitan yellow mosaic against a royal blue background, was redone in 1784 in an off-white colour with blue panelling, and the large wooden pillars that obstructed one's view were removed from the two-by-two boxes [...] The two administrative boxes are dressed by a painted curtain with military or naval attributes.*

Military influence added to the highly particular and exclusionary racial geography of the auditorium. Soldiers from metropolitan France—a contested force that locals both relied upon and resented—helped characterize anything one might call the 'theatrical experience' in colonial Saint-Domingue. Segregation from (what are assumed to be) white civilian theatre patrons—the very same patrons that soldiers were sent to the colonies to protect and help thrive—informed the experiences of civilian and soldier spectators alike.

Court proceedings, records and other civilian administrative sources also reveal the military's reach into the judicial, legislative and religious festivals and public ceremonies in the colonies. For example, in a court document reprinted in Moreau de Saint-Méry's *Loix et constitutions*, the clerk describes the complete military involvement in (and control of public performances and celebrations of) religious holidays and national events, such as a Corpus Christi procession in spring, 1769:

> La Procession s'est mise en marche; la Cour suivant immédiatement le S. Sacrement porté par le Préfet Apostolique et Curé; assisté de deux Vicaires; et était le Dais porté le côté gauche par deux Grenadiers de la Légion de Saint-Domingue, et le côté gauche par deux Grenadiers des Milices de cette Ville, les cordons d'icelui tenus par les deux Marguilliers en exercice, et les deux qui sont sortis de charge l'année dernière; la Compagnie de Grenadiers de ladite Légion, les Officiers à la tête, formant une haie à la droite, et la Compagnie des Grenadiers des Milices une haie à gauche du Dais, en dedans de laquelle étaient les Huissiers du Conseil marchant

sur deux files en avant de la Cour, et au milieu d'eux le premier Huissier sa baguette à la main; à la suite du Conseil marchait en même ordre le Siège Royal du Cap, pareillement entre deux haies de Soldats, prolongées en arrière par la Compagnie de Maréchaussée du Cap, et fermée par la Troupe de Police; marchaient en avant du S. Sacrement toutes les Troupes et Milices de la Ville sur deux haies, dans l'ordre suivant, La Légion de Saint-Domingue, les Gendarmes, les Carabiniers, les Dragons à pied, et les Compagnes des sieurs Papillon, Crebassa [...] à l'Église, a été chantée la Grand'Messe.

The procession set out; the court followed immediately after the holy sacrament, which was carried by the apostolic prefect and the priest with two curates assisting him. The [procession] canopy was carried by two grenadiers of the Legion of Saint-Domingue on its right side, and by two grenadiers of this town's militia on its left; its cords were held by the two current churchwardens along with the two who had exercised the charge last year; the grenadier company of said legion, their officers in front, formed a double line to the right, and the grenadier company of the militia a double line to the left of the canopy, inside which the Conseil's bailiffs marched in two lines in front of the court with the first bailiff, baton in hand, at their center. After the Conseil, the lower court of Le Cap marched in the same order, similarly between two double lines of soldiers, followed by the company of the maréchaussée *and finally by that of the police. In front of the holy sacrament, all of the troops of the town's militia marched in two double lines in the following order: the Legion of Saint-Domingue, the Gendarmes, the Carabiniers, the Foot Dragoons, and the companies of Sieurs Papillon, Crebassa [...] [in] the church, high mass was performed.*[32]

In this performance of power and intra-departmental cooperation, specific military units and grades are paired with representatives of the colony's governmental and religious institutions. The military initiates and endorses the celebration, controls the speed, order and the flow of people in a performance that symbolically sanctions the island's

[32] 'Procès-Verbal du Cérémonial, observé par le Conseil Supérieur du Cap, à la Procession et à l'Office du jour de la Fête-Dieu. 15 Mai 1769', in Moreau de Saint-Méry, *Loix et constitutions*, 5: 245–46; original trans. by Gene E. Ogle, in Ogle 'The Trans-Atlantic King and Imperial Public Spheres: Everyday Politics in Pre-Revolutionary Saint-Domingue', in David Patrick Geggus and Norman Fiering (eds), *The World of the Haitian Revolution* (Bloomington, IN: Indiana University Press, 2009), pp. 79–96.

civil and spiritual cultures. As Gene Ogle, Lauren Clay and others have demonstrated, the relationship between the military and the judiciary in Saint-Domingue was fraught, which makes this performance even more illustrative of the colony's anxieties and power strategies.[33] Although it is difficult to speculate about how this performance was received by residents, the procession proves that the military played an important role in religious life as well as in performances of the structural relationships between and among colonial institutions. In addition, and as with the military archive, the account of the Corpus Christi celebration confirms the erasure of black and mixed-race agency and bodies from (accounts of) representations of what were deemed at the time to be the most important collective celebratory experiences in the French colony.[34]

Lastly, there are military memoirs penned by soldiers who served in the colonial Caribbean, such as the text by de Rouville which introduced this chapter. It should be no surprise to learn that theatre features prominently in the colonial experiences of soldiers. For example, in his *Essai sur La Situation de Saint-Domingue à cette époque*, de Rouville details the urban planning of Port-au-Prince (where he spent most of his time) and of Cap-Français, to which he was often sent on mission. He describes the architecture of different theatres around the island, comparing that in Port-au-Prince, which he insists is 'fort simple' (*very simple*) and embedded into local white Creole culture and customs, with the one in Cap-Français, which he associates with Le Cap's metropolitan *French* political and military institutions.[35]

---

[33] Many colonists complained that soldiers were uncontrollable and that they basically had free range to do what they pleased. The most famous testimony of this was from Hilliard D'Auberteuil, who viewed the military's influence in Saint-Domingue as brutal, unnecessary and corrupt. He was constantly getting into trouble with soldiers, even claiming to have been beaten and 'left for dead' in 1772 by a group of officers, who were then investigated by colonial authorities (that is, officers) and found not guilty. See Gene E. Ogle, 'Natural Movements and Dangerous Spectacles: Beatings, Duels, and "Play" in Saint-Domingue', in John Smolenski and Thomas J. Humphrey (eds), *New World Orders: Violence, Sanction, and Authority in the Colonial Americas* (Philadelphia, PA: University of Pennsylvania, 2007), pp. 226–48 (238).

[34] This is not to say that enslaved and free people of colour did not participate in the event but that their presence was dismissed, downplayed and largely unrecorded in official documentation at the time.

[35] De Rouville, *Essai* in *Éloge historique*, 105. De Rouville added that the theatre in Port-au-Prince staged mostly *opéra-comiques* and other musical works, given that 'ces sortes de pièces' were 'les seules estimées à cause

De Rouville's narration of violent intra-military performances in the assassination of Mauduit-Duplessis provides an alternative reading to the organized, grandiose, deliberate performances of civil–martial solidarity and spectacle in the eyewitness reports from earlier decades. Although both texts ground colonial experiences in events occurring to—and perpetuated by—exclusively white participants, the orderly lines, collaboration and orchestrated turn-taking of different units, grades and squadrons in the Corpus Christi celebration devolve into the violent chaos of a revolutionary moment in de Rouville's account. By 1791, residents of Port-au-Prince were witness to a procession of enlisted soldiers dragging the body of the aristocratic Mauduit-Duplessis down the street, the colonel's head leading the way on a pike that the soldiers used to threaten any sympathizers of the nobility left in the military ranks. The cortege then arrives at the bottom of a hill near the harbour, and Mauduit-Duplessis's corpse is 'turned over' to a crowd of local women. One of the women, the wife of a fisherman, sits on the headless colonel's chest, takes out a fishing knife, cuts off the 'marks of his virility' and triumphantly marches away with them in her hand.[36] French soldiers inflicting harm and fear on other French soldiers and class war carried out within the military—a supposed 'band of brothers'—this is a very different military procession, performance and representation from what is recounted in institutional military archives. Mauduit-Duplessis's gruesome death obviously did not make it into official obituaries, which concentrate on his valour during the American Revolution when, as a young engineer and friend of George Washington, he instigated the strategic reconfiguration of Fort Mercer (New Jersey) and helped defeat the Hessian forces at Red Bank.[37]

de la musique que les créoles aiment passionnément' (*those kinds of works [were] the only ones wanted because of the music, which the Creoles love with passion*) (106).

[36] De Rouville, *Éloge historique*, 41–42.

[37] See the 'Map and Description of Fort Mercer, Red Bank, Gloucester County, New Jersey', *Encyclopedia of Greater Philadelphia/Library of Congress*. https://philadelphiaencyclopedia.org/. The death scene in de Rouville's text also differs from Marsollier de Vivetières's play, in which the colonel perishes with dignity (and after many proclamations) when wounded by several mutinous soldiers (Marsollier de Vivetières, *La Mort du Colonel Mauduit*, 8.32–33).

Archiving the repertoire

Not all colonial performances were influenced by military culture, and it is essential not to overrepresent military–theatrical interactions merely because it was the goal of this chapter to find them. There are facts that call into question the potency and pervasiveness of the military-theatrical complex such as the cost of boxes at the theatre, which were prohibitively expensive for many officers.[38] Other mitigating factors include the reality that the majority of (but not all) theatre directors and theatre journalists were civilians;[39] that the white Creole population, which was often antagonistic to the military, was at the origin of many theatrical projects on the island; and, most essentially, that there were numerically more civilians (including women) than soldiers at the theatre. The military's actual role in theatrical life is difficult to qualify or quantify, and we should not overemphasize its imprint merely because the armed forces were particularly adept at writing things down. Those caveats aside, it is clear from many kinds of documents that the relationship between the military and public theatre or the military and public performances and festivals was different in French Caribbean colonies than in metropolitan France, and especially in Paris. Members of the military constituted an important subsection of colonial theatre audiences. Soldiers and sailors in Saint-Domingue were often far from the places they considered home, and thus attended performances and events on the island while on active duty. This was unlike the situation in Paris, for example, where many military men at theatres would have been on leave and/or far from the battle front, and thereby (re)inserted into civilian circles, social groups and metropolitan behavioural norms.[40]

From an empirical position, military documents provide data. They help describe how theatres were funded on the island and they may

---

[38] Lesueur, *Les Troupes coloniales*, 255.

[39] Laurence Marie notes, however, that the Spectacles column was probably edited between 1768 and 1771 by Henri Duchemin-Despaletz, a former lieutenant in the Quercy Cavalry Regiment. See Laurence Marie, 'Writing about Theatre in Saint-Domingue (1766–1791): A Public Voice on a Public Space?', in Jeffrey M. Leichman and Karine Bénac-Giroux (eds), *Colonialism and Slavery in Performance: Theatre and the Eighteenth-Century French Caribbean*, Oxford University Studies in the Enlightenment (Liverpool: Liverpool University Press, 2021), pp. 139–65 (140).

[40] This is not to say that Parisian theatre audiences were docile, but that the professional demographics of male spectators in Paris were very different from the colonial context.

complicate purely market-driven rationales of eighteenth-century theatre management.[41] Military documents can also help reveal the power networks (and their associated tensions) that were at play in French colonies, and they provide new comparative frameworks for studying theatrical life at the time. Rather than viewing theatres in Port-au-Prince, Léogane or Cap-Français as inferior but emulative models of Parisian tastes and practices, military documents can speak to the specificity of colonial theatrical experiences. What is more, military documents can illuminate other flows of theatre professionals and dramatic texts: the comparison mentioned earlier, Brest–Le Cap, but potentially, with further inquiry, Bordeaux–Port-au Prince, Brest–Le Cap–Port-au-Prince, Kingston–Le Cap or Saint-Pierre–Havana, to name just a few.

From a critical perspective, military documents provide information on the colonial theatrical archive—the 'supposedly enduring materials' that build knowledge about theatrical practices, institutions and relationships during the violent years of French colonialism in the Caribbean. They provide evidence of a concerted effort to uphold, foster and police predominantly white-centric colonial practices and experiences such as public theatre, as well as the associated assumptions, tensions and impossibilities inherent to those processes. Documents from military sources, as well as those written by civilians, provide glimpses of 'embodied memory'—a 'repertoire' of performances, gestures, orality, movement and practices that often elude the institutional archives and traditional historiographies of both colonial theatre and colonial military practices.[42] Accounts of social performances and embodied acts at the time can be put into dialogue with institutional archives and other sources to reveal a more holistic vision of theatre and performance, and of their articulations with power, coloniality, repression and violence in the eighteenth-century Caribbean.[43]

---

[41] Military documents may soften the more rigorous claims of commercial pressure and financial bottom lines that have been made recently by Lauren Clay or Andrei Pesic, for example.

[42] Taylor, *Archive and the Repertoire*, 20.

[43] Combining archival information with testimony on the performances of soldiers can help enable us construct something like a colonial military–theatrical séance (to borrow Christian Biet's term)—a device that binds certain groups and identities to the same physical space and at least some of the same experiences and stimuli while also highlighting their differences, tensions and anxieties. See Christian Biet, 'Séance, performance, assemblée et représentation: Les jeux de regards au théâtre (XVIIe–XXIe siècle)', *Littératures classiques*, 82.3 (2013), pp. 79–97.

In conclusion, more analysis of military–theatrical overlaps will dislodge eighteenth-century French theatre studies from normative models of theatrical experience, such as the ones espoused by Enlightenment *philosophes* at the time, which, through an implied ideal spectatorial experience and a persistent emphasis on dramatic textuality, continue to this day.[44] Military documents show that French colonies, and especially Saint-Domingue, boasted rich theatrical cultures that were both encouraged and complicated by a high concentration of soldiers and sailors. Military documents reveal eager soldier-spectators and grandiose displays of military might, but also deeply aggressive performance environments, an exclusionary society with racism embedded into every theatrical (and non-theatrical) practice, intense rivalries among theatre patrons and between mixed-race and white military units, and violent performances of military brutality and disaccord. These tensions combined with other features of colonial life to constitute the performance ecosystem of eighteenth-century Saint-Domingue. Overall, this line of inquiry decentres French theatre studies from Paris's state-sponsored venues and exposes several of the most important power relations and social anxieties that informed and complicated any sort of collective performance experience in the French colonial Caribbean.

Bibliography

Baron, Bruno. 'Élites, pouvoirs et vie municipale à Brest, 1750–1820' (PhD thesis, Université de Bretagne occidentale, 2012).

Bennett, Susan. *Theatre Audiences: A Theory of Production and Reception* (New York: Routledge, 1997).

Berkovich, Ilya. *Motivation in War: The Experience of Common Soldiers in Old-Regime Europe* (Cambridge: Cambridge University Press, 2017).

Biet, Christian. 'Séance, performance, assemblée et représentation: Les jeux de regards au théâtre (XVIIe–XXIe siècle)', *Littératures classiques*, 82.3 (2013), pp. 79–97.

---

[44] Eyewitness testimony of military behaviours and practices in the theatre support criticism of the link between ideal spectatorship and a largely white, heterosexual, male-centred perspective. For more information on this line of inquiry see, among others, Judith Mayne, *Cinema and Spectatorship* (New York: Routledge, 1993); see also Susan Bennett, *Theatre Audiences: A Theory of Production and Reception* (New York: Routledge, 1997).

Cheney, Paul. *Cul de Sac: Patrimony, Capitalism, and Slavery in French Saint-Domingue* (Chicago and London: University of Chicago Press, 2017).

Clay, Lauren R. *Stagestruck: The Business of Theater in Eighteenth-Century France and its Colonies* (Ithaca, NY and London: Cornell University Press, 2013).

Delafosse de Rouville. *Éloge historique du Chevalier Mauduit-Duplessis, suivi d'un Essai sur La Situation de Saint-Domingue à cette époque* (Senlis: Tremblay, 1817).

Fouchard, Jean. *Le théâtre à Saint-Domingue* (Port-au-Prince: Imprimerie de l'État, 1955).

Girod-Chantrans, Justin. *Voyage d'un Suisse dans différentes colonies d'Amérique pendant la dernière guerre, avec une table d'observations météorologiques faites à Saint-Domingue* (Neuchâtel: Société Typographique, 1785).

Hilliard d'Auberteuil, Michel-René. *Considérations sur l'état présent de la colonie française de Saint-Domingue. Ouvrage politique et législatif; Présenté au Ministre de la Marine*, 2 vols (Paris: Grangé, 1776–77).

Kerdraon-Duconte, Nolwenn. 'Théâtre et pouvoir à Brest au XVIIIe siècle: Le costume et l'uniforme', *Annales de Bretagne et des Pays de l'Ouest*, 119.2 (2012), pp. 143–72.

Kernéis, Auguste-Aimé, 'Contribution à l'Histoire de la ville et du port de Brest', *Société académique de Brest*, 36 (1912), pp. 97–285.

Lesueur, Boris. *Les Troupes coloniales d'Ancien Régime: Fidetilate per Mare et Terras* (Paris: SPM Kronos, 2014).

Lesueur, Boris. 'Les troupes coloniaux aux Antilles sous l'Ancien Régime', *Histoire, Économie et Société*, 28.4 (2009), pp. 3–19.

'Map and Description of Fort Mercer, Red Bank, Gloucester County, New Jersey', *Encyclopedia of Greater Philadelphia/Library of Congress*, https://philadelphiaencyclopedia.org/

Marie, Laurence. 'Writing about Theatre in Saint-Domingue (1766–1791): A Public Voice on a Public Space?', in Jeffrey M. Leichman and Karine Bénac-Giroux (eds), *Colonialism and Slavery in Performance: Theatre and the Eighteenth-Century French Caribbean*, Oxford University Studies in the Enlightenment (Liverpool: Liverpool University Press, 2021), pp. 139–65.

Marsollier de Vivetières, Benoît-Joseph. *La Mort du Colonel Mauduit ou Les Anarchistes au Port-au-Prince, fait historique en un acte et en prose* (Paris: Cailleau, 1800).

Mayne, Judith. *Cinema and Spectatorship* (New York: Routledge, 1993).

McClellan, James E. *Colonialism and Science: Saint Domingue and the Old Regime* (Chicago: University of Chicago Press, 1992; 2010).

Moreau de Saint-Méry, Médéric Louis Élie. *Description topographique, physique, civile, politique et historique de la partie française de l'isle Saint-Domingue*, 2 vols (Philadelphia, PA: Moreau de Saint-Méry, 1797).

Moreau de Saint-Méry, Médéric Louis Élie. *Loix et constitutions des colonies françoises de l'Amérique sous le Vent suivies d'un tableau raisonné des différentes parties de l'administration*, 6 vols (Paris: Moreau de Saint-Méry, 1784–90).

Ogle, Gene E. 'Natural Movements and Dangerous Spectacles: Beatings, Duels, and "Play" in Saint-Domingue', in John Smolenski and Thomas J. Humphrey (eds), *New World Orders: Violence, Sanction, and Authority in the Colonial Americas* (Philadelphia, PA: University of Pennsylvania Press, 2007), pp. 226–48.

Ogle, Gene E. 'The Trans-Atlantic King and Imperial Public Spheres: Everyday Politics in Pre-Revolutionary Saint-Domingue', in David Patrick Geggus and Norman Fiering (eds), *The World of the Haitian Revolution* (Bloomington, IN: Indiana University Press, 2009), pp. 79–96.

Pesic, Andrei. 'The Flighty *Coquette* Sings on Easter Sunday: Music and Religion in Saint-Domingue, 1765–1789', *French Historical Studies*, 42.4 (2019), pp. 563– 93.

Pichichero, Christy. *The Military Enlightenment: War and Culture in the French Empire from Louis XIV to Napoleon* (Ithaca, NY and London: Cornell University Press, 2017).

Powers, David M. *From Plantation to Paradise? Cultural Politics and Musical Theatre in French Slave Colonies, 1764–1789* (East Lansing, MI: Michigan State, 2014).

Prospectus pour l'Année 1776, 1984, Archives nationales d'outre-mer (ANOM) COL F3 160 F10 F21.

Ravel, Jeffrey S. *The Contested Parterre: Public Theatre and French Political Culture, 1680–1791* (Ithaca, NY and London: Cornell University Press, 1999).

Scott, James C. *Seeing Like a State: How Certain Schemes to Improve the Human Condition Have Failed* (New Haven, CT and London: Yale University Press, 1998).

Stoler, Ann Laura. 'Colonial Archives and the Arts of Governance', *Archival Science*, 2 (2002), pp. 87–109.

Tableau des tous les officiers des troupes du Roy dans les Isles du Vent de l'Amérique, Archives nationales (AN), D2A 18 (1741).

Taylor, Diana. *The Archive and the Repertoire: Performing Cultural Memory in the Americas* (Durham, NC and London: Duke University Press, 2003).

Tribout de Morembert, Henri. *Le théâtre à Metz* (Paris: Publications de la société d'histoire du théâtre, 1952).

Nine

Uncovering Connections between Theatre and Slavery: Runaway Advertisements in Colonial Saint-Domingue and Beyond

Julia Prest

Scholars of colonial-era Caribbean theatre have tended not to engage deeply with the links between public theatre and the local enslaved population. This is for a number of reasons. One such is that these links are not always immediately apparent: advertisements in newspapers announcing upcoming performances in the local playhouses (a staple diet for many of us) make almost no mention of the contributions, direct or indirect, that enslaved people made to these performances. This, perhaps unwittingly, has led to the somewhat circular claim that sources dealing with such matters are almost entirely lacking. Another reason for the disinclination to engage with enslaved people in colonial-era theatre research is that they are often seen, somewhat conveniently, as peripheral to matters theatrical—part of the background against which public theatre unfolded rather than as an integral part of that story. This, in turn, allows scholars to avoid the uncomfortable topic of slave 'ownership' among theatremakers. Theatremakers are supposed to be decent people, a force for good—or, at least, definitely *not* a force for harm. Instead, the undeniably important—and more comfortable—topic of enslaved characters in theatrical works is popular among scholars, as evidenced, for example, in the number of chapters dealing with enslaved characters in a recent, important, edited volume entitled *Colonialism and Slavery in Performance*.[1]

I contend, however, that it is the duty of theatre scholars specializing in the colonial-era Caribbean (and other slave societies) to engage with—and actively seek—connections between the enslaved population and theatre practice, and that these connections *can* be uncovered, at

---

[1] Jeffrey M. Leichman and Karine Bénac-Giroux (eds), *Colonialism and Slavery in Performance: Theatre and the Eighteenth-Century French Caribbean*, Oxford University Studies in the Enlightenment (Liverpool: Liverpool University Press, 2021).

least to some degree, with some shifts in approach and methodology. In my monograph, *Public Theatre and the Enslaved People of Colonial Saint-Domingue*, I seek to put enslaved people at the centre of the story, rather than leaving them half-glimpsed and barely heard at its periphery.[2] Sometimes this can be done by returning to more familiar theatre sources ready to see what is barely there; sometimes it requires rereading them alongside, and in conversation with, less familiar, non-theatrical sources. At other times, as Saidiya Hartman points out, the process demands a different response: that we 'imagine what cannot be verified'.[3] In this chapter I explore the potential, as well as the limitations, when researching links between theatre and real-life slavery, of one particular source type that is found across the colonial Caribbean and contemporary slave societies (particularly in the USA): the runaway advertisement.

The runaway advertisement

What is a runaway (or fugitive) advertisement (or notice) and how can it be approached by the modern scholar seeking to uncover the lives of enslaved people? Runaway advertisements appeared regularly in local, colonial newspapers under headings such as *Esclaves en mar[r]onage* (maroon/runaway slaves) or *Runaway*, sometimes with a reward prominently displayed.[4] Advertisements served to announce publicly the news of an enslaved person's disappearance by or on behalf of the slave 'owner', to dissuade others from harbouring or otherwise helping the fugitive, and to invite their capture and return. It is deeply ironic, then, that a print form seeking to reassert individual runaways as dehumanized property should provide some of the most detailed and, if one reads between the lines, humanized descriptions of those

---

[2] Cham: Palgrave Macmillan, 2023.

[3] Saidiya Hartman, 'Venus in Two Acts', *Small Axe*, 12.2 (June 2008), pp. 1–14 (12). She proposes this method as a means to writing a 'critical fabulation' (11). For an excellent example of a critical fabulation, see Marisa J. Fuentes, *Dispossessed Lives: Enslaved Women, Violence, and the Archive* (Philadelphia: University of Pennsylvania Press, 2016), Chapter One.

[4] Hunt-Kennedy points out that in the Anglophone press (though not in Saint-Domingue), these advertisements were often accompanied by an image of an able-bodied black man moving quickly, carrying a stick: Stefanie Hunt-Kennedy, *Between Fitness and Death: Disability and Slavery in the Caribbean* (Urbana, Chicago and Springfield: University of Illinois Press, 2020), pp. 106–08.

individuals in existence. Advertisements for runaways usually include a first name, and I shall return to the question of names below. They often include the approximate age and supposed ethnic origins of the individual and sometimes other physical details. Alongside an approximate height, build is sometimes mentioned as well as other features that might help identify the individual in question. These might include 'country marks' (scars resulting from initiation practices and other rituals in the individual's community in Africa) as well as scarring, disfigurements or disabilities that will have resulted, in most instances, from accidents and punishments. Many advertisements include details of the enslaved individual's linguistic abilities,[5] and/or of any special skills that they might have had, including musical talent (especially on the violin) or a trade such as carpentry. Some include details of what the person was wearing when they ran away and of what they took with them.

The following advertisement is fairly typical of those found in Saint-Domingue in the last quarter of the eighteenth century:

> Un Negre créole, nommé *Pierre-Michel*, âgé de 22 ans, taille de 5 pieds 3 à 4 pouces, parlant François, étampé sur le sein droit FOUGERIT, est parti maron du 10 au 12 du mois dernier. Ceux qui le reconnoîtront, sont priés de le faire arrêter & d'en donner avis au Sieur *Fougerit*, Charpentier du Roi, au Cap, à qui ce Negre appartient.[6]

> *A Creole* nègre *called* Pierre-Michel, *aged 22 years, five foot three to four inches tall, speaks French, branded FOUGERIT on his right breast, ran away between 10th and 12th of last month. Those who recognize him are asked to have him detained and to inform M. Fougerit, King's Carpenter, in Le Cap, to whom this* nègre *belongs.*[7]

---

[5] Writing about the US context, Waldstreicher notes that multilingual slaves were the most successful at escaping: David Waldstreicher, 'Reading the Runaways: Self-Fashioning, Print Culture and Confidence in Slavery in the Eighteenth-Century Mid-Atlantic', *William and Mary Quarterly*, 56.2 (April 1999), pp. 243–72 (259).

[6] *Affiches américaines* (4 September 1782), p. 334.

[7] In my translations of runaway advertisements I have chosen to retain the French term *nègre* (and *négresse*) owing to its ambiguity of meaning (the word usually designated an enslaved person but could also be used to designate a person of African ancestry), but above all to draw attention to—and not elide—the violence inherent in the language of these

Fundamentally, of course, these advertisements were tools of colonial (re-)enslavement, but how exactly did this work? It is understood that the majority of fugitives returned to their 'masters' after a few days or were recaptured without recourse to such advertisements.[8] Running away for a short period of time (sometimes known in French as *petit marronnage*) was a common occurrence and distinct from the long-term *grand marronnage* of more established maroon communities that formed, for instance, in the mountainous areas of Jamaica and Saint-Domingue, among other places. In Saint-Domingue the rural police force, known as the *maréchaussée* and composed mostly of free people of colour, was constantly on the lookout for runaways and needed no prompting from special advertisements. Our source type thus documents the relatively small number of individuals who were able—and who chose—to place such advertisements in the public space of the local, colonial newspaper. It also documents a small proportion of enslaved individuals who were able (at least for a short time)—and who chose—to take matters into their own hands and seek their own freedom by running away or, to put it another way, freeing themselves. The bravery that it took to do this should not be underestimated given the likelihood of recapture and the punishments that were meted out, particularly for those who ran away for more than a few days.[9]

Jean-Pierre Le Glaunec has suggested that the function of the runaway advertisement was also to reassert, in print, the master–slave relationship, and especially its racially informed power differential, in response to a clear challenge to that relationship: this person belongs to me—and remains within my control—even though they have run away temporarily (or, from the point of view of the colonial reader, even if my slaves also run away temporarily, they will remain my property

---

advertisements. This is in line with Thomas's suggestions in Chapter Three of this volume.

[8] Jean-Pierre Le Glaunec, 'Précisions/imprécisions, ou comment re-présenter l'esclave en fuite', *Écrire l'histoire: Histoire, littérature, esthétique*, 3 (2009), pp. 23–33 (24) and Jonathan Prude, 'To Look Upon the "Lower Sort": Runaway Ads and the Appearance of Unfree Laborers in America, 1750–1800', *The Journal of American History*, 78.1 (June 1991), pp. 124–59 (129).

[9] These punishments were explicitly set out in the French slave code known as the 'Code Noir' (originally 1685). See Bernard Moitt, *Women and Slavery in the French Antilles, 1635–1848* (Bloomington and Indianapolis: Indiana University Press, 2001), pp. 16, 102, 105, 133, 137–39 and 175 for examples of actual punishments meted out in the 'French' Caribbean.

and within my control).[10] A rhetorical re-enslavement. Michel-Rolph Trouillot notes that these discrete advertisements about individuals also served to deny the possibility that running away—or freeing oneself—could be a mass phenomenon. As he puts it, 'to acknowledge resistance as a mass phenomenon is to acknowledge the possibility that something is wrong with the system'.[11]

Some scholars understand these advertisements to be early slave narratives,[12] while Le Glaunec reads them not just as narratives, but also as 'interconnected short stories' and even 'short, though incomplete, biographies'.[13] In his view, the enslaved individual's presence in print sits in tension with their absence from the master's house or plantation.[14] As a print genre, as David Waldstreicher observes, the advertisements were pivotal in the close reciprocal relationship that was established between print (in this case newspapers) and enslavement: each kept the other in business.[15] The advertisements also provide clues about who ran away and why. They often feature newly arrived slaves or enslaved people who have recently been sold to a new 'master'. Enslaved people often ran away in an attempt to maintain ties of family, kin or shipmates.[16] Although it is inseparable from the violence of its ultimate purpose, this level of detail offers some important insights into the lives of some individuals who would otherwise slip through the record. The advertisements are, of course, biased in form, content and purpose, but when read carefully they can yield important information and hint at more.[17] They provide glimpses into the lives and experiences of a group of people who were so often denied their humanity as well as their voice and place in the record. Fuentes rightly cautions against overascribing

---

[10] Jean-Pierre Le Glaunec, *Esclaves mais résistants dans le monde des annonces pour esclaves en fuite: Louisiane, Jamaïque, Caroline du Sud (1801–1815)* (Paris: Karthala/CIRESC, 2021), pp. 33, 182 and 185–95.

[11] Michel-Rolph Trouillot, *Silencing the Past: Power and the Production of History* (Boston, MA: Beacon Press, 2015), p. 84.

[12] Waldstreicher, 'Reading the Runaways', 271.

[13] Jean-Pierre Le Glaunec, '"Writing the Runaways": Descriptions, Inscriptions and Narrations in the Runaway Slave "Advertisements" in *Le Moniteur de la Louisiane*, 1802–1814', *Cahiers Charles V*, 39 (December 2005), pp. 205–36 (227, 229 and 230). For Le Glaunec, enslaved runaways are storytellers writing their own narratives by running away (231).

[14] Le Glaunec, 'Writing the Runaways', 212.

[15] Waldstreicher, 'Reading the Runaways', 268.

[16] Le Glaunec, 'Writing the Runaways', 215 and 217.

[17] For a good example of a rereading of such an advertisement in light of other sources, see Waldstreicher, 'Reading the Runaways', 265–68.

agency and resistance to enslaved people as a matter of course.[18] But the act of leaving one's 'master' is clear evidence of some personal agency and of non-compliance with local systems of slavery—and the unequal power relations on which that system depended—despite the considerable personal risks involved.[19] Fugitive slaves thus occupy a fascinating grey area somewhere between enslavement and freedom.

Runaway databases

One of the first scholars to make possible more widespread engagement with these advertisements was Lathan A. Windley who, in 1983, published a four-volume compilation of runaway advertisements from colonial Virginia, *Runaway Slave Advertisements: A Documentary History from the 1730s to 1790*.[20] This was followed by other, similar publications dealing with other regions, including *Blacks Who Stole Themselves: Advertisements for Runaways in the Pennsylvania Gazette, 1728–1790*,[21] and *'Pretends to Be Free': Runaway Slave Advertisements from Colonial and Revolutionary New York and New Jersey*.[22] The digital age has seen a small explosion of online database projects also relating primarily to the United States of America. These include the North Carolina Runaway Slave Notices, 1750–1865 database,[23] the Texas Runaway Slave Project,[24] the Geography of Slavery in Virginia database,[25] and the Documenting Runaway Slaves project, which looks at Mississippi newspapers from

---

[18] Fuentes, *Dispossessed Lives*, 9–10.

[19] Crystal Nicole Eddins argues that in Saint-Domingue these advertisements provide evidence of a 'liberation consciousness' before the Revolution: see her article 'Runaways, Repertoires, and Repression', *Journal of Haitian Studies*, 25.1 (Spring 2019), pp. 4–38.

[20] Lathan A. Windley, *Runaway Slave Advertisements: A Documentary History from the 1730s to 1790* (Westport, CT: Greenwood, 1983).

[21] Billy G. Smith and Richard Wojtowicz (eds), *Blacks Who Stole Themselves: Advertisements for Runaways in the Pennsylvania Gazette, 1728–1790* (Philadelphia: University of Pennsylvania Press, 1989).

[22] Graham Russell Hodges and Alan Edward Brown (eds), *'Pretends to Be Free': Runaway Slave Advertisements from Colonial and Revolutionary New York and New Jersey* (New York: Taylor and Francis, 1994; 2019). For a full survey of these publications and their particular approaches to the material, see Le Glaunec, *Esclaves mais résistants*, 15–21.

[23] <http://libcdm1.uncg.edu/cdm/landingpage/collection/RAS>; follow 'NC slave notices' icon.

[24] <https://digital.sfasu.edu/digital/collection/RSP>.

[25] <http://www2.vcdh.virginia.edu/gos/>.

1790–1860.[26] Outside the USA and on a much smaller scale, there is the Runaway Slaves in Britain website and database, which covers a small corpus from the period 1700–1780.[27] To my knowledge, there were no print datasets or online databases dealing with the Caribbean context until the welcome appearance of www.marronnage.info, launched in 2009 and initially devoted to advertisements from Saint-Domingue between 1766 and 1791. The site was later expanded to include some announcements pertaining to Guadeloupe, Louisiana, South Carolina, Jamaica, French Guiana and Lower Canada and renamed *Le marronnage dans le monde atlantique: sources et trajectoires de vie*.

Ideally, scholars seeking to uncover the lives of enslaved people by means of newspaper advertisements for runaways would, of course, work through the newspapers in question one by one, page by page, in digital or print form. This method would ensure the best chance of identifying all relevant announcements; it would also give the researcher a more complete sense of the broader context in which the announcements were made. For scholars of the theatre, it is important not just to know, but also to see (and experience) that the announcements about upcoming theatre performances appear in the same publication as announcements about runaways. This tells us that both types of advertisements were likely to be of interest to—and read by—many of the same readers. In other words, many people who were interested in what was going to be performed at the local theatre were also interested in news of enslaved runaways. It is also enlightening to see what else people would have been reading and thinking about on the same day.[28]

Reading the whole newspaper, or at least reading theatre announcements alongside runaway announcements, can also—with some prior knowledge or some careful cross-referencing—reveal links between theatremaking and slave 'ownership'. Many of the theatremakers who announced upcoming performances, notably benefit performances that they organized independently of the standard subscription performances, also submitted runaway notices. Occasionally their theatre

[26] <http://runawayslaves.usm.edu/about.html>.
[27] <https://www.runaways.gla.ac.uk>.
[28] Le Glaunec notes that in *Le Moniteur de la Louisiane*, new announcements for runaways appeared on the second page of the newspaper (and sometimes also the third), straight after the insert featuring upcoming performances at the theatre in New Orleans. Similarly, the second page of the *Courrier de la Louisiane* included announcements about upcoming balls and plays alongside new runaway announcements (*Esclaves mais résistants*, 43 and 45).

announcements and runaway advertisements even appeared in the same edition of the newspaper, as happened on 13 December 1786. On the front page of this edition, we read:

> Les Comédiens du Cap donneront, Samedi 16 du courant, au bénéfice du sieur Dubuisson, LA BELLE ARSENE, opéra en quatre actes, musique de *Monsigny*, dans lequel madame *Marsan* remplira le rôle de *la Belle Arsene*: on ne négligera rien pour rendre ce spectacle aussi brillant qu'il est susceptible de l'être.[29]

> *The actors of Le Cap will perform, on Saturday 16th of this month, for the benefit of Sieur Dubuisson, LA BELLE ARSENE, an opera in four acts with music by* Monsigny, *in which Madame* Marsan *will take the role of* la Belle Arsène. *Nothing will be spared in order to make this spectacle as brilliant as it can be.*

Three pages later, the second item in the 'Esclaves en marronage' list reads:

> *Michel & Janvier*, de la taille de 5 pieds, étampés AF, sont partis marrons dans la nuit du 7 au 8 du courant, ayant emporté quatre avirons étampés V. En donner avis à M. *Dubuisson*, comédien au Cap, à qui ils appartiennent.[30]

> Michel and Janvier, *five feet tall, branded AF, ran away the night of 7th to 8th of this month, taking with them four oars marked V. Notify* M. Dubuisson, *actor in Le Cap, to whom they belong.*

The fact that Dubuisson submitted both a theatre announcement and a runaway announcement to the same edition of the newspaper tells us that the actor and fireworkmaker was thinking about his upcoming performance of *La Belle Arsène* at the same time that he was thinking about Michel and Janvier. The fact that Dubuisson explicitly identifies himself in the runaway advertisement as an actor and slave 'owner' also underscores the inseparability of slave 'ownership' and theatremaking in the colony, even if Michel and Janvier laboured not as Dubuisson's domestic servants but, more probably, on his charcoal processor or at another labour-intensive operation.[31]

---

[29] *Supplément aux affiches américaines* (13 December 1786), p. 577.
[30] *Supplément aux affiches américaines* (13 December 1786), p. 580.
[31] See *Supplément aux affiches américaines* (5 April 1786), p. 177.

Although desirable, reading the entire run of a newspaper is extremely time-consuming, and therefore not always possible. A searchable online database such as www.marronnage.info enables researchers to find valuable information quickly (or sometimes to confirm a lack of information), and this option does not preclude then reading the relevant advertisements in context in the newspaper itself. For theatre researchers interested in Saint-Domingue, some of the information found in www.marronnage.info can be cross-referenced with the performance database www.theatreinsaintdominge.org, which is based on theatre announcements from the same newspapers: the *Affiches américaines* and its sister publication, the *Supplément aux affiches américaines*, both of which are available in digital format via the Digital Library of the Caribbean and the University of Florida (the print version is held in the Bibliothèque de France).[32] The trick is to learn how to get the most out of each database in the first place. After some experimentation using www.marronnage.info, I found, for instance, that the best way of finding the highest number of enslaved people with certain names was to use the search box for words included in the advertisement rather than the search box for names. Users of the *Marronnage dans le monde atlantique* database can search by words featuring in the advertisement, by name, sex, colony or state, by newspaper and date range, or (when everything is working smoothly) a combination of these parameters. Results (which also include lists of recaptured slaves—or 'jail lists'—when these are available), are given in chronological order and include, for the majority of sources, both machine-readable transcriptions of the originals and high-quality, downloadable JPEGs of the relevant portion of the source.

Names given to enslaved people

Researchers engaging with runaway advertisements quickly become aware of the range of names given to enslaved people. As outlined by Vincent Cousseau, the naming of enslaved people in the colonial Caribbean was a complex phenomenon.[33] For him, plantation lists represent the most full and accurate source of information about names that were used by

---

[32] <https://www.theatreinsaintdominge.org> also draws on some additional newspapers.
[33] Vincent Cousseau, 'Nommer l'esclave dans la Caraïbe XVIIe–XVIIIe siècles', *Annales de démographie historique*, 131 (2016), pp. 37–63.

colonials on a daily basis.[34] In these and other colonial records, enslaved people have a personal name—and sometimes two personal names—but never a family name. The absence of a family name served to weaken family ties by rendering them invisible in the record. Enslaved people born in Africa will have been named there, usually with an African name but sometimes, in 'Christianized' regions, with a Christian name.[35] African-born people will have then been allocated a new name or set of new names by colonials at various points in their life: usually, on their arrival in the Caribbean; if and when they were baptized; and, sometimes, when they passed from one owner to another. The majority of enslaved people born in the Caribbean will have been named by their 'master' (or his representative) at birth. Many members of both groups subsequently acquired additional, semi-official names that have also made their way into plantation records and runaway advertisements—often these are nicknames or diminutives aimed at distinguishing between people with the same name working alongside one another.

The repeated act of naming, officially and unofficially, was a repeated reassertion of the master's control over the enslaved person; it also explains why in some of the runaway advertisements we find two different names for a single person, as will be seen below. Generally, the name given in a runaway advertisement is the name by which the enslaved person is known *by the person placing the advertisement*—a common name used in the context of the enslaved person's labour. In practice, most, perhaps all, enslaved people will have been known, at least by some of their circle, by an additional common name—a chosen personal name that does not feature in the written record.[36]

Cousseau classifies the main types of common names that do appear in the records in four main categories: birth or baptismal names such as Julie or Pierre; diminutives (for example, Nanette or Jeannot); names indicating a person's origin (perhaps an African name or a name associated with an ethnic group, such as Sama, or with a place, such as l'Espagnol); and nicknames or monikers, which include names from antiquity as well as biblical and mythological names (for instance, Vénus, Gracieuse, Cuisinier).[37] This last category includes names from antiquity that I suggest may have been familiar to colonials in the Caribbean primarily via the theatre and notably, in the case of Saint-Domingue, via Voltaire's plays.

---

[34] Cousseau, 'Nommer l'esclave', 38.
[35] Cousseau, 'Nommer l'esclave', 43.
[36] Cousseau, 'Nommer l'esclave', 39.
[37] Cousseau, 'Nommer l'esclave', 41.

These include two tragedies, *La Mort de César* and *Zaïre*, which were both performed in the colony and available to buy (as well as being known by reputation). A search for 'César' in www.marronnage.info brings up 187 documents relating to Saint-Domingue, some of which deal with overlapping Césars.[38] Cousseau briefly examines the choice of César as a name, which he suggests may have been 'une manifestation ironique de mépris et de la vanité satisfaite de pouvoir commander à un *César*' (*an ironic manifestation of scorn and of vanity satisfied in being able to command a* Caesar).[39] Similarly, a search for 'Zaïre' in Saint-Domingue produces 34 documents, with an additional Zaïre in Jamaica and one in Louisiana (to whom we shall return briefly below). Although the choice of name does not prove any direct link with the theatre, this can sometimes be found elsewhere. Bernard Camier and Laurent Dubois have explored the curious case of a free black man called Jolicœur who, in an article published in the press in 1793, drew explicitly on the text of Voltaire's play to support the freeing of an enslaved woman called Zaïre.[40] Jolicœur notes that he has seen the play performed on more than one occasion, and likens the personal qualities of his Zaïre to those of Voltaire's heroine. In so doing, he references one of the most famous lines of the play (taken from IV.2) in order to elicit sympathy from his readership: in his rendering, 'Ah, Zaïre, vous pleurez!' (*Ah, Zaïre, you are weeping!*). Clearly, then, in the minds of at least some people living in the colony, links were made between a theatrical name and an enslaved person. If the choice of name did not necessarily indicate anything about the individual granted that name, it could be used and understood subsequently in terms that did bridge the theatrical and the personal.

Names that are indisputably theatrical in origin also appear in runaway advertisements, notably Scapin, Arlequin and Figaro. Both Scapin and Arlequin (who is discussed at length in Chapter Four of this volume in relation to Amsterdam and Paramaribo) are comical figures from the Italian commedia dell'arte tradition. Traditionally, Scapin (or Scapino) was a cowardly servant, although he is a successful

---

[38] An additional six documents come up for Louisiana and Guadeloupe (plus a stray one for South Carolina, which does not appear to feature anyone named César) when the search is expanded to all regions, while a search for 'Caesar' in the Jamaican press produces 21 documents. Additional Caesars are found in South Carolina and one in Louisiana.

[39] Cousseau, 'Nommer l'esclave', 53.

[40] Bernard Camier and Laurent Dubois, 'Voltaire et Zaïre, ou le théâtre des Lumières dans l'aire atlantique française', *Revue d'histoire moderne et contemporaine*, 54.4 (2007), pp. 39–69.

schemer and trickster in Molière's *Les Fourberies de Scapin*, which would have been the primary referent for French audiences (and four performances of the play are documented in Saint-Domingue).[41] Arlequin (or Arlecchino) was particularly well known for getting himself out of scrapes, often by running away and sometimes using magical means, including transforming himself and/or others.[42] No fewer than 23 different works featuring Arlequin in their title are known to have been performed in Saint-Domingue, often on several occasions. Figaro was known to audiences in Saint-Domingue thanks to local performances of Paisiello's and especially Beaumarchais's versions of *Le Barbier de Séville*, in which Figaro helps his social superior secure the hand of his beloved. But the character increased in popularity after news of Beaumarchais's *Mariage de Figaro* (and the controversy that surrounded it) reached the colony in 1784. Its eagerly anticipated premiere in the colony took place in June 1785, but this was preceded by a new local piece, created by the author Clément, called *Figaro au Cap-Français* (1785).[43] Figaro was undoubtedly best known as the figure who outwitted his master in *Le Mariage de Figaro*. Clearly the lower-class protagonists of these works were well known in the colony, and this is reflected in the fact that enslaved people were sometimes named after them.

A search for 'Scapin' across all territories in the database produces only five documents, all of them in Saint-Domingue and all for the same person (who, interestingly, later takes the name Étienne). However, if, prompted by the search box, one then searches for 'Scapin (Coffé)' and 'Scapin (Koffi)', this produces an additional two hits, both in Louisiana and both almost certainly for the same person (despite the variation in spelling, the descriptions of the individual are almost identical). In the Scapin (Koffi) announcement, the enslaved man is reported to have escaped in the company of an enslaved woman called Zaïre:

> Un Nègre nommé Scapin ou koffi, nation Aoula, taille de cinq pieds, six pouces, ayant des barres sur chaque joue, le petit doigt d'un pied coupé, étampé M. V. Une Négresse nommé Zaire, nation

---

[41] For performance statistics and further information about them, see <https://www.theatreinsaintdomingue.org>.

[42] For more on the significance of Arlequin as a magical (and black-masked) figure, see Chapter Four in this volume and Prest, *Public Theatre and the Enslaved*, Mitigated Portrayals chapter.

[43] In addition, Maillot's one-act comedy, *Figaro, directeur des marionnettes* and Pariseau's *Le Repentir de Figaro* were performed on several occasions in the colony. I discuss *Figaro au Cap-Français* in *Public Theatre and the Enslaved*, Mitigated Portrayals chapter.

Congo, taille de quatre pieds cinq à six pouces, la peau rougeâtre, partie avec un grand bidon de fer blanc à anse.[44]

A nègre called Scapin or Koffi, of the Aoula nation, five foot six inches tall, with line marks on both cheeks, the little toe of one foot severed, branded M. V. A négresse called Zaïre, of the Congo nation, four foot five to six inches, reddish skin, left with a large tin can with a handle.

A search for Arlequin, similarly, produces eight documents in Saint-Domingue for several enslaved Arlequins, including 'Jean-Pierre, dit Arlequin' and 'Pierre, dit Arlequin' (who may be the same person).[45] The same search also brings up an enslaved man in Jamaica called Jemmy but 'known by the name of HARLEQUIN'.[46] Jean-Pierre and Pierre are almost certainly baptismal names; Jemmy is probably Jimmy, a derivation of James, perhaps written to convey the influence of a Scottish accent,[47] while Arlequin/Harlequin are clearly nicknames. We cannot know for sure, but it is not impossible that the choice of nickname, which in these instances post-dates the baptismal name, arose partly in response to some of the enslaved person's characteristics or behaviour. Certainly, it confirms that the colonials responsible for naming enslaved people held the Arlequin figure somewhere in their minds as they did so.

Figaro is the most popular name of the three. A search for his name produces 21 documents in Saint-Domingue—some of them for overlapping Figaros and all but one of them post-dating the Parisian premiere of *Le Mariage de Figaro*. This search also brings up one runaway Figaro in Jamaica, five in Louisiana (one of them explicitly identified as being from Saint-Domingue) and one in French Guiana. One of the fugitive Figaros in Saint-Domingue is identified in his advertisement as a domestic servant, like his namesake. The advertisement for one of the Figaros in Louisiana uses a somewhat unusual formulation: 'il se nomme

---

[44] *Le Moniteur de la Louisiane* (9 April 1808).
[45] *Affiches américaines* (11 September 1781) and *Affiches américaines* (27 May 1786). In one instance, the change is in the other direction. We read in *Supplément aux affiches américaines* (24 July 1782), p. 281 of '[u]n Negre Congo, nommé Scapin, qui a pris le nom d'Etienne' (*a Congo nègre called Scapin who has taken the name Étienne*).
[46] *The Royal Gazette* (17 March 1804).
[47] For more on the close ties between Scotland and Jamaica, see T.M. Devine (ed.), *Recovering Scotland's Slavery Past: The Caribbean Connection* (Edinburgh: Edinburgh University Press, 2015).

Figaro' (*he calls himself Figaro*).[48] This young man (around 14 years old) is described as being 'presque brut'—a designation indicating that he has only recently arrived from Africa, and which would strongly suggest that he is unbaptized. Although Figaro is clearly a name known to the person who placed the advertisement in the *Moniteur de la Louisiane*, the choice of wording suggests that it may have been chosen—or at least influenced by—the enslaved teenager himself. If this is the case, we wonder what, if anything, the name Figaro meant to this newly arrived enslaved African?

We must also ask ourselves what the name meant to the people who named enslaved people—their masters or the master's overseer. Whereas César and Zaïre are tragic heroes of high social standing who lived in the past, Scapin, Arlequin and Figaro are (broadly) servant figures living in some kind of present. They are, moreover, figures known for their ability to outwit others, particularly those of a higher social standing including, when necessary, their own masters. The advertisement cited above for Scapin and Zaïre provides some insight into the pair's habits: '[c]es deux esclaves ont l'habitude de se louer en ville, & d'y travailler en cachette' (*these two slaves are in the habit of hiring themselves out in town and of working there in secret*).[49] Of course, no enslaved person needed to be nicknamed Scapin, Arlequin or Figaro in order to try to outwit their master by running away and taking paid work elsewhere; nor is the use of such a nickname firm evidence that any of them did so. But, given that other non-baptismal (nick)names such as La Petite Margot (*Little Margot*), La Grande Jeanneton (*Big Jeanneton*) or Jeanne Borgnesse (*Jeanne One-Eye*), Amant Bras Coupé (*Amant One-Arm*) did refer to personal characteristics, it is not impossible that these names were also meaningful in some way.[50] Certainly, they demonstrate a clear—if general—intersection between theatre and slavery in the minds of enslavers in the colony.

Slave-owning theatremakers

Against this backdrop, and with the Dubuisson example in mind, I now turn to the results of a set of targeted searches for explicit links between the theatre and local slavery. My first set of searches within the www.marronnage.info database was for a series of theatre-related

---

[48] *Le Moniteur de la Louisiane* (15 July 1807).
[49] *Le Moniteur de la Louisiane* (9 April 1808).
[50] Examples taken from Cousseau, 'Nommer l'esclave', 42.

terms: *acteur, actrice, comédie* (which brought up results for *comédien* and *comédienne* as well) and *spectacle*. I then ran additional searches for the surnames of all performers and directors whose names had come up in order to find any additional results in which they were not necessarily identified explicitly by their links to the theatre. I also ran searches for additional names of individuals (with variants in spelling) in whom I am particularly interested. Finally I tried some additional key word searches for terms including *perruquier* (wigmaker) and *décorateur* (set designer), but there are no doubt other terms that would have yielded more results. What follows is an analysis of a small sample of my larger findings.

We begin with the following richly textured announcement from 1788:

> Théodore, carteronne de la Martinique, âgée d'environ 25 à 30 ans, marquée de beaucoup de taches de petite vérole & de rousseurs sur le visage: elle a ci-devant appartenu à la demoiselle Leroi, d'abord comédienne, & qui a tenu ensuite une guinguette au Carenage: en donner des nouvelles, ou l'arrêter & la remettre au sieur Leris, négociant au Cap-Français, rue du Vieux-Cimetière, à qui elle appartient actuellement.[51]

> *Théodore, quadroon from Martinique, aged around 25 to 30 years, lots of marks from small pox and redness on the face: she belonged before to Mlle Leroi, formerly an actress who later ran a dance hall in Le Carenage. Send news of her or detain her and return her to M. Leris, merchant in Cap-Français, rue du Vieux-Cimetière, to whom she now belongs.*

Most obviously, we learn from this that the female actor, Mlle Leroi (also spelled Leroy), who went on to run a dance café, once 'owned' the enslaved woman who has recently run away from her current 'owner'. The fact that Leroi features so prominently in the advertisement suggests that she is thought to be (or to have been) well known to readers of the newspaper—something that is presumably owing to her regular engagement with the public via her dance café, but also—and especially—to her earlier career as a prominent actor. Performances featuring Leroi are announced sporadically in the local press between 1771 and 1784.[52] Her debut role in the colony was as the protagonist

---

[51] *Supplément aux affiches américaines* (15 March 1788), p. 758.
[52] It appears that Leroi spent time in France between 1776 and 1778—a journey

in Voltaire's tragedy, *Sémiramis*.[53] She appears to have specialized in tragedy since we also have announcements for her performing in Racine's *Andromaque* and de la Harpe's *Le Comte de Warwick*, as well as organizing performances featuring Racine's *Athalie*, de la Touche's *Iphigénie en Tauride*, Longepierre's *Médée*, Voltaire's *Œdipe*, Le Mierre's *La Veuve du Malabar*, Voltaire's *Le Fanatisme ou Mahomet le prophète* and his *Mérope ou la Mérope française*.[54] Although this is not stated in the press announcements, it is likely that Leroi appeared in some—perhaps all—of the performances that she organized, especially in her preferred genre of tragedy. She also performed in some comedies in the later stages of her career and organized performances that included *opéras-comiques*.

Of the many works with which Leroi is associated, the most significant for an investigation of colonialism and slavery are *La Veuve du Malabar* and *Le Fanatisme ou Mahomet le prophète*. Although the primary target of Le Mierre's five-act tragedy *La Veuve du Malabar*, premiered in France in 1770 and revived in 1780, was organized (Catholic) religion (here allegorized, interestingly, as Hinduism), its colonial setting and justification of French rule has obvious resonances with Saint-Domingue. Moreover, its critique of *sati*—the self-sacrifice of widows on their husband's funeral pyre—as a cruel practice opens up the broader question of other forms of cruelty practised in the name of a supposedly higher purpose, be it religion, the state or colonialism. It was not unusual for metaphors of slavery to be used in plays of the time, but the references to Indian women being enslaved to their husbands and to the rigours of *sati* unite notions of slavery and cruelty in ways that were obviously applicable in Saint-Domingue.[55] If *La Veuve du Malabar* invites French audiences in France to sympathize with

---

that took over a year to arrange. See Jean Fouchard, *Artistes et répertoire des scènes de Saint-Domingue* (Port-au-Prince: Imprimerie de l'État, 1955; 1988), pp. 53–54.

[53] *Supplément aux affiches américaines* (31 August 1771), p. 374. For more on performances of *Sémiramis* in Saint-Domingue, including a local parody of the work, see Julia Prest, 'From Tragic Hero to Creole Businesswoman: Voltaire's Sémiramis and her Parodies in 18th-century France and Saint-Domingue', in Margaret Geoga and John Steele (eds), *The Allure of the Ancient: Receptions of the Ancient Middle East, ca. 1600–1800* (Leiden: Brill, 2022), pp. 259–83.

[54] Information retrieved from <http://www.theatreinsaintdomingue.org>.

[55] For an interesting discussion of *La Veuve du Malabar* in the context of the colonization of India, see Binita Mehta, *Widows, Pariahs, and Bayadères: India as Spectacle* (Lewisburg, PA: Bucknell University Press, 2002), pp. 57–67.

(female) victims of oppressive religious practices, in Saint-Domingue it may have inadvertently invited sympathy with (female) victims of other cruel practices. As an enslaved woman, Théodore will not have escaped such cruelty.

Similarly, Voltaire's five-act tragedy *Le Fanatisme ou Mahomet le prophète* (1741) also criticizes fanatical Christianity through the lens of another religion—this time Islam. Here too, fanatical religion is sometimes described as a form of enslavement, but in this play the link between metaphorical and real forms of enslavement is even clearer as the play, which is set in Mecca, features two enslaved prisoners in key roles: Palmire (whom Mahomet is seeking to marry alongside his existing wives) and Séide (who, we learn in the course of the play, is in fact Palmire's brother). In II.1, for instance, Palmire refers to her 'prison cruelle' (*cruel prison*), which Séide calls 'ce lieu d'esclavage' (*place of slavery*), and she makes explicit references to their 'fers' (*irons*). Although their enslavement is of a very different kind from that practised in Saint-Domingue, the play nonetheless associates enslavement with cruelty and injustice, and it is difficult to imagine that performers and audience members alike did not perceive those local resonances at all. We wonder how Leroi reconciled her 'ownership' of Théodore and other domestic servants with these moving, theatrical accounts of the suffering of enslaved characters.

Although there is no record of Corneille's tragedy *Théodore, vierge et martyre* (1646) having been performed in Saint-Domingue, the work will certainly have been known to Leroi, and it seems possible, then, that the name Théodore was Leroi's choice. Whatever the significance or otherwise of Théodore's name, Leroi's 'ownership' and subsequent selling of Théodore to a local merchant confirms again what can no longer be overlooked: that actors in the colonial Caribbean 'owned' and traded in enslaved people. Théodore, who is of mixed racial ancestry (as indicated by the designation *carteronne*) and born in the Caribbean, was almost certainly Leroi's domestic servant. If Théodore worked for Leroi while the actor was still performing, she will have undertaken tasks that took her to the playhouse and brought her into contact with other theatremakers and their enslaved domestics. Théodore may even have overheard portions of the works in which Leroi performed. We must ask ourselves what Théodore—or any other domestic servant 'belonging' to Leroi at the time of their performances—might have made of *La Veuve du Malabar* or *Le Fanatisme ou Mahomet le prophète*.

The runaway advertisement featuring Leroi's name prompted a search for further references to the (former) actor in the press beyond those that come under the 'Spectacles' rubric. One such is found in the 'For Sale' section of the local newspaper in 1785:

> Madame *Leroy*, ci-devant actrice, prévient le public qu'ayant pris à ferme la Guinguete [sic] de madame *Bertrand* au Grigri, elle a un negre excellent cuisinier & patissier ainsi que billard & jeu de boule, ladite dame s'efforcera de contenter les personnes qui viendront chez elle.[56]

> Mme Leroi, *former actress, informs the public that, having rented Mme* Bertrand's *dance café in the Grigri, she has a* nègre—*an excellent cook and pastry-maker—as well as a billiard table and set of boules. The aforementioned lady will make every effort to content those who come to see her.*

Leroi appears rather coy about the act of selling here—indeed, were this not in the 'For Sale' section of the newspaper, one would assume that it is an announcement for the reopening of the dance café under new management. Nontheless, she is clearly involved in the buying or selling of the enslaved cook and pastrymaker.

Returning to the runaway announcement with which this discussion began, we must ask what can we glean or, following Hartman, imagine, about Théodore's life. As noted above, Théodore is of mixed racial ancestry and Caribbean-born. Was she the child of an enslaved woman and a white master? She seems to have grown up in the French colony of Martinique and will therefore have travelled by boat to Saint-Domingue at some point. Was her very existence an unwelcome reminder to her master of an illegitimate child that he did not want to recognize, as was often the case? Did she move to Saint-Domingue with another 'master' before being sold to Leroi? What qualities did Leroi perceive in Théodore when she made the choice to buy her? When did Théodore contract smallpox and what are the red marks on her cheeks? If Théodore was in Leroi's possession prior to 1785, what contact did Théodore have with the strong tradition of theatremaking in the town of Le Cap? Did Théodore have any children and, if so, where were they when the advertisement was posted? Why did Théodore run away at this moment in time? Where did she go, what did she do and was she recaptured and returned to Leris? If so, what punishment did she receive? It may be possible to answer some of these questions by undertaking further research. But the fact that we cannot answer all of them should not prevent us from asking them in the first place. On the contrary, it is all the more important to ask questions to which we have no clear answers precisely because the alternative is to leave Théodore and other enslaved people

---

[56] *Supplément aux affiches américaines* (11 May 1785), p. 216.

'belonging' to theatremakers where they have been consigned for so long: in obscurity.

Other advertisements involving people connected to the theatre are even more chilling. A male instrumentalist named Schubert, who put on three benefit performances at the playhouses in Port-au-Prince and Saint-Marc in 1785 and 1787, posted the following advertisement in June 1787:

> Angélique, Arada, âgée d'environ 14 ans, ayant sur chaque joue un bouton de la grosseur d'une noisette, coupée en croissant, louche de l'oeil gauche, ayant sur le ventre des marques en fleurs, marronne du 2 du courant. En donner avis au *Sieur Schubert, Musicien attaché au Spectacle*, dans la maison de M. Faure, Inspecteur de Police.[57]

> *Angélique, of the Arada nation, aged around 14 years, with a crescent-shaped mark the size of a hazelnut on each cheek, a squint in her left eye, and flower marks on her stomach, ran away the 2nd of this month. Please contact* Sieur Schubert, a musician working at the theatre, *at the home of M. Fauré, Police Inspector.*

Angélique's youth and femininity, combined with Schubert's detailed account of the country marks on her body as well as her disability remind us of how vulnerable young enslaved women were. While Théodore was older and better able, as a woman of mixed race born in the Caribbean, to blend in and perhaps to pass as free after her escape, Angélique's prospects, as a young, black, African woman, were less favourable. All of which makes her decision to leave especially courageous and determined.

If one has to read between the lines to perceive the possible sexual abuse of Angélique (which cannot be proven, only suggested), the cruel physical punishments meted out in the name of Jean-Baptiste Lesueur Fontaine, director of the colony's largest and most successful playhouse (alongside other professional activities), are clearly visible to all readers of the local newspaper. My combined searches brought up a series of advertisements for a particularly determined runaway called Phaëton. The third of these reads as follows:

> *Phaëton*, grand, maigre, étampé DALIGRAND, est parti marron le 20 du courant, avec deux nabots & une chaîne aux deux pieds;

---

[57] *Affiches américaines* (14 June 1787), my emphasis.

> ceux qui en auront connaissance, sont priés de le faire conduire à M. *Fontaine*, Directeur du Spectacle du Cap.[58]
>
> Phaëton, *tall and thin, branded DALIGRAND, ran away the 20th of this month with two iron rings and a chain on both feet; those who know anything are asked to have him taken to M.* Fontaine, *Director of the Theatre in Le Cap.*

Phaëton, who has already run away and been recaptured on at least two occasions, has now been subject to one of the harshest punishments meted out to male runaways: the *nabot* (a heavy, steel ring cold-riveted to the foot). The rings and chain on his feet are punishments that are also aimed (unsuccessfully, as it turns out) at preventing Phaëton from being able to run away again. If Fontaine did not personally apply the rings and chain, they were nonetheless applied in his name and are details that he chooses to mention in a public announcement. He also chooses to identify—and be identified—as a man of the theatre, thus linking theatremaking, slave 'ownership' and extreme cruelty and violence in a single sentence. Rather than being an advertisement for Phaëton's return, this is perhaps an advertisement of the pride Fontaine took in his cruelty towards enslaved people.

There are many other examples of actors, directors, theatre musicians and stage hands advertising for the return of enslaved fugitives.[59] I would like to end with one—a runaway advertisement that provides the name of a wigmaker for the theatre who does not appear in any of the theatre advertisements that are the staple of theatre researchers and who—along with his enslaved assistants and employees—might otherwise be overlooked. It was not, then, a search for the name 'Simon' that brought me to this advertisement, but rather the more general search for *comédie* (theatre):

> Un Negre créole, nommé *Jean-Baptiste*, âgé de 12 à 13 ans, sans étampe, bien pris dans sa taille, ayant un oeil plus petit que l'autre, est parti maron depuis deux mois de chez le Sr *Simon*, Perruquier de la Comédie, où il étoit en apprentissage. Ceux qui le reconnoîtront, sont priés de le faire arrêter & d'en donner avis au Sr *Joseph Prevost*, Habitant à Plaisance: il y aura bonne récompense.[60]

---

[58] *Supplément aux affiches américaines* (29 September 1784).
[59] More of them are discussed in Prest, *Public Theatre and the Enslaved*.
[60] *Supplément aux affiches américaines* (16 October 1782), p. 398.

> *A Creole* nègre *called* Jean-Baptiste, *aged between 12 and 13 years, no brand, nicely proportioned, one eye smaller than the other, ran away two months ago from the house of Sr* Simon, *wigmaker at the theatre, where he was an apprentice. Those who recognize him are asked to have him detained and to inform Sr* Joseph Prévost, *a planter in Plaisance. There will be a substantial reward.*

It is reasonable to assume that Jean-Baptiste, as an apprentice to a wigmaker who identifies himself publicly as working at the local theatre in Le Cap, will have helped dress the hair of some actors in the months prior to his disappearance. Again, we must ask what happened to Jean-Baptiste. Being Caribbean-born and having no brands on his body will have increased his chances of passing as free, even as a young man of African (rather than mixed) ancestry. As a trainee wigmaker, Jean-Baptiste may well have been able to find paid work elsewhere in his trade. Having found Simon and Jean-Baptiste in a search for *comédie*, I then searched for '*Simon*' and found another young apprentice who once worked for Simon and may also have helped behind the scenes at the playhouse:

> Un Negre Sénégalois, nommé Dick, âgé de 16 à 17 ans, sans étampe, travaillant ci-devant chez M. Simon, Perruquier. Ceux qui le reconnoîtront, sont priés d'en donner avis au Sieur Simon, ou à M. Delaire, à qui il appartient: il y aura récompense.[61]

> *A Senegalese* nègre *called Dick, aged 16 to 17 years, no brand, who formerly worked for M.* Simon, *wigmaker. Those who recognize him are asked to inform Sieur Simon or M. Delaire, to whom he belongs. There will be a reward.*

The case of Simon, which led us to Jean-Baptiste and then Dick, shows how information about theatre that is not included in theatre sources may be found—or hinted at—elsewhere. Although theatre announcements quite often include the names of set designers and painters, they do not mention wigmakers. Runaway advertisements, on the other hand, include whatever information the person writing the advertisement wishes to mention—including overlooked theatre-related professions and hints of the involvement of enslaved people in local theatre productions.

Our examination of a sample of runaway advertisements has confirmed that a wide range of theatremakers, including theatre

---

[61] *Supplément aux affiches américaines* (5 June 1782).

directors, actors, musicians and wigmakers, 'owned', and traded locally, in enslaved people. Using this source type has also enabled us to uncover individuals with a connection to the theatre who do not feature in theatre announcements or other records. It has confirmed, moreover, that these theatremakers opted to be identified as slave 'owners'—and sometimes as proudly cruel slave 'owners'—in the public context of the local newspaper. Most of them identify in these advertisements precisely as *slave-owning theatremakers*. Indeed, many of the same individuals who advertised upcoming theatre performances that they organized for their benefit (a prime source for theatre researchers) also advertised in the same newspaper for the return of enslaved runaways (a source—or portion of the source—less commonly used by theatre researchers). It is also worth noting the seemingly obvious fact that a number of enslaved people 'belonging' to theatremakers challenged their status as property by running (or driving, walking or rowing) away. Although the advertisements are written with the goal of identifying and recapturing the runaways, they are also, in the absence of better accounts, a useful source of information about the lives and personalities of people who otherwise fall between the archival cracks. Reading between the lines, we can begin to piece together some details of the lives of some enslaved people. Sometimes these details can be fleshed out by other sources, such as 'For Sale' advertisements and notarial documents; they can also be read alongside theatre works that were being prepared and performed by some of the same theatremakers in the colony. Returning to Trouillot's point about the individual versus the collective in runaway notices, the personalized, exceptional nature of the notices can help us to get to know more enslaved individuals, while the sheer volume of notices (coupled with the knowledge that they reflect only a small portion of the people who chose to free themselves in this way) allows the modern researcher to see what the colonials of course knew too: that this *was* a mass phenomenon and that there *was* indeed something very wrong with the system.

Of course, the picture remains very far from complete. We still do not know how enslaved people experienced their lives as the 'property' of theatre professionals, how much they had to do with daily life at the theatre or what precise contributions they made to theatre production. The absence of direct testimony from enslaved people in this regard remains a huge obstacle for the theatre researcher. Nonetheless, runaway advertisements do ultimately contribute to our understanding of slavery and theatre in two important ways: first, they make slave 'ownership', the suffering of enslaved individuals and their wish to escape a real, integrated and unavoidable part of

Saint-Domingue's theatre history, rather than a mere backdrop to it. Reading about Théodore, Angélique, Phaëton, Jean-Baptiste, Dick and others and their links to individuals whose theatremaking we study more readily makes them part of that story. Second, they do at least hint at the contributions of enslaved people to that history, whether as apprentice wigmakers or hairdressers, helping to craft the visual impact on which theatre relies so heavily, or as personal domestic servants running errands for theatremakers, sometimes, no doubt, to and from the playhouse. Although the information we glean is frustratingly thin, it is also valuable for, as Fuentes reminds us, we should not 'let our desires for empirical substantiation remand these fleeting [...] lives back into oblivion'.[62]

Bibliography

Affiches américaines and *Supplément aux affiches américaines* (Port-au-Prince and Cap-Français: Imprimerie Royale, 1766–91).

Camier, Bernard and Laurent Dubois. 'Voltaire et Zaïre, ou le théâtre des Lumières dans l'aire atlantique française', *Revue d'histoire moderne et contemporaine*, 54.4 (2007), pp. 39–69.

Cousseau, Vincent. 'Nommer l'esclave dans la Caraïbe XVIIᵉ–XVIIIᵉ siècles', *Annales de démographie historique*, 131 (2016), pp. 37–63.

Devine, T.M. (ed.). *Recovering Scotland's Slavery Past: The Caribbean Connection* (Edinburgh: Edinburgh University Press, 2015).

Documenting Runaway Slaves. <http://runawayslaves.usm.edu/about.html>.

Eddins, Crystal Nicole. 'Runaways, Repertoires, and Repression', *Journal of Haitian Studies*, 25.1 (Spring 2019), pp. 4–38.

Fouchard, Jean. *Artistes et répertoire des scènes de Saint-Domingue* (Port-au-Prince: Imprimerie de l'État, 1955; 1988).

Fuentes, Marisa J. *Dispossessed Lives: Enslaved Women, Violence, and the Archive* (Philadelphia: University of Pennsylvania Press, 2016).

Geography of Slavery in Virginia. <http://www2.vcdh.virginia.edu/gos/>.

Hartman, Saidiya. 'Venus in Two Acts', *Small Axe*, 12.2 (June 2008), pp. 1–14.

Hodges, Graham Russell and Alan Edward Brown (eds). *'Pretends to Be Free': Runaway Slave Advertisements from Colonial and Revolutionary New York and New Jersey* (New York: Taylor and Francis, 1994; 2019).

---

[62] Fuentes, *Dispossessed Lives*, 138.

Hunt-Kennedy, Stefanie. *Between Fitness and Death: Disability and Slavery in the Caribbean* (Urbana, Chicago and Springfield: University of Illinois Press, 2020).

Le Glaunec, Jean-Pierre. *Esclaves mais résistants dans le monde des annonces pour esclaves en fuite: Louisiane, Jamaïque, Caroline du Sud (1801–1815)* (Paris: Karthala/CIRESC, 2021).

Le Glaunec, Jean-Pierre. 'Précisions/imprécisions, ou comment re-présenter l'esclave en fuite', *Écrire l'histoire: Histoire, littérature, esthétique*, 3 (2009), pp. 23–33.

Le Glaunec, Jean-Pierre. '"Writing the Runaways": Descriptions, Inscriptions and Narrations in the Runaway Slave "Advertisements" in *Le Moniteur de la Louisiane*, 1802–1814', *Cahiers Charles V*, 39 (December 2005), pp. 205–36.

Leichman, Jeffrey M. and Karine Bénac-Giroux (eds). *Colonialism and Slavery in Performance: Theatre and the Eighteenth-Century French Caribbean*, Oxford University Studies in the Enlightenment (Liverpool: Liverpool University Press, 2021).

Le Marronnage dans le monde atlantique: sources et trajectoires de vie. <http://www.marronnage.info>.

Mehta, Binita. *Widows, Pariahs, and Bayadères: India as Spectacle* (Lewisburg, PA: Bucknell University Press, 2002).

Moitt, Bernard. *Women and Slavery in the French Antilles, 1635–1848* (Bloomington and Indianapolis: Indiana University Press, 2001).

Le Moniteur de la Louisiane, (excerpts retrieved on <http://www.marronnage.info>).

North Carolina Runaway Slave Notices, 1750–1865. <http://libcdm1.uncg.edu/cdm/landingpage/collection/RAS>.

Prest, Julia. 'From Tragic Hero to Creole Businesswoman: Voltaire's Sémiramis and her Parodies in 18th-century France and Saint-Domingue', in Margaret Geoga and John Steele (eds), *The Allure of the Ancient: Receptions of the Ancient Middle East, ca. 1600–1800* (Leiden: Brill, 2022), pp. 259–83.

Prest, Julia. *Public Theatre and the Enslaved People of Colonial Saint-Domingue* (Cham: Palgrave Macmillan, 2023).

Prude, Jonathan. 'To Look Upon the "Lower Sort": Runaway Ads and the Appearance of Unfree Laborers in America, 1750–1800', *The Journal of American History*, 78.1 (June 1991), pp. 124–59.

The Royal Gazette (excerpts retrieved on <http://www.marronnage.info>).

Runaway Slaves in Britain: Bondage, Freedom and Race in the Eighteenth Century. <https://www.runaways.gla.ac.uk>.

Smith, Billy G. and Richard Wojtowicz (eds). *Blacks Who Stole Themselves: Advertisements for Runaways in the Pennsylvania Gazette, 1728–1790* (Philadelphia: University of Pennsylvania Press, 1989).

Texas Runaway Slave Project. <https://digital.sfasu.edu/digital/collection/RSP>.

Theatre in Saint-Domingue, 1764–1791: Plays, Ballets and Operas. <https://www.theatreinsaintdomingue.org>.

Trouillot, Michel-Rolph. *Silencing the Past: Power and the Production of History* (Boston, MA: Beacon Press, 2015).

Voltaire, François-Marie Arouet dit. *Zaïre, Le Fanatisme ou Mahomet le prophète [...]*, ed. Jean Goldzink. Paris: Flammarion, 2004.

Waldstreicher, David. 'Reading the Runaways: Self-Fashioning, Print Culture and Confidence in Slavery in the Eighteenth-Century Mid-Atlantic', *William and Mary Quarterly*, 56.2 (April 1999), pp. 243–72.

Windley, Lathan A. *Runaway Slave Advertisements: A Documentary History from the 1730s to 1790*, 4 vols (Westport, CT: Greenwood, 1983).

Ten

Knowledge Exchange Theatre and the Colonial Caribbean: Creating *Placeholder*

Catherine Bisset, Flavia D'Avila and Jaïrus Obayomi

> Leaving a mark that they can't wash out is perhaps the most powerful form of resistance of all.
>
> Mama in *Placeholder*

Practice-as-research in Theatre Studies is a term used to designate a research methodology used by artists interrogating the nature of artistic processes and output.[1] Research-based theatre, on the other hand, usually attends to work involving applied or participatory theatre practices instead.[2] The TDF Theatre Dictionary defines 'applied theatre' as 'what happens when a group of people working in community use the techniques of drama and theatre to address a social issue', which is also referred to as participatory theatre or theatre in education (TIE, for short).[3]

John O'Toole and Judith Ackroyd use the term 'performed research' to describe theatremaking used as a tool to share research undertaken in other fields, like social sciences or STEM (science, technology, engineering, mathematics), which places theatre praxis not at the centre of the research, but rather as a means for disseminating findings and data.[4] George Belliveau and Graham W. Lea also use the term 'research-informed play', which many playwrights and dramaturgs could find problematic as it can be generally understood that a great

---

[1] Simon Ellis, 'A Definition', Practice-as-Research blog (5 January 2016) <https://practiceasresearchblog.wordpress.com/category/definition/>.

[2] See George Belliveau and Graham W. Lea (eds), *Research-Based Theatre: An Artistic Methodology* (Bristol: Intellect, 2016).

[3] TDF Theatre Dictionary, 'Applied Theatre' (2013) <http://dictionary.tdf.org/applied-theatre/>.

[4] Foreword to Belliveau and Lea, *Research-Based Theatre*, xi. See also Johnny Saldaña, *Ethnotheatre: Research from Page to Stage (Qualitative Inquiry and Social Justice)* (Walnut Creek, CA: Left Coast Press, 2011).

deal of research goes into writing a play, particularly commissions, as part of artistic practice-as-usual.[5] Often, also, collaborations of this nature have trouble deciding where to position the artwork within research documentation, asking whether it should stand on its own, be used as an appendix or as a component of the whole project, standing on the same level as the commentary, thesis or dissertation.

All these variations on collaborations between theatre and research are therefore extremely fluid. Although it overlaps with all these different ways of creating work, ultimately the term we coin here, knowledge exchange theatre (KET), does not coincide entirely with any of them. We propose KET as a means to achieve a three-dimensional understanding of research. As such, the term implies that the research lives elsewhere, in this case in the field of history, broadly conceived. The art is there to serve the research, and the research is there to enhance the art.

Our new piece of knowledge exchange theatre, *Placeholder*, is a solo show that takes as its starting point the idea that the gaps in the archives, the lacunae in the texts and the holes in the narrative, are themselves acts of violence and suppression. This piece of theatre was created as part of the activities of the Colonial-Era Caribbean Theatre and Opera Network (CECTON) and had its premiere at the Scottish Storytelling Centre in Edinburgh in November 2021, as part of the Being Human Festival programme,[6] and a second performance at the Byre Theatre in St Andrews in February 2022. Running at approximately 60 minutes, both performances were livestreamed and included a Q&A with the creative team and Julia Prest, Professor of French and Caribbean Studies at the University of St Andrews.

Placeholder was written and performed by Catherine Bisset, with dramaturgy by Jaïrus Obayomi and directed by Flavia D'Avila under the banner of her Edinburgh-based production company, Fronteiras Theatre Lab. This project was kindly supported by a Research Network Grant from the Royal Society of Edinburgh and the Collaboration, Research and Development Fund of the City of Edinburgh Council. This chapter has been written collaboratively by the three members of the creative team and offers a reflective, practitioners' account of the process of creating a new piece of theatre that engages with—and seeks in turn to engage its audiences with—the (hi)story of colonial-era Caribbean theatre.

---

[5] Belliveau and Lea, *Research-Based Theatre*, 4.
[6] A video recording of the Being Human performance can be accessed on <https://www.facebook.com/ScottishStorytellingCentre/videos/198420252466623>.

Producing and directing *Placeholder* (Flavia D'Avila)

I had worked on plays inspired by academic research before, including Debbie Cannon's *Green Knight* based on the well known but anonymous Arthurian poem *Sir Gawain and the Green Knight*.[7] This monologue was influenced by Cannon's own doctoral research in Medieval Studies at York University. Another piece, *The Remarkable Deliverances of Alice Thornton*,[8] also written and performed by Debbie Cannon, was based on Dr Cordelia Beattie's rediscovery of the autobiographical writings of Alice Wandesford Thornton (1626–1707) at Durham Cathedral.[9] In both cases, there were clear characters and narratives to follow, which made both pieces reasonably straightforward to adapt. The present piece, however, would be based on research with a focus on methodology, which presented a more challenging endeavour for our team. Despite the more elusive nature of this project, I welcomed an overlap with my own practice-as-research PhD on devising counter colonial syncretic theatre.[10]

In his study of intercultural performances in colonial Mexico, Leo Cabranes-Grant proposes a shift from analyzing results and reception to focussing on the labour that produces intercultural scenarios through dynamic relations in order to fully apprehend intercultural transformations.[11] Like most of the papers shared in the CECTON discussion workshop and conference workshop (in April and August 2021 respectively), Cabranes-Grant's study is historiographical and, by his own admission, inevitably reliant on 'archival materials over embodied manifestations [...] based on someone else's accounts' and therefore 'severely compromised from the start'.[12] Although interculturalism

---

[7] Debbie Cannon, *Green Knight* (May 2021) <https://debbiecannon.org/green-knight/>.

[8] Debbie Cannon, *The Remarkable Deliverances of Alice Thornton* (June 2017) <https://debbiecannon.org/the-remarkable-deliverances-of-alice-thornton/>.

[9] University of Edinburgh, 'Alice Thornton's Books: Remembrances of a Woman's Life in the Seventeenth Century' (6 August 2019) <https://www.ed.ac.uk/history-classics-archaeology/history/research/research-projects/alice-thorntons-books>.

[10] Flavia Domingues D'Avila, 'Countercolonising the Stage: A Syncretic Dramaturgy for Devising' (PhD thesis, Royal Conservatoire of Scotland/University of St Andrews, 2021) <http:syncretictheatre.wordpress.com>.

[11] Leo Cabranes-Grant, 'From Scenarios to Networks: Performing the Intercultural in Colonial Mexico', in Charlotte McIvor and Jason King (eds), *Interculturalism and Performance Now: New Directions?* (London: Palgrave Macmillan, 2019), pp. 29–59 (32).

[12] Cabranes-Grant, 'From Scenarios to Networks', 41.

was not necessarily the aim of our project, I was confident that this clash between real-time physical and intellectual labour in twenty-first-century Scotland and source materials originating from the eighteenth- and nineteenth-century Caribbean could yield an original piece of historiographical speculation.

In one of her seminal essays about reclaiming the stories of enslaved people from historiographical documents, Saidiya Hartman discusses how 'the stories that exist are not about them, but rather about the violence, excess, mendacity [...] that deposited these traces in the archives'.[13] After hearing and reading the work shared by the CECTON scholars, it became clear during our own meeting to discuss possible themes, narratives or characters to pursue, that our focus was to be the unknown.

The dramaturg (Jaïrus Obayomi) and performer-writer (Catherine Bisset) became very interested in what was *not* there, and in those precious nuggets of information that could give us a starting point.[14] The first few clues we followed were advertisements for the return of enslaved runaways (which are discussed in Chapter Nine of this volume),[15] the practice of sending domestic servants to hold seats at the theatre (the placeholders) and the story of a Creole opera singer in Saint-Domingue known by the name of Minette.[16]

Our first production workshop was in September 2021, and its goal was to organize some of Bisset's initial ideas, including the setting and characters. It is not a rule that solo plays should always feature multiple characters—in *The Remarkable Deliverances of Alice Thornton*, for example, Debbie Cannon only plays one character throughout. Nonetheless, Bisset was encouraged to explore more than one character for this piece, considering that the source materials contained so many possibilities for creating this world. Given this was Bisset's first time writing and performing a monologue, I wanted to give her a solid foundation and turned to techniques that have significantly influenced

---

[13] Saidiya Hartman, 'Venus in Two Acts', *Small Axe*, 12.2 (2008), pp. 1–14 (2).
[14] As explored, notably, by Jenna Gibbs, 'Encountering Gaps and Silences in the Archive' (CECTON conference workshop, August 2021). See Chapter Seven of this volume for a revised and updated version of that exploratory paper.
[15] Julia Prest, 'Colonial-Era Theatre and the Enslaved Population: Uncovering Hidden Connections in Saint-Domingue' (CECTON conference workshop, August 2021).
[16] Julia Prest, 'Parisian Palimpsests and Creole Creations: Mme Marsan and Dlle Minette play *Nina* on the Caribbean Stage', *Early Modern French Studies*, 41.2 (2019), pp. 170–88.

Figure 2: Catherine Bisset in rehearsal (photograph: Flavia D'Avila)

my directing practice. Dario Fo has been described as 'more than a playwright, [...] a performer who writes'[17] and he pioneered a unique style of solo performance focussed on storytelling with quick changes between characters using mostly his body and voice, and seldom relying on props, set or costume. One striking feature in Fo's work is the use of oppositions in his staging, speech and physicality,[18] a strategy that is also identified in Eugenio Barba's study of theatre anthropology and the practice of the Odin Teatret.[19] To help Bisset develop the skill of fragmenting her voice and her body in both the writing and performance, I invited her to complete a series of exercises to explore movement to different (and contrasting) types of music and play with her balance.

Following this physical work, we began exploring the world we would create for the play. We had settled on the idea of the *placeholder* as a central character and realized that at least some of the show would be set inside a colonial-era Caribbean playhouse. I then asked Bisset to imagine and describe the performance space (the actual venue in which we would perform the show), what it looked and felt like, what it was like being in the audience waiting for the show to begin. I asked her what was the first thing she saw, the first thing she heard and how her other senses were engaged. Was she sitting or standing? I asked her to tell us how the show started. Did the performer on stage make an entrance or were they on stage already as the audience came in? Was there a lighting change? Did the performer come in from the auditorium or were they backstage? I asked Bisset to describe how the presence of the performer changed the atmosphere in the theatre. What was the performer wearing? And then I asked her to say the first line of the show:

> I think I'm being watched.

We then played with that opening line in different contexts, leading in with commonplace openers:

> Once upon a time [...]

---

[17] Antonio Scuderi, 'Unmasking the Holy Jester Dario Fo', *Theatre Journal*, 55.2 (2003), pp. 275–90 (275).

[18] Joylynn Wing, 'Techniques of Opposition in the Work of Dario Fo' (PhD thesis, Stanford University, CA, 1988).

[19] Eugenio Barba, *The Paper Canoe: A Guide to Theatre Anthropology* (London: Routledge, 1995).

It was a dark and stormy night [...]

Hello, good evening and welcome [...]

I had a dream [...]

I never knew [...]

This exercise was effective in revealing the world of the play to us, and Bisset, assisted by Obayomi and Prest, managed to build a rich context from the imagery she obtained through this first workshop.

We followed this up by exploring some of the initial text Bisset had written, playing with punctuation, rhythm, changing focus between vowels and consonants, using the breath in different ways like grunting, whistling or whispering. We discussed what we wanted the piece to achieve (shine a light on the lost stories of enslaved people and free people of colour in the colonial-era Caribbean, including theatre's role in that story) and how we could do that using more than words. It became evident here that music would be important, and we did have some excellent papers in this field on which to draw.[20] I concluded that first workshop by asking Bisset to create a 'trailer' for the show, which helped us decide on the central character and think about key moments in the plot.

We were invited to do a performed reading of an extract from the play at the Edinburgh Multicultural Festival in October 2021, which helped Obayomi and Bisset focus on producing 20 minutes of material in a very short time.[21] I decided to step aside and not intervene with this task, but Bisset produced a dialogue between two characters: Minette and her mother. Minette turned out to be the placeholder of the title. A free woman of colour who had tried her hand at professional opera singing but, beaten down by theatre critics and the social organization of her time and place, had given up on her stage career and found employment as a (free) domestic servant in a white household. Her African-born, Jamaican-raised, enslaved, escaped and now deceased Mama manifests as a ghost to challenge and advise Minette, and to

---

[20] These included Wayne Weaver, 'Constructions of "Race" in the Musico-Theatrical Contexts of Eighteenth-Century Kingston' (CECTON conference workshop, August 2021). See Chapter Six of this volume for a revised and updated version of that paper.

[21] Edinburgh Multicultural Festival, 'Catherine Bisset in *Placeholder*' (2 October 2021) <https://www.youtube.com/watch?v=hFh5ZopY-Yo>.

provide the opposition favoured by Fo and Barba, as discussed earlier. Mama opposes Minette in age, racial ancestry, social status and political views.

Both Minette and Mama were drawn from Prest's research but, through a process of critical fabulation, became new characters in our play. The notion 'critical fabulation' was coined by Hartman to describe her own writing practice, in which she attempts 'to jeopardise the status of the event, to displace the received or authorised account, and to imagine what might have happened or what might have been said or might have been done'.[22] Ronald Bogue stresses 'the efficacy of fabulative works as interventions',[23] and acknowledges how these labour to articulate 'untold, erased and forgotten events [in a] reconfiguration of the past that discloses present junctures of potential transformation'.[24] Minette is based on a real, historical person, but Mama was almost entirely created by Bisset, drawing inspiration from various sources, including her own family history, as she recounts below. The connection between the two characters resulted from the work undertaken in the rehearsal room.

Staging decisions were made based both on practicalities—such as space, budget and performance needs following the reading at the Edinburgh Multicultural Festival—and information drawn from the research. We now knew Minette would begin the show seated in the auditorium. Bisset worked with a microphone at the reading and felt her vocal changes between the characters were more easily attainable if her voice was amplified, particularly for Mama's low register. This informed the choice of our first prop: a tailor's dummy. I thought we could use it as a microphone stand for Mama, which would also symbolize her physical presence on stage. However, as a convention, having Mama speak on the microphone behind the dummy would have restricted Bisset's movement too much, rendering her performance flat. We then opted for a wireless microphone that she could wear for the whole show under her hair, but kept the dummy as part of the set. This decision clarified what the stage itself represented: a dressing room in the theatre. This realization made the rest of the set decisions easy, and we obtained an ornate dressing table with mirrors (Figure 3), a stool and a less ornate wooden chair. I strove less to represent the period accurately with the set and more to represent the opposing ideas in the

---

[22] Hartman, 'Venus in Two Acts', 11.
[23] Ronald Bogue, *Deleuzian Fabulation and the Scars of History* (Edinburgh: Edinburgh University Press, 2010), p. 10.
[24] Bogue, *Deleuzian Fabulation*, 10.

Figure 3: Catherine Bisset in *Placeholder* (1), November 2021 (photograph: Chris Scott)

play, so the size and decorative features of the table clashed with the humble and functional chair.

Other props brought in were a wicker wig stand and rococo powdered wig, an eighteenth-century-style golden mantua (Figure 4) and court shoes painted gold to match. Although Bisset did not write stage directions in her script as we were creating the performance together in the rehearsal room, these props were all suggested by her text, as demonstrated in the following extracts (all Mama's lines, my emphasis in italics):

> These white people got no sense of rhythm! Maybe they scared a dancing because they worry their *wig* will fall off or someting!
>
> So your watcher down there, the one in the enormous white *wig*, is called Madame de Laurent [...]
>
> I heard that the law now says that the free people are no longer allowed to wear *shoes*[25]—that's them making the cage smaller and smaller, that's how much they resent you [...]
>
> If you want to play Nina, then play her—and if you want to go on stage in a *ball gown* made of pure gold—then do it—while you still can.

The only props not mentioned in the text are the trinket dishes and bottles that dress the table, which are there to provide further decoration and another layer of opposition in that the delicate shapes and materials contrast with the rusticity of the cotton outfit Mama wears and with the wicker wig stand. One of the dishes also contains a dollop of red face paint (rouge) that Mama puts on her finger and smears on her skirt, when she explains:

> When I was a washerwoman, I noticed something—the enslavers are obsessed with keeping everyting white, down to their linen and tablecloths, so they made us scrub and scrub until our hands

---

[25] Various sumptuary laws and decrees targeting free people of colour were passed in Saint-Domingue and the colonial Caribbean more broadly. See Robert S. Duplessis, 'Sartorial Sorting in the Colonial Caribbean and North America', in Giorgio Riello and Ulinka Rublack (eds), *The Right to Dress: Sumptuary Laws in a Global Perspective, c.1200–1800* (Cambridge: Cambridge University Press, 2019), pp. 346–71.

Figure 4: Catherine Bisset in *Placeholder* (2), November 2021 (photograph: Chris Scott)

bled—so you know what I used to do? I used to leave a stain on them—maybe just a smudge from my finger.

These lines are spoken towards the end of the play and are followed by the line used as the epigraph of this chapter. This extract encompasses what we wanted to achieve with this play—to recover those smudges and honour the memory of marginalized people from the colonial-era Caribbean who were brave enough to leave these traces behind.

Dramaturging *Placeholder* (Jaïrus Obayomi)

Dramaturgy—something of an obscure theatrical 'dark art'—often seems more at home in an academic context, as a 'concept' at a remove from the real business of theatremaking in the real world. It should hardly be surprising, then, that a project conceived in response to academic research should have specifically engaged a dramaturg!

So much is made of authorial voice in discussions about writing, and often a substantial part of the dramaturg's job (in the theatremaking real world) is listening for that authorial voice, for its distinctiveness as well as its clarity. This was especially true on this project, where there needed to be enough space and faith first for Bisset as writer, and then D'Avila as director, to approach the challenge of filling the historiographic lacunae.

What was, and indeed remains, fascinating about *Placeholder* was the role 'voice', in a variety of senses, has ended up playing in the piece. Within the show, voice plays an important part in both its narrative and its execution. More powerfully still, in relation to the research on which we drew, the presentation and interrogation of voice is really the piece's central premise: the black silence(d) in the archives.

A persistent truism of theatremaking is the stock phrase for a sort of theatrical fatalism—*it is what it is*—used to excuse a myriad of circumstances, sins and setbacks. *This is what we're dealing with? Ah well, it is what it is*. However, at the outset of the project that would become *Placeholder*, for once the truism did not seem applicable. After all, it is incredibly hard to 'Pollyanna' a situation if that situation as yet lacks definition. *It is what it is* really only works when everyone is cognizant of what that *it* might be, and that in turn can only be the case when there is already an existing, concrete *is*. Instead, in relation to our project the phrase's breezy stoicism is easily and necessarily challenged with the (normally unspoken) rebuttal: *What is it?*

Posing the question *What is it?* is a key dramaturgical tool. It is a question that theatremakers frequently ask themselves, even when they might not necessarily self-identify as dramaturgically inclined. In the creation of new work, whether text-based or devised, and regardless of the stimulus, it is often the case that form leads content—a knowledge of a formal *what* leading to a *how* of execution. For which reason, attempting to frame the *what* often works well as a starting point because, by setting up a framework or set of boundaries to work within, the content is bound to follow that framework in order to successfully construct meaning.

Within my own practice, this has been true. Lockdowns, shutdowns and distancing necessitated new ideations of praxis. Within these new practice realities, any work that has been produced for recorded or otherwise spatially, if not temporally, disparate (distant/non-overlapping/shared) media has been influenced by the bounds of the relevant medium. What can be done over a Zoom call with a laptop camera is, by necessity, different from what can be done on stage—and because the frameworks differ, so too does the language of making.

For the first stages of this project, we three did not meet in person and, prior to the project, Bisset and I had never met at all. This scenario differed from creating work across digital platforms during the height of lockdowns in 2020—then I was collaborating, often across significant geographical distance, sometimes across time zones, with people with whom I had physically shared space in the weeks and months prior to the policies of lockdown and social-distancing. The conceived outcome was different, too. Then, the point was to make work for the contemporary conditions, that is to say digitally and distanced, both physically from each other as collaborators and from the audiences, physically and temporally. The way of working echoed the mode of sharing: digital processes for digitally consumed projects. Instead, the process for *Placeholder* was hybridized, starting out from two online workshops and typed conversations across messaging, email and cloud document-sharing platforms, before moving into the in-person sphere, but always with the knowledge (or perhaps assumption) that it would have an in-person audience in the first instance, with digital offerings, whether streamed lived or recorded, as something of a support.

Perhaps that ought not to have had any significant impact on the final outcome, but I would argue that it had an impact on the process because, while we were conceptualizing voice, space and being in relation to the omissions in the archives, conceptually/before form, *Placeholder* was always conceived of as an opportunity to give (speculative) voice to those shrouded in archival silence, in keeping with the goals of the network.

The work's title is something of a pun, alluding to the *lorem ipsum* nature of naming something ahead of its existence, necessitated by a listing deadline for inclusion in the festival programme. It was also a nod to an aspect of the network's research that captured the imagination as well as a distillation of what we felt the project ethos, and our role within it, to be: our speculation and extrapolation from what is in the archives in lieu of those very archives yielding something more *authentic*, as well as our holding a space for historical actors whose archival absence is not analogous to the contemporary reality. Creating work that sought (and seeks) to fill gaps felt like it had to acknowledge that work's ontological truth.

There is a playful irony in the name because the reality of placeholders, regardless of the discourse or context in which they appear, is that they are not dialogic. Within their in-built expiration, they are not interactive, they have a single job and they do not have agency, whereas the piece does these things; there is again a sense of the playful (or perhaps the privileged) in creating a piece that is dialogic while being a monologue. In writing it, Bisset had fleshed out her world with more than one voice, while in performance Bisset and D'Avila played with its form by having Bisset's Minette begin the play out in the audience and invite a response through the Mama character. Placeholder as one voice.

Although I am familiar with practice-as-research as a more usual permutation of the performance-making/academia crossover, it has been largely absent from my own practice. Instead, the chief focal point has been the active praxis (the process in adaptation and/or translation) which has lacked that final step and remained unperformed. Instead, the remit of the project was research-as-practice, which from the outset we understood would require something of a hermeneutical approach to the research material and the silences and scraps in the archives.

It was fairly easy to tease out what was of interest, both to Bisset as writer/performer and to the three of us as a group: virtually everything! There was a strong sense of the possibilities for the piece being wide open, that it very much could be anything both in form and content. As might be expected, this was accompanied by true excitement: it really could be *anything*.

Of course, that vastness of possibility was not uncomplicated, and excitement was tempered by sobering consideration of how boundless the project could be. There is something to be said for defined boundaries and their necessity for meaning and meaningfulness. Instead, rather than a teasing out, there would have to be a narrowing down, perhaps earlier than I as a dramaturgy practitioner, and our group as a whole, might have usually endorsed. One early point of agreement, and thus boundary, was that Bisset would have to be enthused and engaged by whatever the proposed direction was and would, therefore, have to take the lead on identifying and pursuing it, and that any steering by D'Avila or by me would be done to support that end.

There was also trepidation because of the multiple possible lines of pursuit and the awareness that CECTON as a network—albeit, in its current early phase, a small one—is made up of a dozen or so contributors and collaborators. A feeling of wanting to include as many different strands as possible, both in the hope of being equitable and because those numerous strands all felt appealing and viable, was something we acknowledged as a group. What came out of that acknowledgement was a feeling of wanting to do the academic work justice. Still, something that we made clear from the outset to the non-theatremaking members of the network was that our response to their research might well end up not resembling that research especially closely, or that we might pursue a line of enquiry that none had dreamed would be the focus. Our perspective would evolve, of course, as we became better acquainted with the research and found the narrative crux of whatever story or stories we wanted to give voice to. But our perspective would be ours and there would be no guarantee that what is compelling in a research paper or workshop discussion would make the cut to be incorporated into a theatre piece.

With so many possible pathways, I was engaged in discussion with Bisset at a much earlier stage than normal—a fact that perforce changed the role. If a theatremaker approaches me regarding new work, the concept is generally in place—something might be written or, at the very least, the stimulus is broadly known and has done its work. Not so here. Within dramaturgy, the midwifery metaphor is well known: Fiona Graham uses and extends the metaphor when dissecting her time and processes in a New Zealand intra-cultural community,[26] while Katherine Profeta, looking to the work of the psychologist C.J. Nemeth, challenges the trope that the dramaturg 'should serve as uncomplicated midwife'.[27] I, like Profeta, welcome any broadening of the realms in which dramaturgs might be found, and being present at pre-conception is entirely different from the usual way of working, especially with regard to working with text.

In that respect, the process was more akin to one of devising, but with the knowledge that there would be a concrete text produced between idea generation and performance. Of course, there is some contradiction in terms of equating an act of a single author with the spontaneous, improvisatory frameworks of devising with more than one collaborator, and yet it feels the most apt equivalence based on my practice hitherto. For example, working with performers who were dance/movement practitioners or otherwise happy to throw themselves into a largely movement-rooted process in the Syn Festival in 2017, the focus was very much on the meaning of bodies in space. What the group there wanted to explore was ways of being together to draw out and draw upon the ritualistic and the uncanny. While there was a text (my translations of passages of Euripides' *Bacchae*), the movement was very much the starting point and focus, while the process that engendered it was about creating a response to the play as much as a performance of (some) of it. The translated text itself was in no way overlooked, but it was secondary to the means of creating dialogue with the play essentialized to the themes and ideas the group wanted to explore. The

---

[26] Fiona Graham, 'Dramaturge as Midwife: The Writing Process within a New Zealand Community Theatre Project', *Journal of Writing in Creative Practice*, 2:2.1 (2009), pp. 209–16.

[27] Katherine Profeta, *Dramaturgy in Motion: At Work on Dance and Movement Performance* (Madison: University of Wisconsin Press, 2015), p. 20.

words of the play were not the way in, instead they overlaid the physical exploration, adding another layer of meaning.

In answer to the *what is it?* posed above, an early format suggestion went hand-in-hand with a stripped-back aesthetic, simply a stage (or more aptly a space) with a microphone in the manner of stand-up comedy or slam poetry—the simplicity of amplification (in a literal sense to accompany the metaphorical), direct address and the possibility of fielding a less conventionally structured narrative format. This would offer two possible benefits for Bisset: first, that of forgoing a standard structure and of writing episodically instead; and second, the potential to tackle a broader range of concepts addressed by the network's research into the colonial-era Caribbean.

Writing and Performing *Placeholder* (Catherine Bisset)

To say this project was a daunting task for me is an understatement. This was only my second attempt at writing a script and my first at drafting a full play. During the first lockdown in 2020, I was part of a collaborative verbatim project supported by Stellar Quines Theatre Company, so some of the lessons learned from this first foray into script-writing were transferable. Working with verbatim quotations had raised major questions particularly around the extent to which wider contextual information can completely shift the meaning and interpretation of factual data, and also how juxtaposing several pieces of information in particular sequences can change not only the meaning of the text but also the impact of the message. Another pertinent issue raised by the verbatim project was addressing the idea of voice. The resulting script was stitched together using direct quotations, so voice—and indeed the manipulation of voice—were central components of the work.

Now I was faced with research outputs where the verbatim perspectives of the main subjects of the historical evidence were (mostly) missing, so voice became even more important. The challenge, however, was how to represent properly those who were not permitted to speak. One path was to read beyond the research papers provided by CECTON during our conference workshop to uncover additional accounts from enslaved people themselves from other sources, if and where they existed.

I found some of these in the Library of Congress Archives,[28] where they keep materials related to slavery in America, including photographs,

---

[28] Library of Congress Research Guides, 'Slavery in America: A Resource Guide' (17 January 2019) <https://guides.loc.gov/slavery-in-america>.

manuscripts, recorded oral histories, and books—thankfully all open access. Among the archives are extraordinary and rare tape-recordings of formerly enslaved people (some of whom were, astonishingly, still alive in the 1930s) who describe in their own words their lived experience. Whilst the experience in the Caribbean and in Saint-Domingue may have been different, it did help fill in some of the holes in the archives.

One of the first questions in my mind was what are we trying to achieve and what would success look like? Early online discussions with D'Avila and Obayomi raised several possibilities as to the overarching purpose of this project. A fairly obvious purpose was described in the brief: to effectively communicate ongoing research into the colonial-era Caribbean theatre to a wider, non-specialist audience. This helped control my tendency to wander into areas that interested me but were outside the parameters of the project. Having said that, the wider research I conducted on the Haitian Revolution ended up being invaluable in placing the workshop papers within a wider context, introducing me to other key historical figures and filling in some more gaps. Another purpose, for me, was simply to tell an interesting story to which the audience could relate on a human level. My goal was to conceal the historiographical evidence within the story, instead of lecturing the audience about it.

I could also draw extensively on my background in research and analysis in the criminological field and as an analyst at the Scottish Government. I am no stranger to extracting messages and themes from research findings and communicating them to as wide an audience as possible. But working in collaboration with D'Avila and Obayomi was critical to filling in the gaps in my theatrical writing experience.

One method I often deploy at work to make sense of policies is called Theory of Change.[29] The model consists of first defining the end goal, change or outcome that you want to achieve and then working backwards to identify the evidence-informed actions needed to achieve that outcome. I wondered if his would work in playwriting, if knowing how the story would end would help us create a series of logical scenes that would propel the narrative towards that conclusion. But before I could experiment with the Theory of Change framework, I first needed to familiarize myself with the research to get a sense of the material I had to play with and view it through the lens of a narrative.

Early on, D'Avila had provided a useful description of solo shows from a performance perspective, so I knew more than one character

---

[29] Center for Theory of Change, 'Setting Standards for Theory of Change' (2021) <https://www.theoryofchange.org/what-is-theory-of-change/>.

or voices could tell the story—if my acting skills were up to it. I was embarking on this endeavour mindful of several constraints. First, I had very little knowledge of the topic area and I had not engaged with academic texts for a long time. I was also working within a very tight timescale, which gave me only a few weeks to come up with something coherent.

Participants in the conference workshop had presented on a range of fascinating but highly specific topic areas including the use of blackface in Cuba, runaway notices, the use of placeholders who held the seats for their employers in the theatre, the composer Samuel Felsted and the military and the theatre. As I revisited them, I found that one of the starkest messages emerging was the dearth of archival evidence in this field, which I found both depressing and, from a writer's perspective, rather disconcerting. Fortunately, Julia Prest had emailed me an article a few months earlier, which focussed on the life of an actor-singer known as 'Demoiselle Minette' (a successful and ambitious mixed-race opera singer) and that of her white rival, Madame Marsan.[30] I revisited the article, which reviewed fascinating evidence that gives a glimpse into Minette's operatic career in the late 1700s. While likely pale-skinned, having only one black great-grandparent, Minette would have been classified as a free woman *of colour* irrespective of her outward appearance. In terms of her career, Minette was clearly exceptional, being one of only two non-white solo performers in Saint-Domingue at the time. Minette would not have been equal to white people, but she had privileges.

A critic's review of one of her performances, suggesting that Minette was extremely talented but also highlighting Minette's complex and precarious social position (thus illustrating what she represented in the wider social structure in Saint-Domingue at the time) really interested me. A highly flattering review, which nonetheless concludes with a swipe at her wearing inappropriately lavish clothing when performing peasant roles. Prest notes that 'in the context of 1780s Saint-Domingue these comments about Minette's costuming acquire additional resonance given the increasingly harsh measures, including sumptuary laws, that were being passed in order to try to clip the wings of the free people of colour'.[31] This critic's review seemed highly pertinent in terms of clearly illustrating the prejudices that even a highly accomplished pale-skinned free woman of colour faced in the colonial era.

We do not know how the reviews affected Minette, nor do we know for sure what other types of discrimination she faced. I thought about

---

[30] Prest, 'Parisian Palimpsests'.
[31] Prest, 'Parisian Palimpsests', 177.

my personal experiences of being a member of a mixed-race minority. I was also aware that theatre reviews, and their power to make or break a performer, have as much influence on an artist's career today as they did in the late 1700s, so this was another way for the play to connect directly to the present. One of the first decisions I made was that the character of Minette could read out the review on stage, to show the possible consequences for the person it criticizes and to pose the question: do critics know or care what impact they have on the lives of performers?

Moreover, the record rarely accounts for how an event impacted on ordinary individuals as told through their own lived experience, and I was clear that this needed to be at least speculated upon in the play itself. A possibility that D'Avila, Obayomi and I discussed was that Minette might have considered giving up her career in response to these put-downs and this idea led to the outline of the narrative: Minette gave up singing, but something or someone persuades her to return to the stage. Now I had arrived at this decision, I drafted a brief description of the ending into a Theory of Change framework and started to consider what events (informed by the historiographical research) might drive Minette's change of heart and her return to the theatre.

Theatre-making thrives in emotional manipulation, and perhaps the most moving topic addressed at the conference workshop was that of runaway notices, which raised some difficult realities. Firstly, that information about enslaved people is so scarce that runaway notices are a valuable source of information.[32] Secondly, that the horrific injuries inflicted on them were dispassionately listed in such notices. The idea that historians were trying to reconstruct these people's lives by interpreting the types of injuries they were carrying was extremely sobering. Thirdly, the notices revealed that Minette's theatre director partner owned enslaved servants, and according to contextual knowledge about free people of colour, that Minette almost certainly did too. Moreover, these notices were posted not far from the theatre advertisements, alongside the latest show and ticket details. This was all fodder for subverting any notion that creatives have always been well-meaning lefties fighting for human rights.

Engagement with this material led to the creation of the second character in the play—Minette's enslaved mother. The research tells us that mother of the historical Minette was not enslaved, but it would not have been implausible for our Minette as many free people of colour were the children of enslaved women and their white masters. This

---

[32] See Chapter Nine in this volume for more on how they can be used by the theatre researcher.

relationship would represent the wider social structure of the time rather than being faithful to the details of Minette's actual life. It is the complexity of Minette's social status and the tensions played out between these social groups, perhaps deliberately engineered by the plantocracy to divide and rule, which lent itself to the tense dynamic between the two characters.

As the performer and writer I had to keep one eye firmly on finding a character that I could feasibly play, and since my heritage is half Jamaican and half English, Mama immediately became a serious contender for the lead character. Another discussion that caught my attention was that about (usually) mixed race people (mostly men) who sometimes held seats for their employers in the theatre. Although historical Minette, as far as we know, was never a placeholder, I began to play around with the notion of taking some artistic licence with Minette's real life to allow me to incorporate both her and those placeholders into the script. Under other circumstances, she might have taken up a role as a domestic servant and placeholder to maintain her relationship with the stage.

Doing my own research, I came across the group of poorer whites living in Saint-Domingue often referred to as *petits blancs*.[33] I found the jealousy and acrimony that clearly existed within this social group, which was positioned between the rich white plantocracy and the enslaved, compelling. The *petits blancs* came to be represented by a character who is referred to in the script as 'Mistress Anxiety'. She never speaks in the play but her very presence is key to driving the arc of Minette's story.

Another useful discovery was Joseph Boulogne, the Chevalier de Saint Georges, the remarkable but largely overlooked conductor and composer sometimes known (unhelpfully and inaccurately) as the 'Black Mozart'.[34] The son of an enslaved mother and a white father, Boulogne was by all accounts quite an extraordinary character. Born in Guadeloupe, he was sent to Paris to be educated and became a conductor of a prestigious symphony orchestra in Europe. There is evidence that the Chevalier may have played a concert in Saint-Domingue (certainly his music was performed there on several occasions), which provided

---

[33] Molly M. Hermann, 'The French Colonial Question and the Disintegration of White Supremacy in the Colony of Saint-Domingue, 1789–1792' (MA dissertation, University of North Carolina, 2005).

[34] Julian A. Ledford, 'Joseph Boulogne, the Chevalier de Saint-George and the Problem with Black Mozart', *Journal of Black Studies*, 51.1 (2020), pp. 60–82.

me with the idea for the setting of the play. *Placeholder* opens on the night of his concert in Port-au-Prince with Minette in the audience.

The conclusion I drew at the end of this initial journey was that the violence of slavery had another long-term consequence—the almost complete absence of the voices of enslaved people and their children in the archives, no matter how successful they were. In my mind this had to become a major consideration in terms not just of the themes in the play, but also in driving the wider purpose of both the play and the performance. Finally, as the play had to be set in Saint-Domingue, where Minette had lived, I also decided to set it during the build-up to the Haitian Revolution, which provides the backdrop to the narrative and also serves one of the key themes that emerged from the script: how divide and rule has to be destroyed for resistance to succeed.

I used the lack of evidence about the lives of enslaved people as an underlying theme in the play and explored it as an extension of their dehumanization. Most importantly, I wanted to view the notion of being absent from the historical records from their perspective. Mama appears as a memory in Minette's imagination, to tell her:

> the thought of dying never bothered me much, but what really bothered me was the thought of being forgotten, being consigned to the dustbin of history.

To Mama, being forgotten or lost in time is even worse than slavery and death. She embodies the absence of lived experience in historical literature. Of course, Mama is fully aware of being silenced. Her ability to understand her position beyond the immediacy of the violence and degradation she suffers gives her an acute awareness of the consequences of slavery, and she also speaks to the future position of most black and mixed-raced people.

Mama's fear of being erased also gave me the idea for the key point of tension in the relationship between the characters. Minette has given up on her flourishing opera career, whereas her mother points out that Minette has a responsibility to use any small advantage she has as a free woman of colour. Mama instructs Minette to leave a mark on behalf of the millions of others who will be forgotten:

> you can be remembered, and not just as some placeholder holding a seat for a white woman, but as a real human being.

A workshop paper on the use of blackface was as fascinating as it was depressing, and I wondered how black people themselves would have experienced it, should they have ever been forced to watch such a thing.[35] Lane noted that blackface performances seemed to suggest that white actors believed they could possess black people, which indicated to me that black people were seen as empty, devoid of any feelings, personality, intelligence or soul, which made them open to cruel imitation and ridicule. It also seemed to me that it was perfectly possible that blackface was used to remind enslavers and the wider white population that black people were not quite human, which in turn facilitated and justified their ongoing mistreatment. Mama manifests this in a monologue performed in front of a mirror to represent the cruel distortion of physical appearance that blackface also inflicts.

In many fields of research, and certainly in the social sciences, the absence of evidence from those who were directly involved in events or the topic under investigation would be discussed as an acknowledged limitation of the research, as it is in the present volume. History as I was taught it at school, however, ignored the impact of voices missing from historical records and this seemed highly problematic to me. In the context of slavery, the resounding silence of any enslaved voices or even second-hand accounts emerged as secondary violence against not just enslaved people but also their living descendants. *Placeholder* complements academic research that seeks to hear those voices once more and brings them to a wider audience.

Together, theatre and research can open possibilities of engagement on both an educational and emotional level, as demonstrated by the feedback received after the *Placeholder* performances. We asked our audiences in Edinburgh, St Andrews and online to fill out an anonymous questionnaire after watching the show, and out of a total of 68 respondents, 35 indicated that their understanding of the colonial-era Caribbean increased 'a lot' and 24 indicated that it had increased 'a bit'. In other words, the play had a positive educational impact on 86% of respondents. The feedback also demonstrated an overwhelmingly positive response towards increased interest in the subject matter and specifically, in Saint-Domingue and the Haitian Revolution (90%). Most importantly, perhaps, a compelling 96% of respondents agreed that theatre was an effective way of communicating about the colonial-era Caribbean.

The emotional impact of the piece can also be observed in the audience's freetext feedback. The words 'moving', 'captivating' and

---

[35] Jill Lane, 'Problems of Comparison: National Approaches to Caribbean Blackface' (CECTON conference workshop, August 2021). See Chapter Five of this volume for an updated version of this paper.

'powerful' are used repeatedly by respondents. One audience member highlighted *Placeholder* as 'one of the most genuine and successful collaborations between researchers and practitioners I have come across', and another called it 'a model collaboration'. A representative of the City of Edinburgh Council remarked, 'you have achieved more with this play than any policy or manifesto would'.[36] *Placeholder* has also had an impact in the theatre sector: it was shortlisted as runner-up for Production of the Year at Framework Theatre's inaugural Scottish Emerging Theatre Awards in December 2021, and received a 4-star review.[37] Catherine Bisset was also longlisted for the 2022 Alfred Fagon Award—the leading award for black British playwrights—for Best New Play.

Placeholder will continue to develop with support from a Create: Inclusion grant from Creative Scotland, which has enabled the team to conduct a consultation on innovative ways of integrating captioning and British Sign Language into the show. Our experiment in Knowledge Exchange Theatre has thus moved beyond a productive exchange of knowledge between academic research and theatre practice. In its modest way, *Placeholder* has changed—and will continue to change—many people's understanding of one of the most complex and uncomfortable periods of theatre history and, indeed, of human history.

Bibliography

Barba, Eugenio. *The Paper Canoe: A Guide to Theatre Anthropology* (London: Routledge, 1995).

Belliveau, George and Graham W. Lea (eds). *Research-Based Theatre: An Artistic Methodology* (Bristol: Intellect, 2016).

Bisset, Catherine. *Placeholder*. Performance at Being Human Festival (November 2021) <https://www.facebook.com/ScottishStorytellingCentre/videos/198420252466623>.

Bogue, Ronald. *Deleuzian Fabulation and the Scars of History* (Edinburgh: Edinburgh University Press, 2010).

Cabranes-Grant, Leo. 'From Scenarios to Networks: Performing the Intercultural in Colonial Mexico', in Charlotte McIvor and Jason King (eds), *Interculturalism and Performance Now: New Directions?* (London: Palgrave Macmillan, 2019), pp. 29–59.

---

[36] Beata Skobodzinska, personal email to Flavia D'Avila (2021).
[37] Dominic Corr, '*Placeholder*—Byre Theatre review' (12 February 2022) <https://corrblimey.uk/2022/02/12/the-placeholder/>.

Cannon, Debbie. *Green Knight* (May 2021) <https://debbiecannon.org/green-knight/>.

Cannon, Debbie. *The Remarkable Deliverances of Alice Thornton* (June 2017) <https://debbiecannon.org/the-remarkable-deliverances-of-alice-thornton/>.

Center for Theory of Change. Setting Standards for Theory of Change (2021) <https://www.theoryofchange.org/what-is-theory-of-change/>.

Corr, Dominic. *Placeholder*—Byre Theatre review (12 February 2022) <https://corrblimey.uk/2022/02/12/the-placeholder/>.

Domingues D'Avila, Flavia. 'Countercolonising the Stage: A Syncretic Dramaturgy for Devising' (PhD thesis, Royal Conservatoire of Scotland/University of St Andrews, 2021) <http:syncretictheatre.wordpress.com>.

Edinburgh Multicultural Festival, 'Catherine Bisset in *Placeholder*' (2 October 2021) <https://www.youtube.com/watch?v=hFh5ZopY-Yo>.

Ellis, Simon. A Definition. Practice-as-Research blog (5 January 2016) <https://practiceasresearchblog.wordpress.com/category/definition/>.

Gibbs, Jenna. 'Encountering Gaps and Silences in the Archive' (CECTON conference workshop, August 2021).

Graham, Fiona. 'Dramaturge as Midwife: The Writing Process within a New Zealand Community Theatre Project', *Journal of Writing in Creative Practice*, 2:2.1 (2009), pp. 209–16.

Hartman, Saidiya. 'Venus in Two Acts', *Small Axe*, 12.2 (2008), pp. 1–14.

Hermann, Molly M. 'The French Colonial Question and the Disintegration of White Supremacy in the Colony of Saint-Domingue, 1789–1792' (MA dissertation, University of North Carolina, 2005).

Lane, Jill. 'Problems of Comparison: National Approaches to Caribbean Blackface' (CECTON conference workshop, August 2021).

Ledford, Julian A. 'Joseph Boulogne, the Chevalier de Saint-George and the Problem with Black Mozart', *Journal of Black Studies*, 51.1 (2020), pp. 60–82.

Library of Congress Research Guides, Slavery in America: A Resource Guide (17 January 2019) <https://guides.loc.gov/slavery-in-america>.

Prest, Julia. 'Colonial-Era Theatre and the Enslaved Population: Uncovering Hidden Connections in Saint-Domingue' (CECTON conference workshop, August 2021).

Prest, Julia. 'Parisian Palimpsests and Creole Creations: Mme Marsan and Dlle Minette play *Nina* on the Caribbean Stage', *Early Modern French Studies*, 41.2 (2019), pp. 170–88.

Profeta, Katherine. *Dramaturgy in Motion: At Work on Dance and Movement Performance* (Madison: University of Wisconsin Press, 2015).

Riello, Giorgio and Ulinka Rublack (eds). *The Right to Dress: Sumptuary Laws in a Global Perspective, c.1200–1800* (Cambridge: Cambridge University Press, 2019).

Saldaña, Johnny. *Ethnotheatre: Research from Page to Stage (Qualitative Inquiry and Social Justice)* (Walnut Creek, CA: Left Coast Press, 2011).

Scuderi, Antonio. 'Unmasking the Holy Jester Dario Fo', *Theatre Journal*, 55.2 (2003), pp. 275–90.

Skobodzinska, Beata. Personal email to Flavia D'Avila (2021).

TDF Theatre Dictionary, Applied Theatre (2013) https://www.tdf.org/on-stage/theatre-dictionary/search-by-letter/applied-theatre/>.

University of Edinburgh, Alice Thornton's Books: Remembrances of a Woman's Life in the Seventeenth Century (6 August 2019) <https://www.ed.ac.uk/history-classics-archaeology/history/research/research-projects/alice-thorntons-books>.

Weaver, Wayne. 'Constructions of "Race" in the Musico-Theatrical Contexts of Eighteenth-Century Kingston' (CECTON conference workshop, August 2021).

Wing, Joylynn. 'Techniques of Opposition in the Work of Dario Fo' (PhD thesis, Stanford University, CA, 1988).

Index

abolition of slavery, abolitionism 104, 111n3, 112–13, 116, 117
abolition of slave trade 95, 112
actors 3, 63n7, 68, 69, 91, 94, 95, 99, 113, 117–18, 123, 127, 143–44, 171, 187, 212, 219, 221–22, 224, 225–26, 248, 252
Africa, African people 3, 27, 51, 62, 69–71, 94, 100, 104, 105, 111–12, 114, 119–20, 122, 123, 131, 140, 147, 149, 162, 171, 175, 207, 214, 218, 223, 237
African-descended people 3, 12, 19, 22–23, 29, 38, 94, 140, 141–42, 143n28, 146, 149n46, 151–52, 168, 172, 174, 225
African Grove Theatre 171, 173
Afro-Caribbean culture 9, 13, 70, 120, 131, 162, 175
Aldridge, Ira 171
American Civil War 13, 117n26, 171, 176–77, 178
American Company 142–43
American Revolution 28, 199
Americas 22, 24, 26, 31, 42, 137, 151, 155
    Central America 26, 47
    South America 18, 26, 30, 31, 47
Anansi 87n1, 104–05
Anglicans, Anglicanism 12, 141, 151, 154
anticolonialism 107, 112, 114, 115, 116n26, 117, 123, 167

archives, the archive 4, 6, 7, 9, 13, 14–15, 63, 66–68, 73, 75, 164–69, 184–88, 190, 191, 193–94, 198, 199, 201, 246–47
    construction of 6, 52, 69, 165, 166–67, 177–78, 185
    see also gaps and absences
Atlantic Ocean 87, 106, 107, 169, 190, 192
Atlantic revolutions 25
Atlantic world 1, 2, 20, 21, 24, 25, 29, 112, 116, 125, 126, 142, 169
audiences, audience response 3, 8, 9, 10, 13, 15, 22, 45, 49, 63n7, 65–66, 68, 92, 94–96, 99, 100, 102, 115, 121, 128, 130, 135, 143n31, 145, 146, 148, 149, 151n51, 152, 162–63, 166, 174, 178, 200, 202n44, 216, 220–21, 232, 236, 243, 244, 247, 251, 252–53

Bakhtin, Mikhail 89
Barbados 10, 19, 27, 28, 30, 31, 46, 48, 75, 177
Bassnett, Susan 78, 79–80
Being Human Festival 232
Belize 25, 26
Bénac, Karine 8–9
Bhabha, Homi 89
Bisset, Catherine, *Placeholder* 14–15, 231–53

257

blackface performance 12, 97–98, 106, 111–31, 143n28, 248, 251–52
  see also minstrelsy; racial impersonation; *teatro bufo*
Bolingbroke, Henry 19, 23n10
Boulogne, Joseph (Chevalier de Saint Georges) 250–51
Brazil 26, 43, 111, 112, 167
Britain, British people 8, 13, 19, 22, 27, 31, 48, 49, 76, 111, 112, 127, 135, 136n5, 138–40, 146, 149–50, 151, 154, 168, 169, 174, 187, 211, 253
  London 2, 40, 116, 118, 137, 143, 144, 161, 169, 171–73, 175
  see also England; Scotland
British Atlantic 13, 127, 161, 162
British Caribbean 8, 19, 20, 22, 23, 27, 28, 31, 48–49, 76, 111, 161, 162, 177
British-Israel paradigm 149–50, 154
Britto, Louis 19, 28, 31
brownface 123
Burnard, Trevor 7, 140n17, 140n18, 140n19, 141n23
Byre Theatre, St Andrews 15, 232

Caribbean region(s) 20, 25, 31, 40, 41, 45, 47, 51, 52, 64n10
  Greater Antilles 28, 29, 47
  Greater Caribbean 20, 22, 25–31, 48, 49, 172
  Greater Southern Caribbean 29–30
  Gulf of Mexico 28, 45, 48, 50
  Leeward Islands 10, 27, 29, 31
  Lesser Antilles 30, 38, 47
  Windward Islands 30, 190
Caribbean Sea 20, 25, 27, 29–31, 47
categories 6n12, 10, 99, 125, 126n57, 141, 166, 214
censorship 112, 118, 173
Chinese language 67, 76, 76n36
Chinese people 67, 76, 76n36, 124
circuits 10, 39, 42–47, 50, 56, 116
circum-Atlantic 2, 125–27

class 69, 70, 101, 105, 115, 118, 119, 121, 122, 140, 151, 168, 199, 216
Clément, *Papa Simon ou les Amours de Thérèse et Janot, Jeannot et Thérèse* 68–69
co-authorship 7, 8, 14
colonial era 20, 30, 62, 66, 76, 81, 164, 168, 248
colonial-era Caribbean 1–15, 23, 61, 64, 66, 74, 81–82, 90, 140, 183, 205, 232, 236, 237–41, 246, 247, 252
Colonial-Era Caribbean Theatre and Opera Network (CECTON) 5, 7–9, 14, 232, 243–44
colonialism 1, 11, 20–21, 38, 39, 76, 88, 89, 112, 201, 220
commedia dell'arte 87–107, 215
Cooper, Frederick 5–6, 87n2, 88, 90n13
Costa Rica 43, 51
Covarrubias, Francisco 112–13
Creole culture 1, 3, 8–9, 11, 68–69, 74–75, 130n70, 135, 139, 189, 198, 198n35, 234
critical fabulation 206n3, 238
Cuba 3, 12, 28, 29, 45, 47–50, 56, 66, 67, 70–71, 75, 76, 99, 111–31, 151, 193, 248
  Havana 3, 10, 39, 41, 43, 44–45, 48–50, 56, 67, 76, 119, 127, 201
  Santa Clara 3
  Santiago de Cuba 3, 46, 49, 122
Curaçao 20, 28, 29

dance, dancers 4, 19, 69, 70, 89, 90, 102, 119, 120–21, 122, 127–28, 131, 162, 175, 183, 219, 222, 245
Davis, Tracy 6, 13n24, 136, 166–67
Delafosse de Rouville 183, 198–99
de la Harpe, Jean-François, *Le Comte de Warwick* 220
de la Touche, Claude Guimond, *Iphigénie en Tauride* 220

INDEX

Dillon, Elizabeth Maddock 1, 88, 90, 103, 104, 136n5
Dissenter churches 141, 153
  Anabaptists 12, 142, 146, 153
  Baptists 153
  Moravians 151, 153
  Quakers 151, 153
Dubuisson, Henri 212, 218
Dwyer, Ted, *Mansong* 178

empire(s) 2, 4, 9, 38, 49, 56, 63, 116, 145, 148
  French 184
  Spanish 111, 117
England, English people 1, 41, 117, 121, 137, 144n32, 193
  see also Britain
enslaved characters 9, 113, 118, 122, 205, 238
enslaved people 14–15, 23, 27, 29, 38, 69, 70, 81, 94, 95, 102, 103–04, 112, 118, 126, 131, 140, 141, 141n23, 143n31, 146, 147, 151, 153–54, 161, 163, 172–75, 184, 186–87, 192, 198n34, 205–27, 234, 237, 238, 249, 250–52
  brandings of 207
  country marks of 207, 223
  disabilities of 207, 223
  for sale 221–22, 226
  injuries of 216–17, 249
  punishments of 208
  skills of 207
  testimony of 246–47, 226
  see also enslaved runaways; slavery
enslaved runaways 205–27
Europe, European people 2, 3, 4, 11, 12, 20, 21, 24, 37–39, 40, 51, 52, 61, 62, 66, 69, 107, 140, 143n28, 143n31, 149, 150n50, 163–64, 171, 185, 193

Fawcett, John, *Obi; or, Three-Finger'd Jack* 161–78

Felsted, Samuel 135–55, 248
Ferrer, Ada 29, 111–12
Ferron de la Ferronnays 187n11, 188–89
fold, the 126–27
France, French people 2, 40n9, 41, 43n23, 45, 46, 68, 144, 151, 173, 183, 184, 186–88, 188n14, 189–93, 196, 198–200, 213, 216, 219n52, 220–21
  Bordeaux 193n26, 201
  Brest 187, 190–93, 201
  La Rochelle 193n26
  Le Havre 45
  Nantes 193n26
  Paris 40, 40n11, 54, 183, 186, 187, 200–02, 217, 250
  Rochefort 187, 190
French Atlantic 1
French Caribbean 2, 4, 8, 19, 20, 22, 23, 64, 111, 208n9
Fuentes, Marisa 165, 177–78, 206n3, 209–10, 227

gaps and absences 2, 6, 9, 13, 14–15, 42n18, 68, 140, 148, 161–78, 185, 209, 214, 226, 232, 243, 247, 251, 252
  see also archives; silencing and erasure
Garrigus, John 7
Gaspar, David Barry 26–27
Geggus, David Patrick 25n18, 26–27
gender 96, 116
Ghana 115, 116, 175
Girod de Chantrans, Justin 195
Glissant, Édouard 73–75
Gottschalk, Louis Moreau 10, 41–42, 45–52, 54–56
Grenada 19
Guadeloupe 10, 39, 45, 48, 186, 190, 211, 215n38, 250
Guatemala 43
Guianas 10, 25, 26, 30
  British 48, 76

Dutch 22, 48
French 186, 190, 211, 217
see also Guyana; Suriname
Guyana 19, 30, 100, 105
see also Guianas (British)

Haiti 3, 4, 48, 49, 51, 64, 66, 75, 111, 112, 183
see also Saint-Domingue
Haitian Revolution 13, 24–25, 29, 51, 102, 169, 172–74, 178, 247, 251, 252
Handel, George Frideric 12, 137–38, 144n32, 147n42, 150, 151
Harlequin, Arlequin 11–12, 13, 87–107, 215–18
Hartman, Saidiya 14, 126, 127, 164–65, 171, 206, 222, 234, 238
Hill, Errol 135n2, 136, 162, 171
Hilliard d'Auberteuil, Michel-René 195, 198n33
humour 54, 99, 113, 114, 119, 122, 129

Iberian America 26
Iberian Atlantic 112, 117
immigrant characters 69–70, 123–24
indigenous people(s) 21–24, 30, 38, 62, 63n7, 167–69
Italian Opera Company 41

Jamaica 1, 3, 7, 12, 13, 27, 28, 66, 71, 76, 116, 135–55, 161–78, 193, 208, 211, 215, 215n38, 217, 237, 250
  Kingston 3, 12–13, 48, 137, 138, 142–45, 147, 149, 151, 153, 154, 161–78, 201
  Montego Bay 3
  Spanish Town 3, 135, 138
  Warwick Crescent 176
Jewish people 12, 91, 94, 141, 142n26, 143–47, 149, 151, 153–54
Jewish Theatre, Paramaribo 91, 95, 96

Jonkanoo 3, 13, 161–62, 164, 166, 174–78

Knowledge Exchange Theatre 14, 15, 232, 253

language, languages 7–8, 9, 11, 24, 38, 50, 56, 61–82, 89, 121–24, 129, 145, 168, 193, 207n7, 253
  accented speech 123, 124, 217
  Creole languages 62, 68, 75–76, 89, 130n70
  dialects 69–70, 129
  monolingualism, fallacy of 62–66
  multilingualism 61–82, 207n5
  see also Chinese language
Latin America 8, 21, 124
Leal, Rine 114–15, 131
Le Glaunec, Jean-Pierre 208–09, 211n28
Leichman, Jeffrey 2
Le Mierre, Antoine-Marin, *La Veuve du Malabar* 220–21
Lhamon, William T. 118, 120–21, 127
Lott, Eric 88n4, 115, 123, 124, 128

Mackendal, François 173
magic, magical practices 12, 13, 89, 90, 92, 99–100, 102–03, 105–06, 107, 216
  see also obeah; vodou
Mahon, James 143–44, 144n32
Mansong, Jack 161, 172, 173
Maretzek, Max 10, 41, 42, 44–45, 47, 48–56
Marollier de Vivetières, Benoît-Joseph, *La Mort du Colonel Mauduit* 183n2, 199n37
Martinique 3, 8, 9, 10, 19, 39, 45, 47, 48, 75, 186, 190, 219, 222
  Saint-Pierre 3, 46, 201
Mauduit-Duplessis, Colonel 183, 192, 199

methodological approaches
  anthropological 166, 194, 236
  Caribbean 2, passim
  collaborative 23, 56, 72, 73, 73n30, 82, 246
  colonial 4, 9, 12, 111–31
  combined 10, 19–32, 106
  comparative 5, 9, 23, 25, 76, 116, 126, 201
  contextual 6, 9, 12, 13, 32, 135–55, 163, 168, 175, 176, 178, 246, 249
  creative 167, 231–53
  decentring 186, 202
  extractive 126, 184, 247
  geographical 4, 10, 19–32, 48–49, 52, 65, 66, 74, 127
  global 20, 24–26, 31, 56
  historiographic 20, 24, 47, 88, 103, 115, 177, 191, 201, 233, 234, 242, 247, 249
  imaginative 68, 105, 128, 206, 222, 236, 238
  imperial 8, 10, 20–23, 26–29, 31, 49, 50, 68, 166–69, 177
  literary 65, 74, 135n3, 147–53, 165, 173
  local 20, 31, 136, 221
  multilingual 11, 61–82
  national 9, 10, 12, 20, 27, 36, 37, 38n5, 111–31, 149
  reading against the grain 14, 162, 165, 169–74, 177, 178, 185, 186n7
  reading along the grain 14, 165, 166, 185, 186n7
  regional 10, 20, 21, 23–25, 28, 29, 31, 32, 63–65, 69–70
  relational 72, 111–31
  scientific 164, 172
  speculative 14, 15, 153, 154, 198, 234, 243, 249
  story-telling 209n13, 236, 244, 247–48, 250
  synchronic 23
  systadial 23
  theoretical 2, 42, 53, 63n7, 64–65, 74–75, 82, 124–31, 163
  trans-imperial 5, 20, 22, 23, 28, 29, 31
  trans-national 20, 30, 170
metropole–colony paradigm 2, 5–6, 11–12, 68, 87, 88, 90, 91, 106, 193
Mexico 10, 21, 43, 45, 49, 50, 233
  Veracruz 28, 48, 49–50, 52, 53
military 13–14, 183–202
  army, soldiers 13, 176, 183–90, 192, 194–202
  documents 163, 183–202
  navy, sailors 13, 29, 176, 186–89, 191–92, 200, 202
  and the theatre 8, 13, 142, 162, 183–202, 248
military-theatrical complex 185, 200
Minette 15, 40n10, 234, 237–38, 244, 248–51
minstrelsy 12, 97, 99, 111–31
misogyny 123
mobility 9, 10, 27, 30, 37–57, 65, 107
monolingualism *see* languages (monolingualism, fallacy of)
Moreau de Saint-Méry, Médéric Louis Élie 194–97
Moten, Fred 127–28
mulata 113, 123
Mulich, Jeppe 5, 10, 29
music, musicians *see* Afro-Caribbean culture; Felsted, Samuel; Gottschalk, Louis Moreau; theatrical genres (*guarachas*; minstrelsy; music theatre; opera; *opéra-comique*; oratorio; *teatro bufo*; zarzuela)

nationalism 112
negrito 112–14, 122–23, 131
  bozal 69–71, 80, 122–23
  catedrático 120, 122–23, 128–29
Netherlands 87, 89–92, 95, 106, 193

Amsterdam 89–91, 94, 97, 106, 215
networks 5, 10, 28, 30, 82, 139, 142, 185, 190, 201
  Caribbean 10, 29
  imperial 20, 28
  trans-imperial 22, 27, 29
  see also Colonial-Era Caribbean Theatre and Opera Network (CECTON)
New Granada 10, 29, 46, 48
newspapers, periodicals 14, 40, 103, 143n28, 146, 162, 171, 205–13, 219, 221–23, 226
Nugent, George 135
Nugent, Maria 135, 141, 150

obeah 13, 161, 169, 170, 172–74

Panama 28, 43
parodies, parody 70–71, 115, 118, 120–23, 220n53
Patti, Adelina 41, 48, 54–55
plantations, plantation economy 24, 26–27, 31, 92, 95–96, 100, 101, 101n45, 105, 106, 111–13, 120, 122, 161, 169, 173, 175, 184, 186, 188, 193n26, 209, 213, 214
postcolonial theories 53, 165
  see also methodological approaches (theoretical)
power structures, power relations 1, 3, 4, 24, 38–39, 41, 43, 47, 50, 52, 54, 57, 61, 67, 75, 79, 80, 87–89, 92, 99, 100, 103–07, 112, 120, 126, 161, 164–65, 167, 169, 174, 176, 184n3, 185, 186n9, 187, 198, 201, 202, 208, 210, 249
practice-as-research 8, 231, 233, 244
public theatre 2–3, 185, 187, 189, 190, 192, 200, 201, 205, 206
Puerto Rico 10, 19, 28, 46, 48

racial counterfeit 117, 228–29
racial difference 12, 52–53, 139

racial impersonation 12, 99, 117–19, 130n70, 131
racial mixing 123, 131
Racine, Jean 220
  Andromaque 220
  Athalie 220
rebellion, rebellions 99–103, 106–07, 112–13, 164, 169, 170, 172–73, 175
resistance 13, 89, 105, 107, 127, 169–72, 174–78, 209, 210, 231, 251
revolution(s) see American Revolution; Atlantic revolutions; Haitian Revolution
Rice, Thomas D. 118, 120–21, 127, 128
Roach, Joseph 2, 125–27
Royal Circus 173
runaway advertisements 14, 205–27, 234, 248, 249

Saint-Domingue 3, 4, 7, 8, 9, 13, 14, 39, 40n10, 41, 45, 47, 64, 68, 69, 71, 95n25, 99n37, 111, 112, 130n70, 144, 151, 171, 173, 183–202, 205–27, 234, 247, 248, 250–51, 252
  Cap-Français 2, 185–89, 198, 201, 219
  Léogane 189, 201
  Port-au-Prince 2, 15, 48, 183, 185, 188–89, 198–99, 201, 223, 251
  Saint-Marc 3, 223
  see also Haiti
Scotland, Scottish people 217, 217n47, 234, 247, 253
Scottish Storytelling Centre, Edinburgh 15, 232
Seven Years' War 184–86, 192
silencing and erasure 6, 9, 13, 53, 54, 62, 63n7, 66–69, 71, 79, 80, 88, 113, 161–78, 198, 230, 242–44, 251, 252
  see also archives; gaps and absences
slavery 12, 14, 23, 24, 26, 54, 87, 94–96, 104, 105, 111, 112, 116, 117,

INDEX

123, 125, 126, 131, 136, 139, 151–54, 164, 167, 169–73, 175–76, 187, 205–27, 246, 251, 252
slaves *see* enslaved people
sound, sounds 62, 63n7, 65, 67–69, 74, 119–21, 126, 131, 152, 167
Spain, Spanish people 70, 111, 113, 114, 116, 118, 123, 131, 141, 151, 193
Spanish Caribbean 8, 11, 20, 22, 23, 28, 31, 49, 63, 72, 130, 131, 141, 168
St Eustatius 20
St Thomas 10, 29, 41, 41n15, 46, 48
sources 5, 9, 11, 13–14, 41, 42n18, 63, 63n7, 67, 68, 71, 79, 104, 135, 149, 154, 159–253
   material 166
   official 13, 40, 103, 166, 168, 188, 189, 198n34, 199
   oral 166, 168, 247
   top-down 13, 163–64, 176, 178
   traces, trace evidence 40, 56, 115, 163–66, 169, 171, 176, 178, 185, 234, 241
   unofficial 166, 169
   see also military documents; runaway advertisements
South Africa 116
Stoler, Ann Laura 5–6, 14, 87n1, 88, 96n27, 166, 184n3, 186n7
Suriname 3, 11, 20, 48, 87, 89–91, 94–95, 99, 100–07, 130n70, 147n42, 167
   Paramaribo 3, 12, 13, 48, 87, 90, 91, 95–97, 99, 102–06, 215
   see also Guianas (Dutch)

Teatro Tacón, Havana 39, 45
Théâtre de la Marine, Brest 190–92
theatre subscriptions 188n14, 189–91, 211
theatrical genres
   comedy 3, 8–9, 89, 90, 113, 143, 150n49, 183, 216n43, 220
   danzón 120–22
   drame 3

   guaracha 114–15, 119, 121
   music theatre 154
   opera 3, 10, 12, 37–57, 63, 64, 67, 68, 82, 118, 121, 137, 212, 251
   opéra-comique 3, 69n20, 143, 198n35, 212
   oratorio 3, 8, 12, 135–55
   pantomime 3, 13, 88–90, 107n61, 121, 161–78
   teatro bufo 12, 113–24, 128–31
   tragedy 220–21
   zarzuela 3, 121, 121n38
   see also minstrelsy
Theory of Change 247–49
Toussaint L'Ouverture 172, 173
translation 8, 11, 62, 63, 66, 72, 207n7, 244, 245
   domesticating 11, 80–81
   foreignizing 11, 80–81
   reparative 76–81
Trinidad 10, 19, 20, 22, 28, 30, 46, 48, 66, 75, 76, 116
Trouillot, Michel-Rolph 64, 167, 177–78, 209, 226

United States of America 1, 19, 41–54, 71, 72, 111–14, 125, 170, 171, 176, 193, 210
   Georgia Lowcountry 27–28
   Louisiana 2, 29, 211, 215–18
   New Orleans 3, 8, 10, 20, 29, 41, 43–49, 51, 63n6, 66, 67, 69, 211n28
   New York 43, 44, 46, 46n37, 54, 115, 119–21, 127, 171, 210
   Philadelphia 116, 121, 127, 169, 173
   South Carolina 27, 47n40, 173, 211, 215n38

Venezuela 19, 28–30, 46
   Caracas 11, 46, 48
vernacular culture 67, 70–71, 104–06, 113, 115, 116–17, 119, 124, 129, 130, 161, 164, 166, 169, 170

Vesey, Denmark 173
Veuves créoles, Des 9
Veuves créoles, Les 8–9
vodou 3, 173
Voltaire 90, 214, 215
   Le Fanatisme ou Mahomet le prophète 220, 221
   Mérope ou la Mérope française 220
   Sémiramis 219–20, 220n53
   Zaïre 215

Walcott, Derek 64, 65, 75, 78
war, wars 10, 11, 46, 48, 94n19, 115, 185
   wars of independence 112–14, 142, 146
   see also American Civil War; Seven Years' War
whiteness 12, 99, 106, 126n57, 131, 136, 139, 142, 144, 151, 153–54, 172
white performance 53, 69n20
Williams, Eric 10, 23, 24, 24n17

9781837645039